VERSES
AND
VERSIONS

OTHER WORKS OF POETRY AND
TRANSLATION BY VLADIMIR NABOKOV

POETRY
Poems and Problems
Stihi

TRANSLATIONS FROM FRENCH TO RUSSIAN
Colas Breugnon by Romain Rolland

TRANSLATIONS FROM RUSSIAN TO ENGLISH
A Hero of Our Time by Mihail Lermontov (with Dmitri Nabokov)
The Song of Igor's Campaign (Anon.)
Eugene Onegin by Alexander Pushkin
Mary (with Michael Glenny)
King, Queen, Knave
The Defense (with Michael Scammell)
The Eye (with Dmitri Nabokov)
Glory (with Dmitri Nabokov)
Laughter in the Dark
Despair
Invitation to a Beheading (with Dmitri Nabokov)
Nabokov's Dozen
The Gift (with Michael Scammell and Dmitri Nabokov)
A Russian Beauty and Other Stories (with Simon Karlinsky and
Dmitri Nabokov)
Tyrants Destroyed and Other Stories (with Dmitri Nabokov)
Details of a Sunset and Other Stories (with Dmitri Nabokov)

TRANSLATIONS FROM ENGLISH TO RUSSIAN
Alice in Wonderland by Lewis Carroll
Speak, Memory
Lolita

VERSES AND VERSIONS

THREE CENTURIES
OF RUSSIAN POETRY
SELECTED AND
TRANSLATED BY

VLADIMIR NABOKOV

EDITED BY BRIAN BOYD
AND STANISLAV SHVABRIN
INTRODUCTION BY
BRIAN BOYD

HARCOURT, INC.
ORLANDO AUSTIN NEW YORK
SAN DIEGO LONDON

Library of Congress Cataloging-in-Publication Data
Verses and versions: three centuries of Russian poetry/selected and
translated by Vladimir Nabokov; edited by Brian Boyd and Stanislav
Shvabrin; introduction by Brian Boyd.
p.   cm.
English and Russian in parallel translation.
Includes index.
Summary: Here, collected for the first time in one volume, are
Nabokov's English translations of Russian verse, presented next to
the Russian originals, as well as two never-before-published poems
written in English by Nabokov himself. Here, also, are some of his
notes on the dangers and thrills of translation.
1. Russian poetry—Translations into English.   2. Russian poetry.
I. Nabokov, Vladimir Vladimirovich, 1899–1977.   II. Boyd, Brian,
1952– .   III. Shvabrin, Stanislav.
PG3237.E5V47   2008
891.71008—dc22   2008013726
ISBN 978-0-15-101264-0

Text set in ITC New Baskerville and Baskerville Cyrillic
Designed by Kaelin Chappell Broaddus

First edition
Printed in the United States of America

K J I H G F E D C B A

What is translation? On a platter
A poet's pale and glaring head,
A parrot's screech, a monkey's chatter,
And profanation of the dead.

CONTENTS

CONTENTS

INTRODUCTION

Translation, like politics, is an art of compromise: inevitable compromise between the resources of From-ish and those of To-ish.* When the unique riches of From-ish—all the accidents of its associations and accidence—have been exploited to the full by a poet of genius, the compromise must be all the greater.

"Vladimir Adamant Nabokov," as he once signed himself, was a man singularly averse to compromise. Artists usually are: Within the work, as nowhere else in life, they can choose their own conditions. Nabokov notoriously eschewed compromise by translating the unquestioned masterpiece of Russian verse, Aleksandr Pushkin's *Eugene Onegin,* into an English version that allows readers to understand the exact sense of Pushkin's lines, especially through notes eight times as long as the poem, but renounces any attempt to provide an equivalent of Pushkin's poetry, his perfect placement

*To follow the lead of Nabokov and the lilt of his friend Dr. Seuss. Nabokov met Theodor Seuss Geisel at a writers' conference in Utah in the summer of 1949. During the conference, Dr. Seuss wrote a butterfly poem for Nabokov; years later, in *Horton Hears a Who!* (1954), he introduced an incidental "black-bottomed eagle named Vlad Vlad-i-koff," after Vladimir Vladimirovich Nabokoff (as Nabokov once spelled his name).

of words, his seemingly effortless mastery of rhythm and rhyme. Rather than trying to replicate Pushkin's landscape in another medium, another place, Nabokov provides detailed signposts to Pushkin's own terrain.

But before 1951, when he arrived at this austerely unpoetic method of translating *Eugene Onegin,* Nabokov had been a brilliant translator of verse into verse, always with a strong loyalty to accuracy of sense, but accepting in this one instance the compromises that must be made to find some match for the verse of From in the linguistic resources and verse conventions of To. He translated from French and English—and even German, of which he knew little—into Russian, from Russian and French into English, and from Russian into French.

Fluently trilingual by the age of seven, he translated at twelve Mayne Reid's Wild West novel *The Headless Horseman* into French alexandrines. That translation does not survive, but much of his prolific early verse and verse translation does, although neither Nabokov himself nor his son, Dmitri, has judged this juvenilia worth publishing. In his last years Nabokov was ruthless in selecting his early verse for his collection *Stihi* (*Poems*), published two years after his death. His first nine years as a poet are represented there by only slightly more poems than the single year of 1923, his last year as predominantly a poet, his first year of real poetic maturity. That year therefore provides the starting point for this collection of Nabokov's verse translations.

There is another reason for choosing 1923. That was the year Nabokov met Véra Slonim, whom he married two years later. Fluent in Nabokov's three languages, and also in German, an avid reader of his verse before they met, and already herself translating and publishing in *Rul'*, the Russian émigré newspaper in Berlin where Nabokov had published most of his early work, Véra remained particularly attached sixty years later to the notion of assembling a volume of her husband's verse translations, and would have edited it herself in her eighties had she had the strength and time.

Nabokov, too, had often thought of collecting his verse translations, even after he had insisted so firmly in *Eugene Onegin* on the need for unyielding literality. In November 1958 the young Jason Epstein, who had eagerly published *Pnin* and *Nabokov's Dozen* for Doubleday, flew from New York to Ithaca to secure Nabokov for the firm he had just joined, Random House, and proposed publishing three books: *Eugene Onegin;* an anthology of Russian poetry, including the masterpiece of Russian medieval poetry, *The Song of Igor's Campaign,* and "some Pushkin, some Lermontov, Tyutchev, possibly Blok & Hodasevich"; and Nabokov's greatest Russian novel, *The Gift.* Nabokov signed an agreement for an "Anthology of Russian Verse" in translation, which he expected to include, apart from the Igor epic, "three short dramas by Pushkin and poems from Lomonosov (XVIII century), through Zhukovski, Batyushkov, Tyutchev, Pushkin, Lermontov, Fet, to Blok."

But after spending a productive spring in Arizona, Nabokov realized by June 1959 that *The Song of Igor's Campaign* had become "a book in itself which cannot be combined with the kind of second half we had planned. That second half . . . would throw the book completely out of balance because it would necessarily lack the copious notes the first half has." Since the second half was "supposed to cover the entire century of Russia's renaissance in poetry, the commentary should have taken at least twice as many pages as that on *The Song.*" Nabokov realized he did not have the time, and Random House happily published *The Song of Igor's Campaign* on its own.

In the wake of *Lolita*'s triumph, Nabokov was kept busy both writing new novels and translating or supervising translations of his old Russian work. In 1968, dissatisfied with Putnam, the publisher of *Lolita,* he was ready to move to McGraw-Hill, which offered a large advance for a multibook contract that included *Ada.* Late in the year he proposed delivering a translation of his first novel, *Mary,* and "An Anthology of Russian Poets" by mid-January 1970. Other books, however, replaced that proposed anthology, and when a second multibook contract was being negotiated with McGraw-Hill late in 1973, Nabokov proposed an "Anthology of Russian Poetry in English" for delivery in 1978. By 1975 he had become too weak to advance the project, and by 1977 he was dead. When Véra recovered from the shock of his death, she wanted to compile the volume herself, but did not know where to turn to or how to find the time.

    Verses and Versions contains the anthology of Russian poets Nabokov proposed to McGraw-Hill, and more. It also includes some of Nabokov's discussions of translation (others are readily available in *Eugene Onegin* and *Strong Opinions*); the entire texts, both notes and translations, from his first anthologies of Russian verse (*Three Russian Poets*, 1944, expanded in the British edition of 1947 into *Pushkin, Lermontov, Tyutchev*); selections of notes and verses from the *Eugene Onegin* commentary, from his talks to fellow Russian émigrés and his still-unpublished Cornell lectures on Russian verse; and his translations of verse, by Mandelshtam and Okudzhava, more recent than he originally intended to include. Still left in the archives: Nabokov's Russian translations, early and late, from English, French, and German (Shakespeare, Baudelaire, Goethe, and others) and from Russian (Pushkin, Tyutchev) into French.

This volume therefore serves three linked purposes: as a treasury of Russian verse, as a workshop in translation, and as another showcase in the library of Nabokov's literary diversity.

First, it is an introduction to the classics of Russian lyric verse—an anthology of texts, translations, and pointed pen-portraits of poets—by the person who has already done more than anyone else to introduce to the Anglophone world the narrative masterpieces of medieval and modern Russian verse, *The Song of Igor's Campaign* and *Eugene Onegin*. Russia's prose and drama have been readily enjoyed and admired outside her borders, but it has taken the greatest writer working in both Russian and English to convince the English-speaking world through his translation and commentary that Pushkin is, as all Russians know, central to the Russian literary pantheon. As Korney Chukovsky writes, thanks to Nabokov's *Eugene Onegin*, "Pushkin, whose genius has until recently been concealed from a 'proud foreign gaze,' has at last become for readers abroad an established classic."

In *Verses and Versions* we can see other sides of Pushkin: his incomparable love lyrics; his verse dramas; his pungent epigrams; his range of emotions, forms, and themes. As translator and commentator, Nabokov places Pushkin in time and space, introducing first the origins of the Russian iamb in Lomonosov, then Pushkin's great predecessor Derzhavin, then Pushkin himself amid his contemporaries, then the successors he inspired even as they established new directions over the century that followed his early death.

To offer the reader maximum access to poems in another language and script, Nabokov first intended his *Eugene Onegin* translation to be published interlinearly, with each line of the translation beneath its transliterated and stress-marked Russian counterpart. He abandoned the idea when he correctly foresaw that the sheer bulk of his text—it turned out to be four printed volumes—would make publication difficult enough even without the extra expense of such an expanse of transliteration. But within the 1,200 pages of his commentary, Nabokov always transliterates and stress marks any Russian verse. And in 1966, for the last Russian verse translation he attempted (and failed) to publish, by the youngish Soviet poet Bulat Okudzhava, he carefully prepared a transliterated and stressed Russian text.

I had intended to follow Nabokov's practice in *Eugene Onegin*, but he himself found that for the sake of readers who know some Russian, from students to native speakers, the publisher of *Poems and Problems* required the originals of his own Russian poems that he translated for the volume to be printed in Cyrillic. For the same reason, we also present the originals of all Russian texts in Cyrillic. For those without Russian but with an interest in the placement of the original words and sounds, the Web site www .nabokovversesandversions.ac.nz contains transliterated and stress-marked texts of all the Russian texts here. Written Russian does not normally indicate stress, but stressed syllables are marked on the Web site transliteration, since even for intermediate students of Russian syllabic stress can often be difficult. Readers with little or no Russian can therefore engage with the originals, in print and on screen, with a reliable sense of the music and magic of their sound.

Had Nabokov lived to complete the anthology of Russian poetry himself, he would no doubt have affixed to each poet an introductory sketch as pithy and witty as those he wrote on Pushkin, Lermontov, and Tyutchev for *Three Russian Poets* in his first years in America. Those introductions are here, along with other astute commentaries, sometimes directed at fellow Russians for whom nothing needs to be explained, sometimes at Anglo-American readers or students of whom nothing can be assumed, sometimes at Anglo-American or Russian scholars.

The selection of poems is also more accidental than it would have been had it been entirely Nabokov's own. Nevertheless, it includes the range of poets he intended for his Russian anthology, like Pushkin, Lermontov, Tyutchev, Fet, and Hodasevich, whom he had already published, and other literary peaks. Nabokov translated poetry over many years, for many reasons and many different audiences: to introduce a new enthusiasm to a wider audience; as a personal tribute, or an exercise in the possibilities of translation, because he thought the model a masterpiece and a challenge (Shakespeare, Goethe, Baudelaire, Rimbaud); to have work to sell to periodical and book publishers in the early 1940s, when he still had no widespread American reputation, and, despite his command of English, found it painful to write fiction other than in Russian; to introduce Russian literature to a wider audience; to teach Russian literature, from 1947 to 1958; to establish his scholarly credentials during his academic years, in his copiously annotated and exact *Eugene Onegin* and *The Song of Igor's Campaign;* and as part of a polemical critique of other translators in the 1950s and '60s (Pushkin, Mandelshtam, Okudzhava).

What follows is not, therefore, Nabokov's selection of the top third or so of the three hundred perfect poems he believed had been written in Russian. He had selected over thirty of those in the poems from Pushkin to Hodasevich that he translated in the 1940s. About as many again in *Verses and Versions* might also sit in his top tier. Others are included simply because he translated them, especially as part of his vast *Eugene Onegin* apparatus. Pushkin's predecessors and contemporaries, and fragments of Pushkin's own minor poetry that merely happen to have some strong association with this or that part of *Eugene Onegin,* are all slightly overrepresented, yet all allow invaluable views of the context, life, and personality of Russia's greatest poet. And throughout the selection of the Pushkin poems in particular we can see Nabokov's particular interest—evident also in his still-unpublished lectures on Russian poetry—in Pushkin's poems about art and the artist, about freedom, and about the freedom of art and artist.

Not included are poems by four older Russian contemporaries Nabokov preferred not to translate but to parody, as he parodied T. S. Eliot in *Lolita, Pale Fire,* and *Ada:* Vladimir Mayakovsky, whom he thought "fatally corrupted by the regime he faithfully served"; Boris Pasternak, whose early poetry he respected but thought marred by clumsy lapses; Marina Tsvetaeva, whom he considered a flawed genius, and compromised in her relationship to Stalin's Soviet Union; and Anna Akhmatova, whom he rated, along with Ezra Pound, as "definitely B-grade," and parodied in *Pnin.*

Second, *Verses and Versions* is a master class in the possibilities and problems of literary translation. Nabokov became not only one of the most renowned writers of the twentieth century, but also the most celebrated translator—even though he ended up not translating *Ulysses* into Russian or *Anna Karenina* into English, as he had at various times intended. His *Eugene Onegin* provoked "what can be called the great debate on translation norms of the 1960s," which embroiled Edmund Wilson, Robert Lowell, George Steiner, and Anthony Burgess, and caused more of an uproar than anything on the subject since the famous polemics of Matthew Arnold and Francis Newman on translating *The Iliad* a hundred years earlier. Nabokov's extreme position on translating *Eugene Onegin* with unflinching literalism still polarizes. Pushkinist Alexander Dolinin writes that "everyone who has tried to teach *Eugene Onegin* in rhymed translations knows all too well that they make it a futile enterprise to convince even the most gullible students that Pushkin, to quote Edmund Wilson, 'is the only modern poet in the class of Shakespeare and Dante.'" But Douglas Hofstadter, writing two years later in his *Le Ton beau de Marot: In Praise of the Music of Language,* saw the eschewal of rhyme in translating rhymed verse as a betrayal; he demonizes "the rabid Nabokov," "the devil," "the implacably Nazistic Nabokov," for his "unrelenting verbal sadism" and "hardball savaging" that "goes way beyond bad taste." Nabokov in reply might have quoted his "Problems of Translation: *Onegin* in English": "To translate an *Onegin* stanza does not mean to rig up fourteen lines with alternate beats and affix to them seven jingle rhymes starting with pleasure-love-leisure-dove. Granted that rhymes can be found, they should be raised to the level of *Onegin's* harmonies"—but no ukulele can ever replicate a Stradivarius.

Although in teaching American students of Russian literature at Cornell and Harvard he developed an uncompromising literalism to allow them to appreciate great originals directly, not via pseudosurrogates, Nabokov had indeed been a superb translator of verse into verse, from four and into three languages. At Cornell he began translating *Onegin* in rhyme (no text survives) before deciding at the beginning of the 1950s that this was "sinful" and hopelessly misleading. Yet even in the *Eugene Onegin* commentary he offers rhymed translations of short poems by Lomonosov, Karamzin, Zhukovski, Batyushkov, and Pushkin. As late as 1959 and 1962, after completing his unversified *Onegin*, he entered *Sunday Times* poetry competitions, translating formally intricate French verse into formally intricate English verse (he signed the 1962 submission "Sybil Shade": In *Pale Fire*, published that year, Sybil, the wife of the poet John Shade, translates English verse into French). Nabokov's early verse translations attain rare heights of fidelity. In a comparative and strictly quantitative study of nineteen translations of *Eugene Onegin*, Russian scholar Ljuba Tarvi assesses Nabokov's verbal accuracy at between 98 and 100 percent, well ahead of the competition, but even in her sole example of his other translations from Russian (Tyutchev's "Silentium") she assigns him an unmatched score for combined verbal and formal equivalence of 97 percent.

But *Verses and Versions* does not pretend to be a collection of perfect or near-perfect translations. Some of Nabokov's translations come close: some of the poems of Pushkin, Lermontov, Tyutchev, Fet, and perhaps especially Hodasevich, which he translated for publication in the 1940s, before the needs of teaching students drove him to total fidelity to sense even at the cost of style. His other translations work as ideal cribs for accessing the originals. But the tribulations of translation, even for a writer with such a command of prose and verse style and history in three languages, are as fascinating as the triumphs. Nabokov's successive tries at translating a particular poem, with and without rhyme, show the sheer magnitude of the task, the impossibility of perfection, the possibility only of offering improved access to the original, but not of creating its image and equal.

Nabokov painstakingly worked and reworked his fiction to a state of serene finality. His translations were different. As he writes in an unpublished note, "Translations fade much more rapidly than the originals, and every time I re-read my versions I tend to touch them up here and there." So *Verses and Versions* is not only an anthology of two centuries of Russian poetry, but also a sampler of the problems and possibilities of literary translation, as demonstrated by someone who wrote and translated in three languages for over sixty years. The prose essays and talks that begin the volume articulate Nabokov's theory of translation, first in the 1940s, before he developed his provocative literalism, then in the 1950s, when he first began to formulate his new principles. Because the poems that follow are arranged chronologically not by the date of Nabokov's translations but according to the poet's date of birth and the poem's date of composition, readers will find themselves moving from a poem translated into a melodious poem, in Nabokov's own early manner, to another translated in his later exact but unpoetic manner, or vice versa. Sometimes the translation shifts to another version of the same poem, the gains and losses of each method bright on the page. Readers should therefore take note of the date of Nabokov's translation in the right-hand margin after the last line: Anything after 1950 is likely to display the unrhymed literalism of his later style.

Having concluded that it was impossible to translate poetry *as* poetry with total fidelity to both sense and verse form,

Nabokov at the end of the 1960s decided to show the exception that proved the rule, by composing a short poem simultaneously in English and Russian, with the same complex stanza structure: a poem about the very act of riding simultaneously on these two separate linguistic tightropes, each swinging to its own time. Even he found he could write only stiltedly under these disconcerting conditions, and he wisely abandoned the effort.

Much more successful was Nabokov's earlier attempt to create in English two stanzas in the strict form that Pushkin created for *Eugene Onegin,* in a poem about his translating *Onegin* (see p. 16). Pushkin's fourteen-line *Onegin* stanza ingeniously reworks the pattern of the sonnet so that, as Nabokov notes, "its first twelve lines include the greatest variation in rhyme sequence possible within a three-quatrain frame: alternate, paired, and closed." The stanza offers an internal variety of pace, direction, and duration that forms part of the poem's magic for Russian readers. To show non-Russian readers the variability of this very variety, Nabokov composes two stanzas in English that, like Pushkin's, modulate tone, pace, subject, imagery, and rhyme quality within the stanza and from stanza to stanza, so that the stanzas are both self-contained and internally changeable, and in the movement from one to another both continuous and contrasting. The first quatrain of stanza one stops and starts, with question and answer after abrupt dismissive imagistic answer; the first quatrain of the second stanza skims on unstopped, like a camera zooming through a fast-forward nightscape. Nabokov knows he cannot combine Pushkin's sense and pattern while transposing exactly Pushkin's precise thought into the different structures and associations of English, but at least he can impart to Anglophone readers a sense of the coruscating enchantment of Pushkin's stanza form.

Third, *Verses and Versions* offers not only an anthology of some of Russia's best poetry and a workshop on translation by a craftsman who worked in multiple directions and multiple modes, but another facet of one of the greatest and most multifaceted writers of the twentieth century—not only a major author in two languages, and in fiction, nonfiction, poetry, and drama, but also, as readers have come to realize, a world-class scientist, a groundbreaking scholar, and a translator.

Nabokov once said that he called the first version of his autobiography *Conclusive Evidence* because of the two *V*s at the center, linking Vladimir the author and Véra the anchor and addressee, as she proves to be by the end of the book. *Verses and Versions* similarly links Vladimir and Véra, who wanted to assemble a book like this as a monument to her husband's multifacetedness. It also pays homage to *Poems and Problems,* which, late in his career, introduced readers to Nabokov's Russian verse as well as his English, and to still another facet of his creativity: his world-class chess-problem compositions.

Pushkin has a special place in the hearts of all Russians who love literature. He has a particularly special place for Nabokov, throughout his Russian work (Pushkin is the tutelary deity of his last and greatest Russian novel, *The Gift,* which even ends with an echo of the ending of *Eugene Onegin,* in a perfect Onegin stanza, cast in prose) and throughout his efforts as an English writer to make Pushkin known. Pushkin is also a byword for the untranslatability of poetic greatness: unquestioned in his preeminence in his native land, yet long almost unrecognized in any other. Flaubert, one of the brightest stars in Nabokov's personal literary pléiade, famously remarked to Turgenev: "He is flat, your poet."

Nabokov himself discusses the untranslatability of one of Pushkin's great love lyrics in the first of his essays on translation. I would like here to consider another great love lyric, "Ya vas lyubíl" ("I loved you"), which Nabokov translated three times, in three different ways: in an awkward verse translation of 1929 and in a literal translation and a lexical (word-for-word) translation, accompanied by a stress-marked transliteration and a note, about twenty years later. None of these quite works (the lexical is not even meant to work, merely to supply the crudest crib); none of these can quite convince the English-language reader that this is one of the great love lyrics—one of the great lyrics of any kind—in any language.

Yet Nabokov is not alone. For the bicentennial of Pushkin's birth—and coincidentally the centennial of Nabokov's—Marita Crawley, a great-great-great-granddaughter of Pushkin and chairman of the British Pushkin Bicentennial Trust, asked herself how she could convince the English-speaking public that Pushkin's genius is as great as Russians claim. She answered herself: She would invite a number of leading poets to "translate" Pushkin poems, or rather to make poems out of Pushkin translations. In a volume for the Folio Society, she includes poets of the stature of Ted Hughes, Seamus Heaney, and Carol Ann Duffy. Duffy took "Ya vas lyubíl":

> I loved you once. If love is fire, then embers
> smoulder in the ashes of this heart.
> Don't be afraid. Don't worry. Don't remember.
> I do not want you sad now we're apart.
>
> I loved you without language, without hope,
> now mad with jealousy, now insecure.
> I loved you once so purely, so completely,
> I know who loves you next can't love you more.

Duffy is a fine poet, but I suspect few will think this one of literature's great lyrics—not that she is not as successful as other poets in *After Pushkin*. What is it that makes Pushkin's poem great?

I offer a plain translation into lineated prose:

> I loved you; love still, perhaps,
> In my heart has not quite gone out;
> But let it trouble you no more;
> I do not want to sadden you in any way.
> I loved you wordlessly, hopelessly,
> Now by timidity, now by jealousy oppressed;
> I loved you so sincerely, so tenderly,
> As God grant you may be loved by someone else.

My translation, if undistinguished, is acceptable, though I almost sinned by ending "As God grant you may be loved again." In Pushkin the last word is *drugím* and means "by another" (in context, "by another man"): "As God grant you may be loved by another." I should not have thought of closing with *again,* and would not have done so had I not been intending to supply a literal translation and a lexical one. On its own, *again* might be ambiguous, might suggest the speaker has perhaps ended up anticipating a complete revival of his own feelings. What is needed is a short, strong, decisive ending, and *again* at first seemed to supply some of this, though without the shift and precision of thought and feeling in Pushkin's *drugím,* where "As God grant you may be loved by another" ended too intolerably limply for me to tack it on to the rest of the translation.

The poem starts with what might seem banal, "Ya vas lyubíl," except that it is in the past, and that gives it its special angle. As Pushkin treats of the near-universal experience of having fallen out of love, he gradually moves from the not unusual—the change from present love to near past, the aftershock of emotions, the shift from desire to tender interest and concern—to the unexpected closing combination, the affirmation of the past love in the penultimate line, "I loved you so sincerely, so tenderly"; then to the selfless generosity of the last line, the hope that she will be loved again as well as *he* has loved her, that in its very lack of selfishness confirms the purity of the love he had and in some sense still has.

Where Duffy's "who loves you next" almost implies a lineup of lovers, Pushkin offers a surprise, yet utter emotional rightness and inevitability. Where Duffy's line becomes a near boast, emphasizing that the speaker's love is unsurpassable, Pushkin's speaker dismisses self to focus on and pray for his former love.

This is what Pushkin is like, again and again. He cuts directly to the core of a human feeling, in a way that makes it new and yet recognizably right and revelatory. He creates a complex emotional contour through swift suggestion, a scenario all the more imaginatively inviting by being unconstrained by character and event. His expression seems effortless and elegant, but his attention and ours is all on the accuracy of the emotion. In this poem Pushkin allows just a shadow of one metaphor, in the verb in the second line, *ugásla*, which can mean "gone out" or "extinguished," where Duffy feels the need to embellish and poeticize the image into "If love is fire, then embers / smoulder in the ashes of this heart," with a pun on "heart" and "hearth." This is inventive translation, but it is not Pushkin's steady focus on feeling. Duffy's lines draw attention to the poet, to the play. In other moods Pushkin can himself be supremely playful, and playfully self-conscious, in his own fashion, but here he offers an emotional directness and a verbal restraint amid formal perfection that is alien to English poetry and that to Duffy feels too bald to leave unadorned.

With your attention now engaged, ready to slow down and savor this poem, I offer below Pushkin's own words, transliterated and stressed, with an italicized word-for-word match below (a "lexical translation" in Nabokov's terms) and my strictly literal translation below that.

Ya vas lyubíl: lyubóv' eshchyó, bït' mózhet,
I   you loved: love   yet,   be   may,
I loved you; love, perhaps, has not yet

V dushé moéy ugásla ne sovsém;
In soul   my   gone-out not altogether
Quite gone out in my heart;

No pust' oná   vas ból'she ne trevózhit;
But let   it [my love] you more   not trouble;
But let it trouble you no more;

Ya ne hochú pechálit' vas nichém.
I   not want   to-sadden you in-any-way
I do not want to sadden you in any way.

Ya vas lyubíl bezmólvno, beznadézhno,
I   you loved   wordlessly, hopelessly.
I loved you wordlessly, hopelessly,

To   róbost'yu,   to   révnost'yu   tomím;
Now   by-timidity,   now   by-jealousy   tormented.
Now by shyness, now by jealousy oppressed;

Ya   vas   lyubíl   tak   ískrenno,   tak   nézhno,
I   you   loved   so   sincerely,   so   tenderly,
I loved you so sincerely, so tenderly,

Kak   day   vam   Bog   lyubímoy   bïty   drugím.
As   give   you   God   loved   to-be   by-another.
As God grant you may be loved by someone else.

Nabokov's note comments perceptively on the sound link between
lyubím and *drugím* in the last line, which makes the inevitability and
the surprise both greater. *Drugím,* coming last, rhyming quietly
and expectedly with *tomím* but also happening to echo the *lyubímoy*
it is linked so closely to in sense, sets off the whole poem's explosive
emotional charge in its final word, without resorting to anything
conventionally "poetic." As Alexander Zholkovsky notes, moreover,
a Russian might well expect a short poem beginning *Ya vas lyubíl,*
"I loved you," and leading up to a rhyme with *tomím* to end with the
word *lyubím,* "(be)loved"; instead it ends with *drugím,* "by another,"
as if to compress the difference between the *ya,* the "I" who used
to love you in the poem's first word, and this *drugím,* this "other" in
the poem's last word, who perhaps *will* love you so well.

Nabokov first tried to translate this poem, uncharacteristically,
in 1929, when he was developing as a Russian writer, and almost al-
ways translating into rather than from Russian. (The occasion was
the centenary of the poem's composition, and since Nabokov was
born a hundred years after Pushkin, he was translating it at the age
at which Pushkin wrote it.) The translation (p. 129) opens with the
eyebrow-raising "I worshipped you." Although not strictly equiva-
lent to Pushkin, this phrase reflects the sense that the speaker has
indeed worshipped the beloved "wordlessly, hopelessly," passively
and distantly rather than actively and intimately, and its stress pro-
vides a reasonably close match for the metrical force of Pushkin's

opening "Ya vas lyubíl." But "I worshipped you" becomes increasingly a liability as the poem progresses and it has to be repeated each time "loved" or "love" would normally return. In general, the translation sacrifices too much sense to keep Pushkin's stresses and his alternating feminine/masculine rhymes. Nabokov chooses the same "ember"/"remember" rhyme that Duffy independently arrives at, but maintains the rhyme where Duffy abandons the effort halfway through. But his rhymes are trite (fashion/passion, true/you) and the whole poem too compliantly follows tired English verse conventions.

By the 1940s Nabokov's verse translations into English were far more assured, and often superb. By the 1950s he had committed himself to literalism, but sometimes with uneasy compromises, if not for the sake of rhyme, then for the sake of rhythm. In the case of "Ya vas lyubíl," his lexical translation often seems closer than the literal translation, not only to Pushkin's words but to his power. The line "now by shyness, now by jealousy oppressed," which I have gladly drawn on, captures the order, the sense, and, except for the tight sound patterns, the impact of Pushkin's "To róbost'yu, to révnost'yu tomím." For some reason Nabokov "improved" this into a literal version, "either by shyness irked or jealousy," supposedly better English and no less accurate, yet in fact both less accurate and more awkward. The last line of the literal version does improve the last line ("as give you God to be loved by another") of the lexical, but only into "as by another loved God grant you be," which has the sense but neither the clarity nor the éclat of Pushkin's line.

Nabokov says he regularly felt the urge to tinker with his translations, and he may well have continued to do so here had he prepared his own *Verses and Versions*. But the difficulties he himself had translating his favorite Russian poet—difficulties he expresses eloquently and ironically in his own voice—are as interesting as, and deliberately more challenging than, his successes. Nabokov uncompromisingly translates the second line of "Ya vas lyubíl" as "not quite extinguished in my soul." I rendered it as "in my heart has not quite gone out." In Russian, *dushá*, "soul," is far more common than its English equivalent and covers much of the territory of the heart as the conventional seat of the emotions. Nabokov, in refusing to compromise on "soul," points to a difference between Russian and English that lies at the core of the difference between an English speaker's and a Russian's sense of self and other and of life and death.

Pushkin famously compared translators to horses changed at the post houses of civilization. In his earlier and more accessible translations, Nabokov makes us feel the posthorses have arrived, that we are meeting Pushkin, Lermontov, Tyutchev, or Hodasevich almost face-to-face. In his later work, translation is not the illusion of arrival but the start of a journey—glimpses of the destination, but also of the bracing rigors of the intervening terrain. Through the contrasting strategies within *Verses and Versions,* as through the special methods of *Eugene Onegin,* Nabokov continues to prod English-speaking readers into persisting on their journey toward the peaks of Russian poetry.

Brian Boyd
December 2006

I. NABOKOV ON TRANSLATION

THE ART OF TRANSLATION
(I: "A FEW PERFECT RULES")

      I thought I might say a few words about this pathetic business of translating, and I thought I might compare the various types of translators to the various types of teachers. I should warn you that I am not a teacher of any language myself—in fact there is a kind of iron curtain painted green, or let us say a green velvet curtain, between Goldwin Smith Hall where I teach literature and the remote Morrill Hall, where the Russian language is taught. But since in my literature classes I am constantly faced with the problem of translating Russian and French into English, I think I have a fair idea of the difficulties an expert in language encounters.

      I am not speaking of the difficulties that the student encounters when taught to say, for example,—this is one of the nicest tongue twisters I could invent: *Vīkarabkavshiesya vīhoholi okoléli u koléblyush-chegosya kolokololitéyshchika*—the martins that had scrambled out died a beast's death at the hesitating maker's of church bells.

      Translation is a controversial subject. In one camp, we have the scholar, the artist, the reader. In the other camp we have the ill-paid drudge, who translates as best he can, the cautious humbug, who does not know the foreign language and cannot write his own, and the publisher who does not give a damn for such niceties and always prefers an adaptation anyway.

Can we do without translators? Can every educated man know at least five foreign languages besides his own?—and as well as his own,—that is the point. English, mainly because of its poetry, obviously heads the list. French and Russian compete for second place. Italian, Spanish and German come next—which makes in all six languages that a man must know in deep and exquisite detail in order to enjoy Shakespeare, Flaubert, Tyutchev, Dante, Cervantes and Kafka. And there are other languages, other great poets in those languages . . . and what about Latin, what about Greek? How then can one do without translators?

I know of one old gentleman now dead, head of a Slavic department in a great university not necessarily in this country who could not utter or write a single Russian sentence without making a mistake, and whose translations from the Russian, published under his name, were written by anonymous natives. This is the common ground where the incompetent teacher and the incompetent translator meet—the man who for years conceals the treasure of his ignorance and lives in solecism as others live in sin.

Three grades of evil can be discerned in the queer world of verbal transmigration. The first, and lesser one, comprises obvious errors due to ignorance or misguided knowledge. This is mere human frailty and thus excusable. The next step to Hell is taken by the translator who intentionally skips words or passages that he does not bother to understand or that might seem obscure or obscene to vaguely imagined readers; he accepts the blank look that his dictionary gives him without any qualms; or subjects scholarship to primness: he is as ready to know less than the author as he is to think he knows better. The third, and worst, degree of turpitude is reached when a masterpiece is planished and patted into such a shape, vilely beautified in such a fashion as to conform to the notions and prejudices of a given public. This is a crime, to be punished by the stocks, as plagiarists were in the shoebuckle days.

The howlers included in the first category may be in their turn divided into two classes. Insufficient acquaintance with the foreign language involved may transform a commonplace expression into some remarkable statement that the real author never intended to make. *"Bien-être general"* becomes the manly assertion that "it is good to be a general"; to which gallant general a French translator of *Hamlet* has been known to pass the caviar. Likewise, in a German edition of Chekhov, a certain teacher, as soon as he enters the classroom, is made to become engrossed in "his newspaper," which prompted a pompous reviewer to comment on the sad condition of public instruction in pre-Soviet Russia. But the real Chekhov was simply referring to the classroom "journal" which a teacher would open to check lessons, marks and absentees. And inversely, innocent words in an English novel such as "first night" and "public house" have become in a Russian translation "nuptial night" and "a brothel." These simple examples suffice. They are ridiculous and jarring, but they contain no pernicious purpose; and more often than not the garbled sentence still makes some sense in the original context.

The other class of blunders in the first category includes a more sophisticated kind of mistake, one which is caused by an attack of linguistic Daltonism suddenly blinding the translator. Whether attracted by the far-fetched when the obvious was at hand (What does an Eskimo prefer to eat—ice cream or tallow? Ice cream), or whether unconsciously basing his rendering on some false meaning which repeated readings have imprinted on his mind, he manages to distort in an unexpected and sometimes quite brilliant way the most honest word or the tamest metaphor. I knew a very conscientious poet who in wrestling with the translation of a much tortured text rendered "is sicklied o'er with the pale cast of thought" in such a manner as to convey an impression of pale moonlight. He did this by taking for granted that "sickle" referred to the form of the new moon. And a national sense of humor, set into motion by the likeness between the Russian words meaning "arc" and "onion," led a German professor to translate "a bend of the shore" (in a Pushkin fairy tale) by "the Onion sea."

The second, and much more serious, sin of leaving out tricky passages is still excusable when the translator is baffled by them himself; but how contemptible is the smug person who, although quite understanding the sense, fears it might stump a dunce or debauch a dauphin! Instead of blissfully nestling in the arms of the great writer, he keeps worrying about the little reader playing in a corner with something dangerous or unclean. Perhaps the most charming example of Victorian modesty that has ever come my way was in an early translation of *Anna Karenin*. Vronski had asked Anna what was the matter with her. "I am *beremenna*" (the translator's italics), replied Anna, making the foreign reader wonder what strange and awful Oriental disease that was; all because the translator thought that "I am pregnant" might shock some pure soul, and that a good idea would be to leave the Russian just as it stood.

But masking and toning down seem petty sins in comparison with those of the third category: for here he comes strutting and shooting out his bejeweled cuffs, the slick translator who arranges Scheherazade's boudoir according to his own taste and with professional elegance tries to improve the looks of his victims. Thus it was the rule with Russian versions of Shakespeare to give Ophelia richer flowers than the poor weeds she found. The Russian rendering of

> There with fantastic garlands did she come
> Of crowflowers, nettles, daisies and long purples

if translated back into English would run like this:

> There with most lovely garlands did she come
> Of violets, carnations, roses, lilies.

The splendor of this floral display speaks for itself; incidentally it bowdlerized the Queen's digressions, granting her the gentility she so sadly lacked and dismissing the liberal shepherds; how anyone could make such a botanical collection beside the Helje or the Avon is another question.

But no such questions were asked by the solemn Russian reader, first, because he did not know the original text; second, because he did not care a fig for botany; and, third, because the only thing that interested him in Shakespeare was what the German commentators and the native Russian radicals had discovered in the way of "eternal problems." So nobody minded what happened to Goneril's lap-dogs when the line

> Tray, Blanche and Sweetheart, see, they bark at me

was grimly metamorphosed into

> A pack of hounds is barking at my heels.

All local color, all tangible and irreplaceable details were swallowed by those hounds.

But, revenge is sweet—even unconscious revenge. The greatest Russian short story ever written is Gogol's "Overcoat" (or "Mantle," or "Cloak," or "She-nel," most properly called a "Carrick"). Its essential feature, that irrational part which forms the tragic undercurrent of an otherwise meaningless anecdote, is organically connected with the special style in which this story is written: there are weird repetitions of the same absurd adverb, and these repetitions become a kind of uncanny incantation; there are descriptions which look innocent enough until you discover that chaos lies right round the corner, and that Gogol has inserted into this or that harmless sentence a word or a simile that makes a passage burst into a wild display of nightmare fireworks. There is also that groping clumsiness which, on the author's part, is a conscious rendering of the uncouth gestures of our dreams. Nothing of these remains in the prim, and perky, and very matter-of-fact English version (see—and never see again—"The Mantle," translated by Claude Field). The following example leaves me with the impression that I am witnessing a murder and can do nothing to prevent it:

GOGOL: . . . his [a petty official's] third or fourth-story flat . . . displaying a few fashionable trifles, *such as a lamp for instance*—trifles purchased by many sacrifices . . .

FIELD: . . . fitted with some pretentious articles of furniture purchased, etc. . . .

Tampering with foreign major or minor masterpieces may involve an innocent third party in the farce. Quite recently a famous Russian composer asked me to translate into English a Russian poem which, forty years before, he had set to music. The English translation, he pointed out, had to follow closely the very sounds of the text—which text was unfortunately K. Balmont's version of Edgar Allan Poe's "Bells." What Balmont's numerous translations look like may be readily understood when I say that his own work invariably disclosed an almost pathological inability to write one single melodious line. Having at his disposal a sufficient number of hackneyed rhymes and taking up as he rode any hitch-hiking metaphor that he happened to meet, he turned something that Poe had taken considerable pains to compose into something that any Russian rhymester could dash off at a moment's notice. In reversing it into English I was solely concerned with finding English words that would sound like the Russian ones. Now, if somebody one day comes across my English version of that Russian version, he may foolishly retranslate it into Russian so that the Poe-less poem will go on being balmontized until, perhaps, "The Bells" become "The Silence."

Something still more grotesque happened to Baudelaire's exquisitely dreamy "Invitation au Voyage" ("Mon enfant, ma soeur, Songe à la douceur . . ."). The Russian version was due to the pen of Merezhkovski, who had even less poetical talent than Balmont. It began like this:

My sweet little bride,
Let's go for a ride;

Promptly it begot a rollicking tune and was adopted by all the organ-grinders in Russia. I like to imagine future French translators of Russian folksongs re-Frenchifying it into

Viens, mon p'tit,
A Nijni

and so on, *ad malinfinitum.*

Barring downright deceivers, mild imbeciles and impotent poets, there exist, roughly speaking, three types of translators. This has nothing to do with my three categories of evil—ignorance, omission, and adaptation—although any of the three types may err in a similar way. These three types are: the scholar who is eager to make the world appreciate the works of an obscure genius as much as he does himself; the well-meaning hack; and the professional writer relaxing in the company of a foreign confrère. The scholar will be, I hope, exact and pedantic: footnotes—on the *same* page as the text and not tucked away at the end of the volume—can never be too copious and detailed. The laborious lady translating at the eleventh hour the eleventh volume of somebody's collected works will be, I am afraid, less exact and less pedantic. But the point is not that the scholar commits fewer blunders than the drudge; the point is that as a rule both he and she are hopelessly devoid of any semblance of creative genius. Neither learning nor diligence can replace imagination and style.

Now comes the authentic poet who has the two last assets and who finds relaxation in translating a bit of Lermontov or Verlaine between writing poems of his own. Either he does not know the original language and calmly relies upon the so-called "literal" translation made for him by a far less brilliant but a little more learned person, or else, knowing the language, he lacks the scholar's precision and the professional translator's experience. The main drawback in this case, however, is the fact that the greater his individual talent, the more apt he will be to drown the foreign masterpiece under the sparkling ripples of his own personal style. Instead of dressing up like the real author, he dresses up the author as himself.

We can deduce now the requirements that a translator must possess in order to be able to give an ideal version of a foreign masterpiece. First of all, he must have as much talent, or at least the same kind of talent, as the author he chooses. In this, though only in this, respect Baudelaire and Poe or Zhukovski and Schiller made ideal playmates. Second, he must know thoroughly the two nations and the two languages involved and be perfectly acquainted with all details relating to his author's manner and methods; also, with the social background of words, their fashions, history and period associations. This leads to the third point: while having genius and knowledge he must possess the gift of mimicry and be able to act, as it were, the real author's part by impersonating his tricks of demeanor and speech, his ways and his mind, with the utmost degree of verisimilitude.

I have at various times tried to translate several Russian poets who had either been badly disfigured by former attempts or who had never been translated at all. The English at my disposal was certainly thinner than my Russian—the difference being, in fact, that which exists between a semi-detached villa and a hereditary estate, between self-conscious comfort and habitual luxury. I am not satisfied therefore with the results attained, but my studies disclosed several rules that other writers might follow with profit.

I was confronted, for instance, with the following opening line of one of Pushkin's most prodigious poems:

Yah pom-new chewed-no-yay mg-no-vain-yay

I have rendered the syllables by the nearest English sounds I could find; their mimetic disguise makes them look rather ugly; but never mind; the *chew* and the *vain* are associated phonetically with other Russian words meaning beautiful and important things, and the melody of the line with the plump, golden-ripe *chewed-no-yay* right in the middle and the *m*'s and *n*'s balancing each other on both sides, is to the Russian ear most exciting and soothing—a paradoxical combination that any artist will understand.

Now, if you take a dictionary and look up those four words you will obtain the following foolish, flat and familiar statement: "I remember a wonderful moment." What is to be done with this bird you have shot down only to find that is not a bird of paradise, but an escaped parrot, still screeching its idiotic message as it flaps on the ground? For no stretch of the imagination can persuade an English reader that "I remember a wonderful moment" is the perfect beginning of a perfect poem. *Yah pom-new* is a deeper and smoother plunge into the past than "I remember," which falls flat on its belly like an inexperienced diver; *chewed-no-yay* has a lovely Russian "monster" (*chúdo*) in it; and a whispered "listen" (*chu!*); and the dative ending of a sunbeam (*luchú*), and many other fair relations among Russian words. It belongs phonetically and mentally to a certain series of words, and this Russian series does not correspond to the English series in which "I remember" is found. And inversely, "remember," though it clashes with the corresponding "pom-new" series, is connected with an English series of its own whenever real poets do use it. And the central word in Housman's "What are those blue *remembered* hills?" becomes in Russian *vspom-neev-she-yes-yah,* a horrible straggly thing, all humps and horns, which cannot fuse into any inner connection with "blue," as it does so smoothly in English, because the Russian sense of blueness belongs to a different series than the Russian "remember" does.

The interrelation of words and non-correspondence of verbal series in different tongues suggest yet another rule, namely, that the three main words of the line draw one another out, and add something which none of them would have had separately or in any other combination. What makes this exchange of secret values possible is not only the mere contact between words, but their exact position in regard both to the rhythm of the line and to one another. This must be taken into account by the translator.

Finally, there is the problem of rhyme. *Mg-no-vain-yay* has over two thousand Jack-in-the-box rhymes popping out at the slightest pressure, whereas I cannot think of one to "moment." The position of *mg-no-vain-yay* at the end of the line is not negligible either, due, as it is, to Pushkin's more or less consciously knowing that he would not have to hunt for its mate. But the position of "moment" in the English line implies no such security; on the contrary he would be a singularly reckless fellow who placed it there.

Thus I was confronted by that opening line, so full of Pushkin, so individual and harmonious; and after examining it gingerly from the various angles here suggested, I tackled it. The tackling process lasted the worst part of the night. I did translate it at last; but to give my version at this point might lead the reader to doubt that perfection may be attained by merely following a few perfect rules.

1941, ca. 1951

PITY THE ELDERLY GRAY TRANSLATOR

Now I have blundered into a situation from which it is psychologically rather difficult to display one's own ability after such an introduction. So let us tackle the question from another angle. Let us see what generally happens, when, say, a good translator goes into action. I have described him in my own verse, and I ask you to pity him.

Pity the elderly gray translator
Who lends to beauty his hollow voice
And—choosing sometimes a second-rater—
Mimes the song-fellow of his choice.
To sacred sense for the sake of meter
His is seldom traitor as traitors go,
But pity him when he quakes with Peter
And waits for the *terza rima* to crow.

It is not the head of the verse line that'll
Cause him trouble, nor is it the spine:
What he really minds is the cursed rattle
That must be found for the tail of the line.

Some words by nature are sort of singlish,
Others have harems of rimes. The word
"Elephant," for example, walks alone in English
But its Slavic equivalent goes about in a herd.
"Woman" is another famous poser
For none can seriously contemplate
An American president or a German composer
In a viable context with that word for mate.
Since rime is a national repercussion
(And a local holiday), how bizarre
That "skies-eyes" should twin in French and Russian:
"*Cieux-yeux*," "nebesá-glazá."

Such boons are irrelevant. Sooner or later
The gentle person, the mime sublime,
The incorruptible translator
Is betrayed by lady rime.
And the poem from the Persian
And the sonnet spun in Spain
Perish in the person's version,
And the person dies insane.

THE ART OF TRANSLATION
(II: "A KIND OF V MOVEMENT")

To begin—I want to say a few words about the art of translation, after which I shall give my versions of four poems by a famous nineteenth-century Russian author. Translation is travel, and may be said to consist of three stages. First—the stage of study and sympathy. If we compare the original poem to a flowerhead, then our first lap is a penetrating descent, a sliding journey down the stem, from the flowerhead to the hidden root. Here we arrive at the next stage—the stage of inspiration. The hidden root is rich, and within its humid heart we find the necessary exhilaration and impetus for our endeavour. The third and final stage is impersonation and expression. It is now an upward journey in another language, from the shared root, up a new stalk, to a new flowerhead; and there we unfold, on the level of the original. It is all a kind of *V* movement: down one stem and up another. This is true translation.

The next question is, how to describe that ideal person, the perfect translator? Let us imagine two fair countries, From and Into, the far hills of From and the translator's homeland Into. The translation is From Into. Now, first of all the perfect translator should know the From language as well as he does the Into language. He should also be acquainted with the manners, traditions, fauna, flora and times of both countries. He should have a special knowledge of the works of his author, John From, and a deep insight into the literature of which he is part. He, John Into, should have genius, style, vision and wit. He should be absolutely honest, should not bypass difficulties, should never let down poor John From (who is generally dead, anyway, and cannot hit back). He should be of the same sex as his author. He should never toady to public or publisher. He should be paid princely sums for his work. Blunders and boners should be punishable by heavy fines; trimmings and omissions by the stocks.

ON TRANSLATING "EUGENE ONEGIN"

1

What is translation? On a platter
A poet's pale and glaring head,
A parrot's screech, a monkey's chatter,
And profanation of the dead.
The parasites you were so hard on
Are pardoned if I have your pardon,
O, Pushkin, for my stratagem:
I traveled down your secret stem,
And reached the root, and fed upon it;
Then, in a language newly learned,
I grew another stalk and turned
Your stanza patterned on a sonnet,
Into my honest roadside prose—
All thorn, but cousin to your rose.

2

Reflected words can only shiver
Like elongated lights that twist
In the black mirror of a river

Between the city and the mist.
Elusive Pushkin! Persevering,
I still pick up Tatiana's earring,
Still travel with your sullen rake.
I find another man's mistake,
I analyze alliterations
That grace your feasts and haunt the great
Fourth stanza of your Canto Eight.
This is my task—a poet's patience
And scholiastic passion blent:
Dove-droppings on your monument.

1954

ONE DAY, EXUBERANT
AND GALLANT

In order to give such readers as have no Russian some notion of the standard modulations in a Russian sequence of iambic tetrameters at the time of their greatest popularity with major and minor poets, i.e. during the first third of the Nineteenth Century, I have devised the following dummy. In no way should it be regarded as a parody of an "Onegin" stanza. Its only purpose is to illustrate the dominant melody—and, incidentally, the rhyme scheme of which more anon—characteristic of such a stanza; but with a different arrangement of rhymes the diagram is good for any piece of verse—elegy, ode, epistle, descriptive or narrative poem, etc.—of that time and that place. It will be noticed at once that what makes the main difference between these Russian patterns of rhythm and those of English poets, is not so much the abundant scudding, with resultant figures of rhythm, as the almost obsessive preponderance of scud III.

The result is a sustained motion and rapidity of flow unusual in the case of English iambic tetrameters.

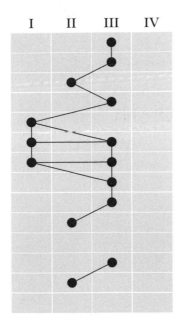

One day, exuberant and gallant,
The next, untalkative, morose;
Now raving of a poet's talent,
Then praising sedentary prose;
Unceremonious; very proper;
Foe of the Ant, but no Grasshopper,
Most unpredictably amused;
On Monday ruffled and confused,
On Tuesday whimsically tidy,
On Wednesday at a fistic fight,
With Iris dancing Thursday night,
Alone in Paradise all Friday,
On Saturday en route to Rose,
In Hell by Sunday. So it goes.

1957

II. NABOKOV: VERSES AND VERSIONS

MIHAIL VASILIEVICH LOMONOSOV
(1711–1765)

ON MIHAIL LOMONOSOV

The godfather of the iambic tetrameter is the famous reformer Lomonosov.

In September, 1739, in a "Letter about the Rules of Russian Versification" (first published in 1778), which Mihail Lomonosov (1711–65) sent (from the German university town of Freiburg, where he was studying metallurgy) to the members of a philologic committee attached to the Academy of Sciences in St. Petersburg, he advocated the total adoption of the metrical system and added as a separate illustrative item the first Russian poem, an ode, entirely and deliberately composed in iambic tetrameters. This is the *Ode to the Sovereign of Blessed Memory Anna Ioannovna on the Victory over the Turks and Tatars and on the Taking of Hotin* (or Khotin, a fortress in Bessarabia, SW Russia, formerly an old Genoese citadel, restored by the Turks with the assistance of French engineers, and stormed by Russian troops on Aug. 19, 1739). . . .

In its preserved form of 1751 *The Hotinian Ode* begins:

> Vostórg vnezápnïy um pleníl,
> Vedyót na verh gorí vïsókoy
> Gde vétr v lesáh shumét' zabíl;
> 4 V dolíne tishiná glubókoy;
> Vnimáya néchto, klyúch molchít,
> Kotórïy zavsegdá zhurchít
> I s shúmom vníz s holmóv stremítsya.
> 8 Lavróvï v'yútsya tám ventsí,
> Tam slúh speshít vo vsé kontsí;
> Daléche dím v polyáh kurítsya.

> A sudden rapture thralls the mind,
> leads to the top of a high mountain
> where wind in woods forgets to sound;
> 4 there is a hush in the deep valley;
> to something listing silent is
> the spring that murmured all the time
> and down the hills with noise went surging;
> 8 there, laurel crowns are being wound;
> there, hastes a rumor to all points;
> smoke in the fields afar is rising.

The fountain is Castalia, on Mt. Parnassus.

[. . .]

Like all Lomonosov's verses, *The Hotinian Ode* has little poetic merit, but prepares the advent of Derzhavin, who was the first real poet in Russia. It should be noted that despite the clumsiness of Lomonosov's idiom, with its obscure banalities and perilous inversions of speech, his iambic tetrameter already includes all the modulations that Derzhavin, Batyushkov, Zhukovski, and Pushkin brought to such perfection.

1951–57

КРАТКОЕ РУКОВОДСТВО К РИТОРИКЕ

Сходящей с поль златых Авроры
Рука багряна сыплет к нам
Брильянтов, искр, цветов узоры,
Дает румяный вид полям,
Светящей ризой мрак скрывает
И к сладким песням птиц взбуждает.
Чистейший луч доброт твоих
Украсил мой усердный стих.
От блеску Твоея порфиры
Яснеет тон нижайшей лиры.

1744

from
A BRIEF MANUAL OF RHETORIC

From golden fields descends Aurora
On us with crimson hand to strew
Her brilliants, sparks, festoons of Flora,
To give the fields a rosy hue;
To hide the dark with her bright cloak
And birds to mellow songs provoke.
Most pure, the ray of blessings thine
Doth ornament my zealous line;
Grows clearer in thy purple's fire
The tone of my most humble lyre.

1951–57

from

ПЕТР ВЕЛИКИЙ, ГЕРОИЧЕСКАЯ ПОЭМА
Песнь первая

[. . .]
Колумбы Росские, презрев угрюмый рок,
Меж льдами новый путь отворят на восток,
И наша досягнет в Америку держава;

[. . .]

1760

from
PETER THE GREAT, A HEROIC POEM
Canto One

Russian Columbuses, despising gloomy fate,
shall open a new path mid ice floes to the east,
and to America our empire shall extend.

1951–57

GAVRILA ROMANOVICH DERZHAVIN
(1743–1816)

ON GAVRILA DERZHAVIN

The greatest Russian poems of the eighteenth century are Derzhavin's majestic odes to his queen and his God.

1951–57

Gavrila Derzhavin (1743–1816) is Russia's first outstanding poet. His celebrated *God: an Ode* (1784), with its curious borrowings from Friedrich Gottlieb Klopstock (German poet, 1724–1803, author of *Messias*, 1748–73) and Edward Young (English poet, 1683–1765, author of *Night Thoughts*, 1742–45), his odes of the same period to *Felitsa* (Catherine II), and such poems of the 1790s as *The Grandee* and *The Waterfall* contain many great passages, colorful images, rough touches of genius. He made interesting experiments in broken meter and assonance, techniques that did not interest the next generation, the iambophile poets of Pushkin's time. Derzhavin influenced Tyutchev much more than he did [Pushkin], whose diction came early under the spell of Karamzin, Bogdanovich, Dmitriev, and especially Batyushkov and Zhukovski.

In his memoirs (1852), Sergey Aksakov (1791–1859), a very minor writer, tremendously puffed up by Slavophile groups, recalls that in December, 1815, Derzhavin told him that the schoolboy Pushkin would grow to be another Derzhavin. Aksakov's recollection was at the time almost half a century old.

Pushkin himself modestly implies a certain act of succession:

> The aged Derzhavin noticed us—
> and blessed us . . .

Not to young Pushkin, however, but to Zhukovski did old Derzhavin address the lines:

> To you in legacy, Zhukovski,
> My antiquated lyre I hand,
> While o'er the slippery grave abysmal
> Already with bent brow I stand.

And not Derzhavin, but Zhukovski did young Pushkin apostrophize in the final stanza of his ode *Recollections at Tsarskoe Selo* (an enthusiastic survey of historical associations, in 176 iambic lines of varying length with alternate rhymes, composed in 1814), which jolted Derzhavin out of his senile somnolence. But let us turn to Pushkin's own notes of 1830 (*Works* 1936, V, 461):

> I saw Derzhavin only once in my life but shall never forget that occasion. It was in 1815 [Jan. 8] at a public examination in the Lyceum. When we boys learned that Derzhavin was coming, all of us grew excited. Delvig went out on the stairs to wait for him and kiss his hand, the hand that had written *The Waterfall*. Derzhavin arrived. He entered the vestibule, and Delvig heard him ask the janitor: "Where is the privy here, my good fellow?" This prosaic question disenchanted Delvig, who canceled his intent and returned to the reception hall. Delvig told me the story with wonderful bonhomie and good humor. Derzhavin was very old. He was in uniform and wore velveteen boots. Our

examination was very wearisome to him. He sat with his head propped on one hand. His expression was inane, his eyes were dull, his lip hung; the portrait that shows him in housecap and dressing gown is very like him. He dozed until the beginning of the examination in Russian literature. *Then* he came to life, his eyes sparkled; he was transfigured. It was, of course, *his* poems that were read, *his* poems that were analyzed, *his* poems that were praised every minute. He listened with extraordinary animation [*s zhivost'yu neobï-knovennoy*]. At last I was called. I recited my *Recollections at Tsarskoe Selo* while standing within two yards of Derzhavin. I cannot describe the state of my soul; when I reached the verse where Derzhavin's name is mentioned [l. 63], my adolescent voice vibrated and my heart throbbed with intoxicating rapture. . . . I do not remember how I finished my recitation [he turned to Derzhavin as he launched upon the last sixteen lines, which were really addressed to Zhukovski, but might be taken to mean Derzhavin]. I do not remember whither I fled. Derzhavin was delighted; he demanded I come, he desired to embrace me. . . . There was a search for me, but I was not discovered.

1951–57

ПАМЯТНИК

Я памятник себе воздвиг чудесный, вечный;
Металлов тверже он и выше пирамид:
Ни вихрь его, ни гром не сломит быстротечный
И времени полет его не сокрушит.

Так!—весь я не умру; но часть меня большая,
От тлена убежав, по смерти станет жить,
И слава возрастет моя, не увядая,
Доколь Славянов род вселенна будет чтить.

Слух про́йдет обо мне от Белых вод до Черных,
Где Волга, Дон, Нева, с Рифея льет Урал;
Всяк будет помнить то в народах неисчетных,
Как из безвестности я тем известен стал,

Что первый я дерзнул в забавном русском слоге
О добродетелях Фелицы возгласить,
В сердечной простоте беседовать о Боге
И истину царям с улыбкой говорить.

О Муза! возгордись заслугой справедливой
И, презрит кто тебя, сама тех презирай:
Непринужденною рукой, неторопливой,
Чело твое зарей бессмертия венчай.

1795

* * *

I've set up to myself a monument,
wondrous, eternal. Stronger 'tis than metals,
higher than pyramids. Neither fleet thunder,
nor whirlwinds, nor the flight of time can break it.

So! I'll not wholly die; a large part of me,
fleeing decay, will after death exist;
my fame will grow, nor will it fade as long
as Slavs are by the universe respected.

Tidings of me will go from White to Black Sea,
where flow Neva, Don, Volga, where Ural
from Riphaeus flows. Tribes countless will remember
how I, unknown, became renowned, because

I was the first in the quaint Russian style
to dare proclaim the virtues of Felitsa,
with simpleheartedness converse of God,
and with a smile to monarchs speak the truth.

O Muse, be justly proud of your achievement
and if by some you're scorned, scorn them yourself,
and with a hand unforced, unhurried, crown
your brow with dawning immortality.

1951–57

GAVRILA DERZHAVIN   33

NIKOLAY MIHAYLOVICH KARAMZIN
(1766–1826)

ON NIKOLAY KARAMZIN

Pushkin had been well acquainted with him in 1818–20, and appreciated him chiefly as a reformer of language and as the historian of Russia . . .

Karamzin's charming, graceful, but now seldom remembered verses (*My Trifles,* 1794) . . . are artistically above his prose fiction.

In his truly marvelous reform of the Russian literary language, Karamzin neatly weeded out rank Church Slavonic and archaic Germanic constructions (comparable, in their florid, involved, and uncouth character, to bombastic Latinisms of an earlier period in western Europe); he banned inversions, ponderous compounds, and monstrous conjunctions, and introduced a lighter syntax, a Gallic precision of diction, and the simplicity of natural-sounding neologisms exactly suited to the semantic needs, both romantic and realistic, of his tremendously style-conscious time. Not only his close followers, Zhukovski and Batyushkov, but eclectic Pushkin and reluctant Tyutchev remained eternally in Karamzin's debt. Whilst, no doubt, in the idiom Karamzin promoted, the windows of a gentleman's well-waxed drawing room open wide onto a Le

Nôtre garden with its tame fountains and trim turf, it is also true that, through those same French windows, the healthy air of rural Russia came flowing in from beyond the topiary. But it was Krïlov (followed by Griboedov), not Karamzin, who first made of colloquial, earthy Russian a truly literary language by completely integrating it in the poetic patterns that had come into existence after Karamzin's reform.

1951–57

ДВА СРАВНЕНИЯ

Что наша жизнь? Роман.—Кто автор? Аноним.
Читаем по складам—смеемся, плачем—спим.

1797

from
TWO SIMILES

Life? A Romance. By whom? Anonymous.
We spell it out; it makes us laugh and weep,
    And then puts us
      To sleep.

1951–57

VASILIY ANDREEVICH ZHUKOVSKI

(1783–1852)

ON VASILIY ZHUKOVSKI
PUSHKIN'S FRIEND

Vasiliy Zhukovski (1783–1852) [was] Pushkin's life-long friend, a prudent mediator in our poet's clashes with the government, and his amiable teacher in matters of prosody and poetical idiom. Zhukovski owned a strong and delicate instrument that he had strung himself, but the trouble was he had very little to say. Hence his continuous quest for subject matter in the works of German and English poets. His versions of foreign poetry are not really translations but talented adaptations remarkably melodious and engaging; and they seem especially so when the original is not known to the reader. Zhukovski at his best communicates to his reader much of the enjoyment he obviously experiences himself in molding and modulating a young language while having his verses go through this or that impersonation act. His main defects are constant tendencies to simplify and delocalize his text (a method consistent with French translatory practice of the time) and to replace with a pious generalization every rough and rare peculiarity. The student who knows Russian will find it profitable to compare, for instance, Zhukovski's *Smaylhome Castle* (*Zamok Smal'gol'm*, 1822) with its model, *The Eve of St. John*, by Walter Scott. It will be seen that Scott's specific details are consistently neutralized. The "platejack" and "vaunt-brace" of quatrain III become with Zhukovski merely "armor of iron" . . . and so on; but, on the other hand, there is in the Russian text a somewhat finer breath of mystery; everything about Scott's rather matter-of-fact adulteress acquires a more romantic and pathetic air with Zhukovski, and what is especially noteworthy, he evolves throughout the piece a set of wonderful, exotic sonorities by employing the least number of words to fill his muscular line and by making his musically transliterated names—*Broterstón* (Brotherstone), *Duglás* (Douglas), *Kol'dingám* (Coldinghame), *El'dón* (Eildon)—resonantly participate in his Russian rhymes and rhythms. . . .

In a five-line inscription, *To Zhukovski's Portrait* . . . , paying deserved tribute to the evocative melody of his friend's poetry, Pushkin said late in 1817 or early in 1818 (ll. 1–2):

> *Egó stihóv plenítel'naya sládost'*
> *Proydyót vekóv zavístlivuyu dal'.* . .

> The captivating sweetness of his verses
> shall cross the envious distance of the ages . . .

1951–57

from
ПЕВЕЦ

[. . .]

И нет певца. . . его не слышно лиры. . .
Его следы исчезли в сих местах;
И скорбно все в долине, на холмах;
И всё молчит. . . лишь тихие зефиры,
   Колебля вянущий венец,
   Порою веют над могилой,
   И лира вторит им уныло:
     Бедный певец!

1811

from
THE BARD

Gone is the bard, and from these haunts his traces
Have disappeared, the voice we heard is still,
And all is melancholy, dale and hill,
And all is mute. Only the quiet zephyrs
    Shaking the withered wreath, when they
    Over the tomb sometimes suspire,
    Are sadly echoed by the lyre:
        Piteous bard!

1951–57

СВЕТЛАНА

[. . .]

Тускло светится луна
   В сумраке тумана—
Молчалива и грустна
   Милая Светлана.
«Что, подруженька, с тобой?
   Вымолви словечко;
Слушай песни круговой;
   Вынь себе колечко.

[. . .]

Вот красавица одна;
   К зеркалу садится;
С тайной робостью она
   В зеркало глядится;
Темно в зеркале; кругом
   Мертвое молчанье;
Свечка трепетным огнем
   Чуть лиет сиянье. . .
Робость в ней волнует грудь,
Страшно ей назад взглянуть,
   Страх туманит очи. . .
С треском пыхнул огонек,
Крикнул жалобно сверчок
   Вестник полуночи.

[. . .]

О! не знай сих страшных снов
   Ты, моя Светлана. . .

from
SVETLANA

II

The moon's light is lusterless
in the darkness of the mist;
silent is and melancholy
dear Svetlana.
Sweet companion, what ails you,
no word uttering?
Hearken to the roundelay,
and take out your ring.

V

Here is the fair one alone;
    sits her at the mirror;
with a secret dread regards
    herself in the mirror;
in the mirror it is dark.
    All around, dead silence;
scarcely with a trembling fire,
    candles pour their luster.
Terror makes her bosom heave,
to glance back she is afraid,
    fear her eyes is dimming . . .
With a crackling spurts the flame,
plaintively the cricket cries,
    messenger of midnight.

EPILOGUE
Never know these frightful dreams,
    You, O my Svetlana!

[. . .]
Как приятный ручейка
    Блеск на лоне луга,
Будь вся жизнь ее светла,
Будь веселость, как была,
    Дней ее подруга.

1808–1812

Let all your life be bright
as on the bosom of a mead
a brooklet's pleasant gleam!

1951–57, 1966–67

from
THEKLA
by Friedrich von Schiller

Schiller's "Thekla" is a short poem of 24 lines, of which part was translated by Zhukovski. Here are the lines he used:

Wo ich sei, und wo mich hingewendet,
    Als mein flücht'ger Schatten dir Entschwebt?
    Hab'ich nicht beschlossen und geendet,
    Hab'ich nicht geliebet und gelebt?

[. . .]

Ob ich den Verlorenen gefunden?
    Glaube mir, ich bin mit ihm vereint,
    Wo sich nicht mehr trennt, was sich verbunden,
    Dort, wo keine Thräne wird geweint.

(You ask) where may I be, whither have I turned
after my fleeting form had vanished from you?
Have I not concluded and terminated things?
Have I not loved and lived?

(You ask) whether I found again the one I had lost?
Believe me, I am united to him
where what has been united cannot be separated,
where no tear is shed.

ca. 1949

ГОЛОС С ТОГО СВЕТА

Не узнавай, куда я путь склонила,
В какой предел из мира перешла. . .
О друг, я всё земное совершила;
Я на земле любила и жила.

Нашла ли их? Сбылись ли ожиданья?
Без страха верь; обмана сердцу нет;
Сбылося всё; я в стороне свиданья;
И знаю *здесь*, сколь *ваш* прекрасен свет.

Друг, на *земле* великое не тщетно;
Будь тверд, а *здесь* тебе не изменят;
О милый, *здесь* не будет безответно
Ничто, ничто: ни мысль, ни вздох, ни взгляд.

Не унывай: минувшее с тобою;
Незрима я, но в мире мы одном;
Будь верен мне прекрасною душою;
Сверши *один* начатое *вдвоем.*

1815

VOICE FROM ANOTHER WORLD

Do not try to find out whither my way has sloped,
into what sphere I have passed when leaving this world.
O friend, all earthly things have I accomplished
on earth I have loved and lived.

Have I found them [the dead]? Have hopes been realized?
Fearlessly believe; no deception awaits the heart;
All has been fulfilled; I am in the land where soul meets soul
and I know *here* how beautiful *your* world is.

Friend, great things on earth are not useless.
Be firm, for *here* you will not be betrayed;
O my dear one, *here* nothing shall remain unanswered
nothing, nothing: neither a thought, nor a sigh, nor a glance.

Do not lose heart: the past is with you;
I am invisible, but our world is one
Let your fair soul remain true to me,
accomplish *alone* what we *both* began.

1951–57

from
К ГЕТЕ

[. . .]
В далеком полуночном свете
Твоею Музою я жил,
И для меня мой *гений Гете*
Животворитель жизни был!

[. . .]

1827

TO GOETHE

In a remote boreal world
I lived because I loved your muse;
and thus for me my genius Goethe
was what gave life to life itself.

1951-57

LORD ULLIN'S DAUGHTER
by Campbell (original)

A chieftain to the Highlands bound
cries: Boatman, do not tarry,
and I'll give thee a silver pound
to row us o'er the ferry.

Now who be ye would cross Lochgyle
this dark and stormy water?
Oh, I'm the chief of Ullva's Isle
and this Lord Ullin's daughter.

And fast before her father's men
three days we've fled together
for should they find us in the glen
my blood would stain the heather.

His horsemen hard behind us ride
Should they our steps discover
then who will cheer my bonny bride
when they've slain her lover?

Oh haste thee, haste! the lady cries.
Though tempests round us gather,
I'll face the anger of the skies
but not an angry father!

Out spake the hardy Highland wight:
I'll go, my chief, I'm ready.
It is not for your silver bright,
but for your winsome lady.

And by my word, the bonny bird
in danger shall not tarry
for though the waves are raging white
I'll row you o'er the ferry.

The boat had left a stormy land
a stormy sea before her
when, ah, too strong for human hand
the tempests gathered o'er her.

And still they rowed amidst the roar
of waters fast prevailing.
Lord Ullin reached that fatal shore
his wrath was changed to wailing.

For sore dismayed, through rain and shade
his child he did discover:
one lovely hand was stretched for aid
and one was round her lover.

Come back, come back, he cries in grief
across this angry water
and I'll forgive your Highland chief,
my daughter, oh, my daughter!

'Twas vain, the high waves lashed the shore
return or aid preventing.
The waters wild went o'er his child
and he was left lamenting.

1804

УЛЛИН И ЕГО ДОЧЬ

Был сильный вихорь, сильный дождь;
Кипя, ярилася пучина;
Ко брегу Рино—горный вождь
Примчался с дочерью Уллина.

«Рыбак, прими нас в твой челнок;
Рыбак, спаси нас от погони;
Уллин с дружиной недалек;
Нам слышны крики; мчатся кони».

«Ты видишь ли, как зла вода?
Ты слышишь ли, как волны громки?
Пускаться плыть теперь беда:
Мой челн не крепок, весла ломки».

«Рыбак, рыбак, подай свой челн;
Спаси нас: сколь ни зла пучина,
Пощада может быть от волн—
Ее не будет от Уллина!»

[. . .]

«Садитесь, в добрый час; плывем».
И Рино сел, с ним дева села;
Рыбак отчалил; челноком
Седая бездна овладела.

[. . .]

Уллин ко брегу прискакал;
Он видит: дочь уносят волны;
И гнев в груди отца пропал,
И он воскликнул, страха полный:

«Мое дитя, назад, назад!
Прощенье! возвратись, Мальвина!»
Но волны лишь ответ шумят
На зов отчаянный Уллина.

OOLLEEN AND HIS DAUGHTER
by Zhukovsky from Campbell

There was a violent gale, a violent rain,
the wild waters roared,
Reeno, the chief of a mountain tribe
came galloping with Oolleen's daughter.

Fisherman, take us in your boat,
fisherman, save us from our pursuers,
Oolleen with his horsemen is not far,
we can hear their shouts, the trampling of their steeds.

Do you see how angry the waters are,
do you hear how loud are the waves?
To set out now would be no good,
my boat is frail, my oars are brittle.

Fisherman, fisherman, bring up your boat!
Look: however angry the waters,
one may expect mercy from them,
but there will be none from Oolleen.

All right, get in, let us hope for the best.
And Reeno got in, and the girl got in.
The fisherman started to row off, the waves raging white
took possession of the boat.

Oolleen came galloping to the beach
and saw his daughter being carried away by the waves,
and in the father's heart anger disappeared
and he cried out, in terror;

Come back, my child, come back!
You are forgiven. Come back, Malveena!
but only waves answered
Oolleen's desperate call.

Ревет гроза, черна как ночь,
Летает челн между волнами;
Сквозь пену их он видит дочь
С простертыми к нему руками.

«О, возвратися, возвратись!»
Но грозно раздалась пучина,
И волны, челн пожрав, слились
При крике жалобном Уллина.

1833

Loud is the tempest and dark as night
the boat slips between waves.
Through their foam he sees his daughter
both her arms are stretched out towards her father.

Come back, come back!
but the abyss parted,
and the waves swallowed the boat
and closed again while Oolleen emitted a piteous cry.

ca. 1948–1949

KONSTANTIN NIKOLAEVICH BATYUSHKOV
(1787–1855)

ON KONSTANTIN BATYUSHKOV

Batyushkov [was a] minor poet and literary pioneer, to whose idiom Pushkin owed at least as much as he did to the style of Karamzin and Zhukovski. . . .

The first edition of Batyushkov's works, in two consecutive volumes, came out in St. Petersburg, 1817, under the title *Essays [Opïtï] in Verse and Prose*. Konstantin Batyushkov was born in 1787. His first published poem, *Mechta,* was composed in 1802, his last, a little masterpiece, in 1821 (or early in 1824, during a lucid interval, after reading the latest edition of Zhukovski's poems—according to Aleksandr Turgenev):

> Do you recall the cry
> Of gray Melchizedek when he prepared to die?
> Man, he exclaimed, is born a slave; a slave
> He must descend into the grave,
> And Death will hardly tell him why
> He haunts the magic vale of tears,
> Suffers and weeps, endures and disappears.

In 1822, Batyushkov attempted to take his own life. He died in 1855, after thirty-three years of insanity.

In his brief heyday of creative endeavor, Batyushkov had translated Gresset, Parny, Boileau, and Tasso and written in the style of his favorite poets. He and Zhukovski were the predecessors of Pushkin, and in [Pushkin's] youth, Batyushkov was his best-loved Russian master. Harmony and precision—these were the literary virtues Pushkin learned from both, although even his boyish verses were more vivid and vigorous than those of his teachers. Later he was critical of Batyushkov, and left some interesting notes in the margin of the *Essays;* but in *Eugene Onegin* there still echoes something of Batyushkov's new-found fluency, certain predilections of idiom and various improved characteristics of his style.

I notice that his name was given four syllables (Bá-ty-úsh-kov) by the only English poet (a very minor one) who mentions him, namely Bernard Barton, in some stanzas (1824) addressed to John Bowring, who translated Batyushkov for his Russian anthology (st. III):

> Derzhavin's noble numbers, soaring high,
>> Replete with inspiration's genuine force,
> And Batiushkov's milder melody,
>> Warm from domestic pleasure's sweetest source.

1951–57

СОВЕТ ЭПИЧЕСКОМУ СТИХОТВОРЦУ

Какое хочешь имя дай
Твоей поэме полудикой:
Петр длинный, Петр большой, но только Петр Великой
Ее не называй.

ca. 1810

ADVICE TO AN EPIC POET

Choose any name to designate
Your half-barbaric song:
Peter the Big, Peter the Long
—But not Peter the Great.

ca. 1948–49

* * *

Ты помнишь, что изрек,
Прощаясь с жизнию, седой Мельхиседек?
Рабом родится человек,
рабом в могилу ляжет,
и Смерть ему едва ли скажет,
зачем он шел долиной чудной слез,
страдал, рыдал, терпел, исчез.

ca. 1821

Do you recall the cry
of old Melchizedek when he prepared to die?
Man, he exclaimed, is born a slave; a slave—
he must descend into the grave
and Death will hardly tell him why
he haunts the magic vale of tears,
suffers and weeps, endures and disappears.

ca. 1948–49

A later parody (Political)

Said old Melchizedek: the tyrant Nero
was born a zero and will die a zero,
and none can tell why in this vale of tears
he governs, grunts, oppresses, disappears.

ca. 1949–58

VILGELM KARLOVICH KYUHELBEKER

(WILHELM VON KÜCHELBECKER)

(1797–1846)

ON VILGELM KYUHELBEKER

Vilgelm Kyuhelbeker was of German descent: Wilhelm von Küchelbecker, according to the dedication Goethe inscribed on a copy of *Werther* he gave him at Weimar, Nov. 22, 1820, N.S. He survived Pushkin almost by a decade (1797–1846). A curious archaic poet, an impotent playwright, one of Schiller's victims, a brave idealist, a heroic Decembrist, a pathetic figure, who after 1825 spent ten years of imprisonment in various fortresses and the rest of his days in Siberian exile. He was Pushkin's schoolmate. . . .

Only at the very end of a singularly sad and futile literary career, and in the twilight of his life, first jeered at by friend and foe alike, then forgotten by all; a sick, blind man, broken by years of exile, Küchelbecker produced a few admirable poems, one of which is a brilliant masterpiece, a production of first-rate genius—the twenty-line-long *Destiny of Russian Poets* (written in the province of Tobolsk, 1845) . . .

A tragic entry in Küchelbecker's diary reads: "If a man were ever unhappy, it is I. Around me there is not one heart against which I might press myself" (Aksha, September, 1842).

1951–57

COMMEMORATING PUSHKIN

To the end of his life [Pushkin] remained deeply attached to what he considered his real home, the Lyceum, and to his former fellow students. He has commemorated these recollections, and the annual reunions on Oct. 19, in several poems. There is something symbolic in the fact that the one he composed for the last anniversary feast he attended was not completed. On the occasion of the Oct. 19 reunion of 1838, his schoolmate Küchelbecker, an exile in Aksha, Siberia, wrote in a wonderful piece:

> At present with our Delvig he is feasting,
> At present he is with my Griboedov . . .

> *On nǐne s náshim Dél'vigom pirúet,*
> *On nǐne s Griboédovïm moím. . .*

1951–57

. . . [H]is remarkable poem *Agasfer, The Wandering Jew* (*Vechnïy zhid*) [was] written in exile, mainly in 1840–42, and published long after his death (1878). Despite its odd archaism, awkward locutions, crankish ideas, and a number of structural flaws, this poem is a major piece of work, with a harshness of intonation and gaunt originality of phrasing that should deserve a special study.

1951–57

УЧАСТЬ РУССКИХ ПОЭТОВ

[. . .]

. . .их бросают в черную тюрьму,
Морят морозом безнадежной ссылки. . .

Или болезнь наводит ночь и мглу
На очи прозорливцев вдохновенных;
Или рука любовников презренных
Шлет пулю их священному челу;

Или же бунт поднимет чернь глухую,
И чернь того на части разорвет
Чей блещущий перунами полет
Сияньем облил бы страну родную.

1845

from
DESTINY OF RUSSIAN POETS

. . . thrown into a black prison,
killed by the frost of hopeless banishment;

or sickness overcasts with night and gloom
the eyes of the inspired, the seers!
Or else the hand of some vile lady's man
impels a bullet at their sacred brow;

Or the deaf rabble rises in revolt—
and him the rabble will to pieces tear
whose wingèd course, ablaze with thunderbolts,
might drench in radiance the motherland.

1951–57

BARON ANTON ANTONOVICH DELVIG

(1798–1831)

ON ANTON DELVIG

Baron Anton Delvig (Aug. 6, 1798–Jan. 14, 1831), one of Pushkin's dearest friends, a minor poet, author of pleasant idyls, folk songs, well-made sonnets, and some excellent dactylic hexameters, curiously combined the classical strain and the folksy one, the amphora and the samovar . . .

Delvig's best poem is the one he dedicated to Pushkin, his schoolmate, in January, 1815 (published the same year in *Russian Museum, Rossiyskiy muzeum,* no. 9). A boy of sixteen, prophesying in exact detail literary immortality to a boy of fifteen, and doing it in a poem that is itself immortal—this is a combination of intuitive genius and actual destiny to which I can find no parallel in the history of world poetry.

1951–57

ПУШКИНУ

Кто, как лебедь цветущей Авзонии,
Осененный и миртом и лаврами,
Майской ночью при хоре порхающих,
В сладких грезах отвился от матери:

Тот в советах не мудрствует; нá стены
Побежденных знамена не вешает;
Столб кормами судов неприятельских
Он не красит пред храмом Ареевым;

Флот, с несчетным богатством Америки,
С тяжким золотом, купленном кровию,
Не взмущает двукраты экватора
Для него кораблями бегущими.

Но с младенчества он обучается
Воспевать красоты поднебесные,
И ланиты его от приветствия,
Удивленной толпы горят пламенем.

И Паллада туманное облако
Рассевает от взоров,—и в юности
Он уж видит священную истину
И порок, исподлобья взирающий!

Пушкин! Он и в лесах не укроется;
Лира выдаст его громким пением,
И от смертных восхитит бессмертного
Аполлон на Олимп торжествующий.

1815

TO PUSHKIN

He—a swan born in blooming Ausonia—
who is crowned with the myrtle and laurel;
who one May night, 'mid hovering choruses,
in sweet dreams from his mother was weaned,

does not quibble in councils; he does not
on his walls hang the flags of the fallen,
or in front of the temple of Ares
deck with enemy rostrums a column.

Fleets with treasures untold from America,
weighty gold that with blood has been purchased
—not for him do those ships in their wanderings
twice disturb the equator;

but since infancy he has been learning
how to sing subcelestial beauty,
and his cheeks are aflame from the greetings
of the wondering crowd.

And the nebulous cloud from his vision
is by Pallas dispelled, and already
as a youth sacred truth he distinguishes,
and the lowering glances of vice.

Pushkin! Even the woods cannot hide him!
With loud singing his lyre will expose him,
and from mortals Apollo will carry
the immortal to cheering Olympus.

1951–57

ALEKSANDR SERGEEVICH PUSHKIN

(1799–1837)

ON ALEKSANDR PUSHKIN

It seems unnecessary to remind the reader that Alexander Pushkin (1799–1837) was Russia's greatest poet but it may be preferable not to take any chances. Apart from numerous short lyrics displaying a precision of expression and a melody of tone that Russian literature had never known before, he wrote epics, ballads, fairy tales, humorous or romantic fantasies (*The Captive of the Caucasus, The Fountain of Bakhchisaray, Count Nulin, The Cottage in Kolomna, The Gypsies, Poltava, The Egyptian Nights, Angelo, The Golden Cockerel, The Bronze Horseman*, etc.), dramas in blank verse (*Boris Godunov* and the diminutive *Mozart and Salieri, The Covetous Knight, The Feast during the Plague, The Guest of Stone, The River Nymph*) and that prodigious "novel" consisting of sonnet-like strophes,—*Eugene Onegin*. He applied the principles of his poetry—an epigrammatical precision and a rhythmical balance difficult to define without examples—to his prose (see his stories and short novels of which the best is *The Queen of Spades*). This precision and balance were quite abandoned by the great but diffuse Russian novelists of the XIXth century.

During his lifetime he was pestered by a fatherly but grossly uncultured Tsar just as his writings were to be rejected later by the well-meaning radical critics of the civic school that dominated public opinion in the Sixties and Seventies. In modern times Marxism had considerable difficulty in adjusting Pushkin to its needs and principles but the question was finally solved on the nationalistic plane. However, for a true appreciation of Pushkin too much is required from the reader to make such readers numerous. His conventional admirers think of him mainly in terms of schoolbooks and Chaikovsky's operas.

His life was as glamorous as a good grammarian's life ought to be. A maze of tragic events led to his fatal duel with a young ex-Chouan, a blond, fatuous adventurer who was hardly aware that the morose black-bearded husband of the pretty woman he courted, dabbled in verse. This Baron d'Anthès, having recovered from the slight wound he had received after shooting Pushkin through the liver returned to France, had a glorious time under Napoléon III, was mentioned by Victor Hugo in one of his poetical diatribes and lived to the incredible and unnecessary age of 90. When an inquisitive Russian traveler once asked the grand old man how he had found it possible to deprive Russia of her greatest poet—"*Mais enfin,*" answered the Baron rather testily, "*moi aussi,* I too am something: *je suis Sénateur!*"

1941–43

ON PUSHKIN'S IDIOM

Pushkin's idiom combined all the contemporaneous elements of Russian with all he had learned from Derzhavin, Zhukovski, Batyushkov, Karamzin and Krïlov; these elements are: 1. The poetical and metaphysical strain that still lived in Church Slavonic forms and locutions; 2. Abundant and natural gallicisms; 3. The everyday colloquialisms of his set; and 4. Stylized popular speech. He made a salad of the famous three styles ("low," "medium elevation," "high") dear to the pseudoclassical archaists, and added to it the ingredients of Russian romanticists with a pinch of parody.

1957

from
МОЕМУ АРИСТАРХУ

[. . .]
Брожу ль над тихими водами
В дубраве темной и глухой,
Задумаюсь—взмахну руками,
На рифмах вдруг заговорю—

[. . .]

1815

from
TO MY ARISTARCH

Whether I roam near tranquil waters,
or in a dense and darksome park,
pensive I grow—throw up my arms
and start to speak in rhyme.

1951–57, 1966–67

from
СОН
(Отрывок)

Ах! Умолчу ль о мамушке моей,
О прелести таинственных ночей,
Когда в чепце, в старинном одеянье,
Она, духов молитвой уклоня,
С усердием перекрестит меня
И шопотом рассказывать мне станет
О мертвецах, о подвигах Бовы. . .

[. . .]

Под образом простой ночник из глины
Чуть освещал глубокие морщины,
Драгой антик, прабабушкин чепец
И длинный рот, где зуба два стучало,—

[. . .]

1816

from
THE DREAM

Ah, can I fail to speak about my mammy
and the enchantment of mysterious nights,
when, in a mobcap, in old-fashioned garments,
she, having turned off specters with a prayer,
would cross me with a most assiduous air
and in a whisper would begin to tell me
about dead men, about Bova's exploits

[. . .]

Beneath the icon a plain earthenware
night lampad dimly brought out her deep wrinkles,
my great-grandmother's mob—a dear antique—
and that long mouth where two or three teeth knocked.

1951–57

ВОЛЬНОСТЬ
Ода

1 Беги, сокройся от очей,
Цитеры слабая Царица!
Где ты, где ты, гроза Царей
4 Свободы гордая певица?—
Приди, сорви с меня венок,
Разбей изнеженную лиру,
Хочу воспеть Свободу миру,
8 На тронах поразить порок.

Открой мне благородный след
Того возвышенного Галла,
Кому сама средь грозных бед
12 Ты гимны смелые внушала.
Питомцы ветреной Судьбы,
Тираны мира, трепещите!
А вы мужайтесь и внемлите,
16 Восстаньте, падшие рабы!

Увы! куда ни брошу взор,—
Везде бичи, везде железы,
Законов гибельный позор,
20 Неволи немощные слезы;
Везде неправедная Власть
В сгущенной мгле предрассуждений
Воссела—рабства грозный Гений
24 И славы роковая страсть.

Лишь там над Царскою главой
Народов не легло страданье,
Где крепко с вольностью святой
28 Законов мощных сочетанье,

LIBERTY: AN ODE, 1817

1   Begone, be hidden from my eyes,
      delicate Queen of Cythera!
      Where are you, where are you, the terror
4   of Kings, the proud chantress of Freedom?
      Arrive; pluck off my garland; break
      the lyre of mollitude! I wish
      Freedom to sing unto the world
8   and smite iniquity on thrones.

      Reveal to me the noble track
      of that exalted Gaul, to whom
      you, 'midst awesome calamities,
12   yourself courageous hymns inspired.
      Nurslings of fickle Destiny,
      you, tyrants of the universe,
      shudder! and you take heart and hearken,
16   resuscitate, ye fallen slaves!

      Alas! where'er my gaze I cast
      —everywhere whips, everywhere irons;
      the perilous disgrace of laws,
20   the helpless tears of servitude.
      Unrighteous Power everywhere
      in condensed fog of prejudices
      has been enthroned—the awesome Genius
24   of slavery, and fame's fatal passion.

      There only on the kingly head
      does not lie the distress of nations
      where firm with sacred liberty
28   is the accord of mighty laws;

Где всем простерт их твердой щит,
Где, сжатый верными руками,
Граждан над равными главами
32   Их меч без выбора скользит

И преступленье с высока
Сражает праведным размахом;
Где не подкупна их рука
36   Ни алчной скупостью, ни страхом.
Владыки! вам венец и трон
Дает Закон, а не Природа,
Стоите выше вы Народа—
40   Но вечный выше вас Закон.

И горе, горе племенам,
Где дремлет он неосторожно,
Где иль Народу, иль Царям
44   Законом властвовать возможно!
Тебя в свидетели зову,
О, мученик ошибок славных,
За предков, в шуме бурь недавних,
48   Сложивший Царскую главу.

Восходит к смерти Людовик,
В виду безмолвного потомства,
Главой развенчанной приник
52   К кровавой плахе Вероломства.
Молчит Закон—Народ молчит,
Падет преступная секира. . .
И се—злодейская порфира
56   На Галлах скованных лежит. . .

Самовластительный Злодей,
Тебя, твой трон я ненавижу,
Твою погибель, смерть детей
60   С жестокой радостию вижу.

where spread to all is their strong shield;
where, grasped by trusty hands, above
the equal heads of citizens
32   their sword without preferment glides,

and from that elevation strikes
wrongdoing with a righteous sweep;
where their arm is unbribable
36   by ravenous avarice or fear.
Rulers! to you the crown and throne
the Law gives and not Nature. Higher
than the People you stand, but higher
40   than you is the eternal Law.

And woe, woe to the races where
imprudently it slumbers; where
either the People or the Kings
44   to dominate the Law are able!
As witness, you I call, O martyr
of glorious errors, who laid down
for ancestors a kingly head
48   in the tumult of recent tempests.

Louis ascends to death, in sight
of mute posterity. His head,
now crownless, he has sunk upon
52   the bloody block of Broken Faith.
The Law is silent; silent is
the People. The criminal blade
now falls and lo! a villainous
56   purple has clothed the shackled Gauls.

Autocratoric Villain! you,
your throne I view with detestation;
your downfall, your descendants' death
60   I see with cruel jubilation.

Читают на твоем челе
Печать проклятия Народы;
Ты ужас мира, стыд природы,
64 Упрек ты Богу на земле.

Когда на мрачную Неву
Звезда полуночи сверкает,
И беззаботную главу
68 Спокойный сон отягощает,
Глядит задумчивый певец
На грозно спящий средь тумана
Пустынный памятник тирана,
72 Забвенью брошенный дворец—

И слышит Клии страшный глас
Над сими страшными стенами,
Калигуллы последний час
76 Он видит живо пред очами. . .
Он видит—в лентах и звездах,
Вином и Злобой упоенны
Идут убийцы потаенны,
80 На лицах дерзость, в сердце страх.

Молчит неверной часовой,
Опущен молча мост подъемной,
Врата отверсты в тьме ночной
84 Рукой предательства наемной. . .
О стыд! о ужас наших дней!
Как звери вторглись Янычары! . .
Падут бесславные удары—
88 Погиб увенчанный злодей!

И днесь учитеся, Цари!
Ни наказанья, ни награды,
Ни кров темниц, ни алтари
92 Не верные для вас ограды.

The Peoples read upon your brow
the stamp of malediction. You
are the world's horror, nature's shame,
64   upon earth a reproach to God.

When down upon the gloomy Neva
the star Polaris scintillates
and peaceful slumber overwhelms
68   the head that is devoid of cares,
the pensive poet contemplates
the grimly sleeping in the mist
forlorn memorial of a tyrant,
72   a palace to oblivion cast,

and hears the dreadful voice of Clio
above yon gloom-pervaded walls
and vividly before his eyes
76   he sees Caligula's last hours.
He sees: beribanded, bestarred,
with Wine and Hate intoxicated,
they come, the furtive assassins,
80   their faces brazen, hearts afraid.

Silent is the untrusty watchman,
the drawbridge silently is lowered,
the gate is opened in the dark
84   of night by hired treachery's hand.
O shame! O horror of our days!
Like animals, the Janizeries
burst in. The infamous blows fall,
88   and perished has the crownèd villain!

And nowadays keep learning, Kings!
Not punishment, not recompenses,
not altars, and not prison vaults,
92   provide you with secure defenses.

Склонитесь первые главой
Под сень надежную Закона
И станут вечной стражей трона
96 Народов вольность и покой.

1817

Be you the first to bow your heads
beneath the Law's trustworthy shelter
and guard eternally the throne
96   shall liberty and peace of Peoples.

1951–57

FROM NOTES TO "VOL'NOST'"/ LIBERTY

LINE 2, *TSITÉRÏ SLÁBAYA TSARÍTSA:*

Cythera, one of the Ionian islands where stood a temple of Aphrodite, or Venus, the frail (*slabaya*, "weak," "delicate") goddess of Love . . .

LINES 22–24:

The "prejudices" refer to the power of the church, to her political use of superstition and directed thought. The "Genius" is an eloquent synonym of "spirit." The definition of "fame" as a "fatal passion" applies to Napoleon—who is waiting in the wings of the poem.

LINES 45–46:

The reference is to Louis XVI beheaded in 1793 during the French regime of Terror.

LINES 57–64:

This stanza refers to "Napoleon's purple" (as Pushkin remarked himself in a marginal note of the autograph which he gave to Nikolay Turgenev in 1817).

LINE 73, CLIO:

The hysterical Muse of History . . .

1951–57

from
К ЩЕРБИНИНУ

[. . .]
Найдем отраду, милый друг,
В туманном сне воспоминаний!
Тогда, качая головой,
Скажу тебе у двери гроба:
«Ты помнишь Фанни, милый мой?»
И тихо улыбнемся оба.

1819

TO SHCHERBININ

pleasure we'll find, dear friend,
in the blurred dream of recollection,
for then, shaking my head,
I'll say to you at the grave's door,
"Remember Fanny, my dear fellow?"—
And softly both we'll smile.

1951–57

from

РУСЛАН И ЛЮДМИЛА
Песнь четвертая

[. . .]

Я не Омер: в стихах высоких
Он может воспевать один
Обеды греческих дружин
И звон и пену чаш глубоких.
Милее, по следам Парни,
Мне славить лирою небрежной
И наготу в ночной тени,

[. . .]

1817–20

from
RUSLAN AND LYUDMILA
(Can. IV, ll. 147–53)

I'm not Omér; in lofty verses
he may alone sing the repasts
of Grecian troops,
the clink and foam of wine cups deep.
Parny I much prefer to follow
and have my casual lyre extol
a naked shape in the night's darkness.

1951–57

***

Наперсница волшебной старины,
Друг вымыслов игривых и печальных,
Тебя я знал во дни моей весны,
4   Во дни утех и снов первоначальных.
Я ждал тебя; в вечерней тишине
Являлась ты веселою старушкой,
И надо мной сидела в шушуне,
8   В больших очках и с резвою гремушкой.
Ты, детскую качая колыбель,
Мой юный слух напевами пленила
И меж пелен оставила свирель,
12   Которую сама заворожила.

[. . .]

1822

THE BOSOM FRIEND OF MAGIC ANCIENTRY
(To His Muse)

The bosom friend of magic ancientry,
the friend of fantasies playful and sad!
I knew you in my springtime's days,
4 in days of games and pristine dreams.
I waited for you; in the vesper stillness
you would appear as a merry old woman
and by me you would sit, in a warm jacket,
8 large spectacles, and with a friskful rattle.
You, rocking the infantine cradle,
with chantings captivated my young hearing
and 'mongst the swaddling bands left a reed pipe
12 o'er which a spell yourself had cast.

1951–57

ПТИЧКА

В чужбине свято наблюдаю
Родной обычай старины:
На волю птичку выпускаю
При светлом празднике весны.

Я стал доступен утешенью;
За что на Бога мне роптать,
Когда хоть одному творенью
Я мог свободу даровать!

1823

LITTLE BIRD

In a strange country I religiously observe
my own land's ancient custom:
I set at liberty a little bird
on the bright holiday of spring.

I have become accessible to consolation;
why should I murmur against God
if even to a single creature
the gift of freedom I could grant!

1974

ДЕМОН

В те дни, когда мне были новы
Все впечатленья бытия—
И взоры дев, и шум дубровы,
И ночью пенье соловья—
Когда возвышенные чувства,
Свобода, слава и любовь
И вдохновенные искусства
Так сильно волновали кровь,—
Часы надежд и наслаждений
Тоской внезапной осеня,
Тогда какой-то злобный гений
Стал тайно навещать меня.
Печальны были наши встречи:
Его улыбка, чудный взгляд,
Его язвительные речи
Вливали в душу хладный яд.
Неистощимой клеветою
Он Провиденье искушал;
Он звал прекрасное мечтою;
Он вдохновенье презирал;
Не верил он любви, свободе;
На жизнь насмешливо глядел—
И ничего во всей природе
Благословить он не хотел.

1823

THE DEMON

In those days when to me were new
all the impressions of existence—
and eyes of maids, and sough of grove,
and in the night the singing of the nightingale;
when elevated feelings,
freedom, glory, and love,
and inspired arts,
so strongly roused my blood;
the hours of hopes and of delights
with sudden heartache having shaded,
then did a certain wicked genius
begin to visit me in secret.
Sad were our meetings:
his smile, his wondrous glance,
his galling speech,
cold venom poured into my soul.
With inexhaustible detraction
he tempted Providence;
he called the beautiful a dream,
held inspiration in contempt,
did not believe in love, in freedom,
looked mockingly on life,
and nothing in all nature
did he desire to bless.

1951–57, 1966–67

***

Изыде сеятель сеяти семена своя.

Свободы сеятель пустынный,
Я вышел рано, до звезды;
Рукою чистой и безвинной
В порабощенные бразды
Бросал живительное семя;
Но потерял я только время,
Благие мысли и труды. . .

Паситесь, мирные народы!
К чему стадам дары свободы?
Их должно резать или стричь.
Наследство их из рода в роды
Ярмо с гремушками да бич.

1823

* * *

A lonely sower of liberty,
I came out too early, before the morning star.

[. . .]

My time, my labors, my
best thoughts were merely lost.

Keep to your pastures, peaceful nations,
what is the gift of liberty to sheep.
To be slaughtered or shorn, that's what they are for,
their inheritance throughout the ages
is a yoke with bells and the goad.

ca. 1949

* * *

Of freedom eremitic sower,
early I went, before the star.
With a hand pure and guiltless
into the enslaved furrows
I cast the vivifying seed;
but all I did was lose my time,
well-meaning thoughts and labors.

Graze, placid peoples!
What are to herds the gifts of liberty?
They have to be slaughtered or shorn.
Their heirdom is from race to race
a yoke with jinglers and the whip.

1951–57, 1966–67

ЕВГЕНИЙ ОНЕГИН
Глава первая

XXXII.

Дианы грудь, ланиты Флоры
Прелестны, милые друзья!
Однако ножка Терпсихоры
Прелестней чем-то для меня.
Она, пророчествуя взгляду
Неоцененную награду,
Влечет условною красой
Желаний своевольный рой.
Люблю ее, мой друг Эльвина,
Под длинной скатертью столов,
Весной на мураве лугов,
Зимой на чугуне камина,
На зеркальном паркете зал,
У моря на граните скал.

XXXIII.

Я помню море пред грозою:
Как я завидовал волнам,
Бегущим бурной чередою
С любовью лечь к ее ногам!
Как я желал тогда с волнами
Коснуться милых ног устами!
Нет, никогда средь пылких дней
Кипящей младости моей
Я не желал с таким мученьем
Лобзать уста младых Армид,
Иль розы пламенных ланит,
Иль перси, полные томленьем;
Нет, никогда порыв страстей
Так не терзал души моей!

from
EUGENE ONEGIN
Chapter I

XXXII

Diana's bosom, Flora's dimple
are very charming, I agree—
but there's a greater charm, less simple,
—the instep of Terpsichore.
By prophesying to the eye
a prize with which no prize can vie
'tis a fair token and a snare
for swarms of daydreams. Everywhere
its grace, sweet reader, I admire:
at long-hemmed tables, half-concealed,
in spring, upon a velvet field,
in winter, at a grated fire,
in ballrooms, on a glossy floor,
on the bleak boulders of a shore.

XXXIII

I see the surf, the storm-rack flying . . .
Oh, how I wanted to compete
with the tumultuous breakers dying
in adoration at her feet!
Together with those waves—how much
I wished to kiss what they could touch!
No—even when my youth would burn
its fiercest—never did I yearn
with such a torturing sensation
to kiss the lips of nymphs, the rose
that on the cheek of beauty glows
or breasts in mellow palpitation—
no, never did a passion roll
such billows in my bursting soul.

XXXIV.

Мне памятно другое время:
В заветных иногда мечтах
Держу я счастливое стремя,
И ножку чувствую в руках;
Опять кипит воображенье,
Опять ее прикосновенье
Зажгло в увядшем сердце кровь,
Опять тоска, опять любовь. . .
Но полно прославлять надменных
Болтливой лирою своей:
Они не стоят ни страстей,
Ни песен, ими вдохновенных;
Слова и взор волшебниц сих
Обманчивы как ножки их.

1823–24

XXXIV

Sometimes I dream of other minutes
by hidden memory retold—
and feel her little ankle in its
contented stirrup which I hold;
again to build mad builders start;
again within a withered heart
one touch engenders fire; again
—the same old love, the same old pain . . .
But really, my loquacious lyre
has lauded haughty belles too long
—for they deserve neither the song,
nor the emotions they inspire:
eyes, words—all their enchantments cheat
as much as do their pretty feet.

1945

НА ВОРОНЦОВА

Полу-милорд, полу-купец,
Полу-мудрец, полу-невежда,
Полу-подлец—но есть надежда,
Что будет полным, наконец.

1824

EPIGRAM

(On Vorontsov)

Half-merchant and half-prince
half-scholar and half-dunce,
half-knave—but there's a chance
he'll be complete for once.

1944–47

from
ЦЫГАНЫ

CTAРИК
[. . .]
Меж нами есть одно преданье:
Царем когда–то сослан был
Полудня житель к нам в изгнанье.
(Я прежде знал, но позабыл
Его мудреное прозванье.)
Он был уже летами стар,
Но млад и жив душой незлобной—
Имел он песен дивный дар
И голос, шуму вод подобный—
И полюбили все его,
И жил он на брегах Дуная,
Не обижая никого,
Людей рассказами пленяя;
Не разумел он ничего,
И слаб и робок был, как дети;
Чужие люди за него
Зверей и рыб ловили в сети;
Как мерзла быстрая река
И зимни вихри бушевали,
Пушистой кожей покрывали
Они святаго старика;
Но он к заботам жизни бедной
Привыкнуть никогда не мог;
Скитался он иссохший, бледный,
Он говорил, что гневный бог
Его карал за преступленье. . .
Он ждал: придет ли избавленье.
И всё несчастный тосковал,
Бродя по берегам Дуная,
Да горьки слезы проливал,
Свой дальный град воспоминая,

from
THE GYPSIES

THE OLD MAN

There is a legend in our midst:
once by some king was sent
to us in banishment a native of the South
(I used to know but have forgotten
his baffling name).
In years he was already old
but young and lively in unrancored spirit.
He had the sublime gift of song,
and a voice like the sound of waters.
And everyone grew fond of him,
and on the Danube's banks he dwelt,
doing no harm to anybody,
with stories captivating people.
He comprehended nothing
and was as weak and timid as a child.
Strangers for him
fishes and beasts would catch with nets.
When froze the rapid river
and winter cyclones raged,
they covered with a furry hide
the old and holy man.
But he to hardships of a poor existence
never was able to grow used.
He wandered, shrunken, pale.
he said a wrathful god
was for a crime chastising him.
He waited for release to come
and went on yearning, hapless one,
while roaming on the Danube's banks,
and bitter tears he shed,
remembering his distant city,

И завещал он умирая,
Чтобы на юг перенесли
Его тоскующие кости,
И смертью—чуждой сей земли
Неуспокоенные гости!

АЛЕКО

Так вот судьба твоих сынов,
О Рим, о громкая держава!..
Певец любви, певец богов,
Скажи мне, что такое слава?
Могильный гул, хвалебный глас,
Из рода в роды звук бегущий?
Или под сенью дымной кущи
Цыгана дикого рассказ?

[. . .]

1824

and on his deathbed he desired
that to his native South be carried
his yearning bones—
even by death, in this strange land,
unrested guests.

ALEKO

So this is the fate of your sons,
O Rome, O resonant empire!
Poet of love, poet of gods,
tell me: what kind of thing is fame?
a tombal rumbling, a praise-giving voice,
a sound that runs from race to race—
or in the shelter of a smoky tent
the tale of a wild gypsy!

1951–57

К ВЯЗЕМСКОМУ

Так море, древний душегубец,
Воспламеняет гений твой?
Ты славишь лирой золотой
Нептуна грозного трезубец.

Не славь его. В наш гнусный век
Седой Нептун Земли союзник.
На всех стихиях человек—
Тиран, предатель или узник.

1826

TO VYAZEMSKI

So 'tis the sea, the ancient assassin
that kindles into flame your genius?
You glorify with golden lyre
Neptune's dread trident?

No, praise him not! In our vile age
gray Neptune is the Earth's ally.
Upon all elements man is a tyrant,
a traitor, or a prisoner.

1951–57

* * *

Во глубине сибирских руд
Храните гордое терпенье,
Не пропадет ваш скорбный труд
И дум высокое стремленье.

Несчастью верная сестра,
Надежда в мрачном подземелье
Разбудит бодрость и веселье,
Придет желанная пора:

Любовь и дружество до вас
Дойдут сквозь мрачные затворы,
Как в ваши каторжные норы
Доходит мой свободный глас.

Оковы тяжкие падут,
Темницы рухнут—и свобода
Вас примет радостно у входа,
И братья меч вам отдадут.

1827

* * *

Deep in Siberian mines
preserve proud patience:
not lost shall be your woeful toil,
and the high surging of your meditations.

Misfortune's faithful sister, Hope,
within the gloomy underearth
shall waken energy and gladness;
the longed-for time shall come.

Love and Friendship shall reach
you through the gloomy bolts,
as now into your penal burrows
my free voice reaches.

The heavy chains shall fall,
prisons shall crumble down, and Freedom
shall welcome you, rejoicing, at the entrance,
and brothers shall return your sword to you.

1951–57

АНГЕЛ

В дверях эдема ангел нежный
Главой поникшею сиял,
А демон мрачный и мятежный
Над адской бездною летал.

Дух отрицанья, дух сомненья
На духа чистого взирал
И жар невольный умиленья
Впервые смутно познавал.

«Прости, он рек, тебя я видел,
И ты недаром мне сиял:
Не всё я в небе ненавидел,
Не всё я в мире презирал».

1827

THE ANGEL

At Eden's door a tender Angel
let sink his radiant head,
while, gloomy and restless, a Demon
flew over hell's abyss.

The spirit of negation, the spirit of doubt
gazed at the stainless spirit
and an involuntary glow of tender feeling
for the first time he dimly knew.

Quoth he: "Forgive me, I have seen you,
and your radiance has not been lost on me:
not everything in heaven I hated,
not everything on earth I scorned."

1951–57, 1966–67

TO DAWE, ESQR.

Зачем твой дивный карандаш
Рисует мой арапский профиль?
Хоть ты векам его предашь,
Его освищет Мефистофель.

Рисуй Олениной черты,
В жару сердечных вдохновений
Лишь юности и красоты
Поклонником быть должен гений.

1828

TO DAWE, ESQR.

Why draw with your pencil sublime
My Negro profile? Though transmitted
By you it be to future time,
It will be by Mephisto twitted.

Draw fair Olenin's features, in the glow
Of heart-engendered inspiration:
Only on youth and beauty should bestow
A genius its adoration.

ca. 1949

ПОЛТАВА
Посвящение

Тебе—но голос музы темной
Коснется ль уха твоего?
Поймешь ли ты душою скромной
Стремленье сердца моего?
Иль посвящение поэта,
Как некогда его любовь,
Перед тобою без ответа
Пройдет, непризнанное вновь?

Узнай, по крайней мере звуки,
Бывало, милые тебе—
И думай, что во дни разлуки,
В моей изменчивой судьбе,
Твоя печальная пустыня,
Последний звук твоих речей
Одно сокровище, святыня,
Одна любовь души моей.

1828

DEDICATION TO THE LONG POEM *POLTAVA*

To you—but will the obscure Muse's voice
touch your ear?
Will you, with your modest soul, understand
the aspiration of my heart?
Or will the poet's dedication,
as formerly his love,
in front of you without response
pass, unacknowledged once again?
Do recognize at least the measures
that pleasing were to you of yore
and think that in the days of separation
in my unstable fate,
your woeful wilderness,
the last sound of your words,
are the one treasure, shrine,
the one love of my soul.

1951–57

АНЧАР
Древо яда

В пустыне чахлой и скупой,
На почве, зноем раскаленной,
Анчар, как грозный часовой,
Стоит, один во всей вселенной.

Природа жаждущих степей
Его в день гнева породила,
И зелень мертвую ветвей
И корни ядом напоила.

Яд каплет сквозь его кору,
К полудню растопясь от зною,
И застывает ввечеру
Густой, прозрачною смолою.

К нему и птица не летит,
И тигр нейдет: лишь вихорь черный
На древо смерти набежит—
И мчится прочь уже тлетворный.

И если туча оросит,
Блуждая, лист его дремучий,
С его ветвей, уж ядовит
Стекает дождь в песок горючий.

Но человека человек
Послал к Анчару властным взглядом:
И тот послушно в путь потек,
И к утру возвратился с ядом.

Принес он смертную смолу,
Да ветвь с увядшими листами,
И пот по бледному челу
Струился хладными ручьями;

THE UPAS TREE
(*Antiaris toxicaria,* Lesch. 1810)

Deep in the desert's misery,
far in the fury of the sand,
there stands the awesome Upas Tree
lone watchman of a lifeless land.

The wilderness, a world of thirst,
in wrath engendered it and filled
its every root, every accursed
gray leafstalk with a sap that killed.

Dissolving in the midday sun
the poison oozes through its bark,
and freezing when the day is done
gleams thick and gem-like in the dark.

No bird flies near, no tiger creeps;
alone the whirlwind, wild and black,
assails the tree of death and sweeps
away with death upon its back.

And though some roving cloud may stain
with glancing drops those leaden leaves,
the dripping of a poisoned rain
is all the burning sand receives.

But man sent man with one proud look
towards the tree, and he was gone,
the humble one, and there he took
the poison and returned at dawn.

He brought the deadly gum; with it
he brought some leaves, a withered bough,
while rivulets of icy sweat
ran slowly down his livid brow.

Принес—и ослабел, и лег
Под сводом шалаша, на лыки,
И умер бедный раб у ног
Непобедимого владыки.

А князь тем ядом напитал
Свои послушливые стрелы,
И с ними гибель разослал
К соседам в чуждые пределы.

1828

He came, he fell upon a mat,
and reaping a poor slave's reward,
died near the painted hut where sat
his now unconquerable lord.

The king, he soaked his arrows true
in poison, and beyond the plains
dispatched those messengers and slew
his neighbors in their own domains.

1941–43

НА КАРТИНКИ К «ЕВГЕНИЮ ОНЕГИНУ»
В «НЕВСКОМ АЛЬМАНАХЕ»

I.

Вот перешед чрез мост Кокушкин,
Опершись жопой о гранит,
Сам Александр Сергеич Пушкин
С мосьё Онегиным стоит.
Не удостаивая взглядом
Твердыню власти роковой,
Он к крепости стал гордо задом:
Не плюй в колодец, милый мой.

II.

Сосок чернеет сквозь рубашку,
Наружу титька—милый вид!
Татьяна мнет в руке бумажку,
Зане живот у ней болит:
Она затем поутру встала
При бледных месяца лучах
И на подтирку изорвала
Конечно «Невский Альманах».

1829

ON THE ILLUSTRATIONS TO *EUGENE ONEGIN*
IN THE *NEVSKI ALMANAC*

I.

Here, after crossing Bridge Kokushkin,
With bottom on the granite propped,
Stands Aleksandr Sergeich Pushkin;
Near M'sieur Onegin he has stopped.

Ignoring with a look superior
The fateful Power's citadel,
On it he turns a proud posterior:
My dear chap, poison not the well!

II.

Through her chemise a nipple blackens;
Delightful sight: one titty shows.
Tatiana holds a crumpled paper,
For she's beset with stomach throes.

So that is why she got up early
With the pale moonlight still about,
And tore up for a wiping purpose
The *Nevski Almanac,* no doubt.

1951–57

ЗИМНЕЕ УТРО

Мороз и солнце,—день чудесный!
Еще ты дремлешь, друг прелестный,—
Пора, красавица, проснись:
Открой сомкнуты негой взоры,
Навстречу северной Авроры,
Звездою севера явись!

Вечор, ты помнишь, вьюга злилась,
На мутном небе мгла носилась;
Луна, как бледное пятно,
Сквозь тучи мрачные желтела,
И ты печальная сидела—
А нынче. . . погляди в окно:

Под голубыми небесами,
Великолепными коврами,
Блестя на солнце, снег лежит;
Прозрачный лес один чернеет,
И ель сквозь иней зеленеет,
И речка подо льдом блестит.

Вся комната янтарным блеском
Озарена. Веселым треском
Трещит затопленная печь.
Приятно думать у лежанки.
Но знаешь: не велеть ли в санки
Кобылку бурую запречь?

Скользя по утреннему снегу,
Друг милый, предадимся бегу
Нетерпеливого коня,
И навестим поля пустые,
Леса, надавно столь густые,
И берег, милый для меня.

1829

WINTER MORNING

A magic day—sunshine and frost—
but you, in dreamland still are lost . . .
Come, open your enchanting eyes
with honeyed indolence replete . . .
Star of the North, arise to meet
Aurora in her wintry skies.

That blizzard yesternight! It spread
dimness and tumult overhead.
The moon through a lugubrious veil
was but a blur of jaundiced gray,
and you were listless . . . But to-day—
well, let the window tell its tale:

Fabulous carpets of rich snow
under the cloudless heavens glow.
Alone the gauzy birches seem
to show some black, while green occurs
among the frost-bespangled firs,
and blue-shot ice adorns the stream.

The room is flooded with a light
like amber, and with all its might
the hot stove crackles. Lolling there
in meditation is no doubt
enjoyable . . . but what about
a sledge behind the chestnut mare?

Sweet friend, together we shall speed
yielding to our impatient steed
on new-born whiteness, fleet and free,
and visit silent fields of snow,
woods that were lush two months ago,
a lakeshore that is dear to me . . .

1944–47

* * *

Я вас любил: любовь еще, быть может,
В душе моей угасла не совсем;
Но пусть она вас больше не тревожит;
Я не хочу печалить вас ничем.

Я вас любил безмолвно, безнадежно,
То робостью, то ревностью томим;
Я вас любил так искренно, так нежно,
Как дай вам Бог любимой быть другим.

1829

* * *

I worshipped you. My love's reluctant ember
is in my heart still glimmering, may be,
but let it not break on your peace; remember,
I should not want to have you sad through me.

I worshipped you in silent hopeless fashion,
shy was my love, jealous, but always true;
I worshipped you with such a tender passion
as I should want all men to worship you.

Le Boulou, Pyrénées orientales, March 1929

NOTE ON "YA VAS LYUBIL"

This elegant little poem is in iambic pentameter with alternate feminine and masculine rhymes and a neat caesura after the second foot. The first quatrain closes with a very euphonious alliteration on "ch" ("ya ne hochú pechálit' vas nichém") and there are further symmetries ("to róbost'yu, to révnost'yu" and "lyubí-moy bït' drugím") in the second stanza where the melody (so restrained in the first three lines of the first stanza) acquires pathetic amplitude. I have given a parsed translation besides my literal one. The apostrophes in the transliteration of the Russian text denote the "softening" of a consonant. The accents are only there to show a non-Russian reader how the verses are scanned.

* * *

I loved you: love, perhaps, is yet
not quite extinguished in my soul;
but let it trouble you no more;
with nothing do I wish to sadden you.

I loved you mutely, without hope,
either by shyness irked or jealousy;
I loved you so sincerely, with such tenderness,
as by another loved God grant you be.

* * *

Ya vas lyubíl: lyubóv' eshchó, bït' mózhet,
V dushé moéy ugásla ne sovsém;
No pust' oná vas ból'she ne trevózhit;
Ya ne hochú pechálit' vas nichém.

Ya vas lyubíl bezmólvno, beznadézhno,
To róbost'yu, to révnost'yu tomím;
Ya vas lyubíl tak ískrenno, tak nézhno,
Kak day vam Bog lyubímoy bït' drugím.

* * *

I you loved: love yet, maybe,
in soul mine has gone out not quite;
but let it you more not trouble;
I not wish to sadden you with anything.

I you loved mutely, hopelessly,
now by shyness, now by jealousy oppressed;
I you loved so sincerely, so tenderly,
as give you God to be loved by another.

ca. 1949

* * *

Что в имени тебе моем?
Оно умрет, как шум печальный,
Волны, плеснувшей в берег дальный,
Как звук ночной в лесу глухом.

Оно на памятном листке
Оставит мертвый след, подобной
Узору надписи надгробной
На непонятном языке.

Что в нем? Забытое давно
В волненьях новых и мятежных,
Твоей душе не даст оно
Воспоминаний чистых, нежных.

Но в день печали, в тишине
Произнеси его тоскуя,
Скажи: есть память обо мне,
Есть в мире сердце, где живу я.

1830

THE NAME

What is my name to you? 'Twill die:
a wave that has but rolled to reach
with a lone splash a distant beach;
or in the timbered night a cry . . .

'Twill leave a lifeless trace among
names on your tablets: the design
of an entangled gravestone line
in an unfathomable tongue.

What is it then? A long-dead past,
lost in the rush of madder dreams,
upon your soul it will not cast
Mnemosyne's pure tender beams.

But if some sorrow comes to you,
utter my name with sighs, and tell
the silence: "Memory is true—
there beats a heart wherein I dwell."

1944–47

НА БУЛГАРИНА

Не то беда, что ты поляк:
Костюшко лях, Мицкевич лях!
Пожалуй, будь себе татарин,—
И тут не вижу я стыда;
Будь жид—и это не беда;
Беда, что ты Видок Фиглярин.

1830

EPIGRAM

The harm is not that you're a Pole:
so are Kosciusko and Mickiewicz;
a Tatar be, for all I care:
likewise no shame can I see there;
or be a Jew, no harm there either;
the harm is you're Vidocq Figlyarin.

1951–57

ТРУД

Миг вожделенный настал: окончен мой труд многолетний.
    Что ж непонятная грусть тайно тревожит меня?
Или, свой подвиг свершив, я стою, как поденщик ненужный,
    Плату приявший свою, чуждый работе другой?
Или жаль мне труда, молчаливого спутника ночи,
    Друга Авроры златой, друга пенатов святых?

1830

THE WORK (TRUD)

Come is the moment I craved: my work of
    long years is completed.
  Why then this strange sense of woe
    secretly harrowing me?
Having my high task performed, do I stand as
    a useless day laborer
  Stands, with his wages received, foreign
    to all other toil?
Or am I sorry to part with my work, night's
    silent companion,
  Golden Aurora's friend, friend of the
    household gods?

from
ДОМИК В КОЛОМНЕ

I

Четырестопный ямб мне надоел:
Им пишет всякой. Мальчикам в забаву
Пора б его оставить.

[. . .]

1830

A SMALL HOUSE IN KOLOMNA

Of the four-foot iambus I've grown tired.
In it writes everyone. To boys this plaything
'Tis high time to abandon . . .

1951–57

from
МОЯ РОДОСЛОВНАЯ

[. . .]

Упрямства дух нам всем подгадил:
В родню свою неукротим,
С Петром мой пращур не поладил
И был за то повешен им.
Его пример будь нам наукой:

[. . .]

Post Scriptum

Решил Фиглярин, сидя дома,
Что черный дед мой Ганнибал
Был куплен за бутылку рома
И в руки шкиперу попал.

Сей шкипер был тот шкипер славный,
Кем наша двигнулась земля,
Кто придал мощно бег державный
Рулю родного корабля.

Сей шкипер деду был доступен,
И сходно купленный арап
Возрос усерден, неподкупен,
Царю наперсник, а не раб.

[. . .]

1830

from
MY PEDIGREE

A stubborn strain has always let us down:
indomitable, after all his kin,
my grandsire did not hit it off with Peter,
and in result was hanged by him.
To us let his example be a lesson . . .

POST SCRIPTUM

Figlyarin, snug at home, decided
That my black grandsire, Gannibal,
Was for a bottle of rum acquired
And fell into a skipper's hands.

This skipper was the glorious skipper
Through whom our country was advanced,
Who to our native vessel's helm
Gave mightily a sovereign's course.

This skipper was accessible
To my grandsire; the blackamoor,
Bought at a bargain, grew up stanch and loyal,
The emperor's bosom friend, not slave.

1951–57

СКУПОЙ РЫЦАРЬ

Сцена II
(*Подвал.*)

Барон

Как молодой повеса ждет свиданья
С какой-нибудь развратницей лукавой,
Иль дурой, им обманутой, так я
Весь день минуты ждал, когда сойду
В подвал мой тайный, к верным сундукам.
Счастливый день! могу сегодня я
В шестой сундук (в сундук еще неполный)
Горсть золота накопленного всыпать.
Не много кажется, но понемногу
Сокровища растут. Читал я где-то,
Что царь однажды воинам своим
Велел снести земли по горсти в кучу,
И гордый холм возвысился—и царь
Мог с вышины с весельем озирать
И дол, покрытый белыми шатрами,
И море, где бежали корабли.
Так я, по горсти бедной принося
Привычну дань мою сюда в подвал,
Вознес мой холм—и с высоты его
Могу взирать на всё, что мне подвластно.
Что не подвластно мне? как некий Демон
Отселе править миром я могу;
Лишь захочу—воздвигнутся чертоги;
В великолепные мои сады
Сбегутся Нимфы резвою толпою;
И Музы дань свою мне принесут,
И вольный Гений мне поработится,
И Добродетель и бессонный Труд
Смиренно будут ждать моей награды.

A SCENE FROM *THE COVETOUS KNIGHT*

Scene 2.
A cellar.

The Baron, *alone.*

Just as a mad young fellow frets awaiting
his rendez-vous with some evasive harlot,
or with the goose seduced by him, thus I
have dreamt all day of coming down at last
in vaulted dimness to my secret chests.
The day was good: this evening I can add
to coffer six (which still is not quite sated)
some recently collected gold: a fistful,
a trifle, you might say, but thus my treasure
a trifle is increased. There is some story
about a Prince who bade his warriors bring
a handful each of earth, which formed a hillock
which swelled into a mountain, and the Prince
from this proud height could merrily survey
the dale white-dotted with his tented army,
the many sails that sped upon the sea.
So bit by bit I have been bringing here
my customary tithe into this vault,
and heaped my hill, and from its eminence
I now survey my vassaldom at leisure.
And who is not my vassal? Like some daemon
from here in private I can rule the world;
let me just wish—and there will rise a palace;
amid the marvels of my terraced lawns
a swarm of Nymphs will airily assemble;
the sacred Nine will come with mask or lute;
unshackled Genius labor as my bondsman,
and noble merit, and the sleepless drudge
wait with humility till I reward them.

Я свистну, и ко мне послушно, робко
Вползет окровавленное Злодейство,
И руку будет мне лизать, и в очи
Смотреть, в них знак моей читая воли.
Мне всё послушно, я же—ничему;
Я выше всех желаний; я спокоен;
Я знаю мощь мою: с меня довольно
Сего сознанья. . .

(*Смотрит на свое золото.*)

Кажется не много,
А скольких человеческих забот,
Обманов, слез, молений и проклятий
Оно тяжеловесный представитель!
Тут есть дублон старинный. . . вот он. Нынче
Вдова мне отдала его, но прежде
С тремя детьми полдня перед окном
Она стояла на коленях воя.
Шел дождь, и перестал и вновь пошел,
Притворщица не трогалась; я мог бы
Ее прогнать, но что-то мне шептало,
Что мужнин долг она мне принесла
И не захочет завтра быть в тюрьме.
А этот? этот мне принес Тибо—
Где было взять ему ленивцу, плуту?
Украл конечно; или, может быть,
Там на большой дороге, ночью, в роще. . .
Да! если бы все слезы, кровь и пот,
Пролитые за всё, что здесь хранится,
Из недр земных все выступили вдруг,
То был бы вновь потоп—я захлебнулся б
В моих подвалах верных. Но пора.

(*Хочет отпереть сундук.*)

I'll whistle, and behold: low-bending, cringing,
in creeps Assassination, blood-bespattered,
and while it licks my hands it will be watching
my eyes to read in them the master's order.
All is to me subjected, I to naught.
I am above desiring; I am tranquil:
I know my domination, and this knowledge
I deem sufficient.

(*Looks into his money-bag*)

It may seem a little,
but what incalculable human cares,
deceptions, tears, entreaties, imprecations,
have weighty representatives here seated!

Where was that old doubloon? . . . Here 'tis. This evening
a widow paid it me—though only after
she'd stood, with her three children, many hours
under my window, on her knees and wailing.
It rained, and ceased to rain, and rained again:
the shamming creature never budged. I might have
sent her away, but a faint something told me
that she had brought the sum her husband owed
and would not care to be in jail next day.
And this one? this was brought me by Thibault:
whom did he get it from, the fox, the loafer?
Stole it, I wager; or perhaps . . . somewhere,
at nightfall, on the highway, in a coppice—
Ah, you! if all the tears, and blood, and sweat,
that have been shed for what is in my keeping,
out of deep earth might suddenly gush forth
we'd have a second flood,—and with a splutter
I'd perish in my trusty vaults.
                    And now—

(*He is about to unlock number six.*)

Я каждый раз, когда хочу сундук
Мой отпереть, впадаю в жар и трепет.
Не страх (о, нет! кого боятся мне?
При мне мой меч: за злато отвечает
Честной булат), но сердце мне теснит
Какое-то неведомое чувство. . .
Нас уверяют медики: есть люди,
В убийстве находящие приятность.
Когда я ключ в замок влагаю, то же
Я чувствую, что чувствовать должны
Они, вонзая в жертву нож: приятно
И страшно вместе.

(*Отпирает сундук.*)

Вот мое блаженство!

(*Всыпает деньги.*)

Ступайте, полно вам по свету рыскать,
Служа страстям и нуждам человека.
Усните здесь сном силы и покоя,
Как боги спят в глубоких небесах. . .
Хочу себе сегодня пир устроить:
Зажгу свечу пред каждым сундуком,
И все их отопру, и стану сам
Средь них глядеть на блещущие груды.

(*Зажигает свечи и отпирает сундуки один
за другим.*)

Я царствую!—Какой волшебный блеск!
Послушна мне, сильна моя держава;
В ней счастие, в ней честь моя и слава!
Я царствую—но кто вослед за мной
Приимет власть над нею? Мой наследник!
Безумец, расточитель молодой,
Развратников разгульных собеседник!

Strange—every time I want to open one
of my good chests, I feel all hot and shaky:
not fear (oh, no! whom should I fear? I have
my gallant sword: one metal guards the other
and answers for it), but a heart-invading
mysteriously enveloping oppression . . .
Physicians claim that there exist queer people
who find in homicide a kind of pleasure;
when I insert and turn the key, my feelings
are similar, I fancy, to what they
must feel when butchering their victims: pleasure
and terror mingled.

> (*Unlocks*)

> This is lovely, lovely . . .

> (*Pours in his gold*)

Go home, you've had your fill of worldly frisking
and served your time with human needs and passions.
Here you will sleep the sleep of peace and power,
as gods do sleep in Heaven's dreamy depth.
To-night I wish to have a feast in secret:—
a candle bright in front of every chest,
and all of them wide-open, and myself
with eyes aglow amid their brimming glory.

> (*Lights candles and proceeds to unlock
> the chests*)

Now I am king! What an enchanted shine!
A mighty realm has now become my manor;
here is my bliss, my blazon, and my banner!
Now I am king!—But who will next enjoy
this bounty when I die? My heir will get it!
A wastrel, a disreputable boy,
by ribald fellow-revelers abetted!

Едва умру, он, он! сойдет сюда
Под эти мирные, немые своды
С толпой ласкателей, придворных жадных.
Украв ключи у трупа моего,
Он сундуки со смехом отопрет,
И потекут сокровища мои
В атласные дирявые карманы.
Он разобьет священные сосуды,
Он грязь елеем царским напоит—
Он расточит. . . А по какому праву?
Мне разве даром это всё досталось,
Или шутя, как игроку, который
Гремит костьми, да груды загребает?
Кто знает, сколько горьких воздержаний,
Обузданных страстей, тяжелых дум,
Дневных забот, ночей бессонных мне
Всё это стоило? Иль скажет сын,
Что сердце у меня обросло мохом,
Что я не знал желаний, что меня
И совесть никогда не грызла, совесть,
Когтистый зверь, скребущий сердце, совесть,
Незваный гость, докучный собеседник,
Заимодавец грубый; эта ведьма,
От коей меркнет месяц и могилы
Смущаются и мертвых высылают? . .
Нет, выстрадай сперва себе богатство,
А там, посмотрим, станет ли несчастный
То расточать, что кровью приобрел.
О, если б мог от взоров недостойных
Я скрыть подвал! о, если б из могилы
Придти я мог, сторожевою тенью
Сидеть на сундуке и от живых
Сокровища мои хранить как ныне! . .

1826–30

With my last sigh, him, him! this vault will hear
come stamping down into its gentle silence,
with crowds of fawning friends, rapacious courtiers;
and having plucked the keys from my dead fist
he will unlock chest after chest with glee,
and all the treasures of my life will stream
through all the holes of tattered satin pockets.
Thus will a sot destroy these holy vessels,
thus mud will drink an oil for kingly brows,
thus he will spend—And by what right, I ask you?
Did I perchance acquire all this for nothing?
Or with the ease of a light-hearted gambler
that rattles dice and grabs his growing winnings?
Who knows how many bitter limitations,
what bursting passions curbed, what inner gloom,
what crowded days and hollow nights—my wealth
has cost me? Or perchance my son will say
that with a hoary moss my heart is smothered,
that I have had no longings, and what's more,
that conscience never bit me? Grizzly conscience!
the sharp-clawed beast that scrapes in bosoms; conscience,
the sudden guest, the bore that does the talking,
the brutish money-lender; worst of witches,
that makes the moon grow dark, and then the grave-stones
move restlessly, and send their dead to haunt us!
Nay, suffer first and wince thy way to riches,
then we shall see how readily my rascal
will toss to winds what his heart-blood has bought.
Oh, that I might conceal this vaulted chamber
from sinful eyes! oh, that I might abandon
my grave and, as a watchful ghost, come hither
to sit upon my chests, and from the quick
protect my treasures as I do at present!

1941–44

МОЦАРТ И САЛЬЕРИ

Сцена I: *Комната.*

Сальери

Все говорят: нет правды на земле.
Но правды нет—и выше. Для меня
Так это ясно, как простая гамма.
Родился я с любовию к искусству;
Ребенком будучи, когда высоко
Звучал орган в старинной церкви нашей,
Я слушал и заслушивался—слезы
Невольные и сладкие текли.
Отверг я рано праздные забавы;
Науки, чуждые музыке, были
Постылы мне; упрямо и надменно
От них отрекся я и предался
Одной музыке. Труден первый шаг
И скучен первый путь. Преодолел
Я ранние невзгоды. Ремесло
Поставил я подножием искусству;
Я сделался ремесленник: перстам
Придал послушную, сухую беглость
И верность уху. Звуки умертвив,
Музыку я разъял, как труп. Поверил
Я алгеброй гармонию. Тогда
Уже дерзнул, в науке искушенный,
Предаться неге творческой мечты.
Я стал творить; но в тишине, но в тайне,
Не смея помышлять еще о славе.
Нередко, просидев в безмолвной келье
Два, три дня, позабыв и сон, и пищу,
Вкусив восторг и слезы вдохновенья,
Я жег мой труд и холодно смотрел,
Как мысль моя и звуки, мной рожденны,
Пылая, с легким дымом исчезали.

MOZART AND SALIERI

Scene I: *A room.*

Salieri

They say there is no justice on the earth.
I know now there is none in Heaven. Plain
as seven simple notes! I have loved the art
from birth; when I was but a little child
in our old church and the organ boomed sublimely,
I listened and was lost—shedding delicious
involuntary tears. I turned away
from foolish pastimes early; found repellent
all studies foreign to my music—ay,
from all I turned with obstinate disdain,
determined thence to dedicate myself
to music, music only. The start is hard,
the first steps make dull going. I surmounted
the initial obstacles; I grounded firmly
that craft that makes the pedestal for art;
a craftsman I became: I trained my fingers
to dry obedient proficiency,
brought sureness to my ear. Stunning the sounds,
I cut up music like a corpse; I tested
the laws of harmony by mathematics.
Then only, rich in learning, dared I yield
to blandishments of sweet creative fancy.
I dared compose—but silently, in secret,
nor could I venture yet to dream of glory.
How often, in my solitary cell,
having toiled for days, having sat unbroken hours,
forgetting food and sleep, and having tasted
the rapture and the tears of inspiration,
I'd burn my work and coldly watch the flame
as my own melodies and meditations
flared up and smoked a little and were gone.

Что говорю? Когда великий Глюк
Явился и открыл нам новы тайны
(Глубокие, пленительные тайны),
Не бросил ли я всё, что прежде знал,
Что так любил, чему так жарко верил,
И не пошел ли бодро вслед за ним
Безропотно, как тот, кто заблуждался
И встречным послан в сторону иную?
Усильным, напряженным постоянством
Я наконец в искусстве безграничном
Достигнул степени высокой. Слава
Мне улыбнулась; я в сердцах людей
Нашел созвучия своим созданьям.
Я счастлив был: я наслаждался мирно
Своим трудом, успехом, славой; также
Трудами и успехами друзей,
Товарищей моих в искусстве дивном.
Нет! никогда я зависти не знал,
О, никогда!—ниже́, когда Пиччини
Пленить умел слух диких парижан,
Ниже́, когда услышал в первый раз
Я Ифигении начальны звуки.
Кто скажет, чтоб Сальери гордый был
Когда-нибудь завистником презренным,
Змеей, людьми растоптанною, вживе
Песок и пыль грызущею бессильно?
Никто! . . А ныне—сам скажу—я ныне
Завистник. Я завидую; глубоко,
Мучительно завидую.—О небо!
Где ж правота, когда священный дар,
Когда бессмертный гений—не в награду
Любви горящей, самоотверженья,
Трудов, усердия, молений послан—
А озаряет голову безумца,
Гуляки праздного? . . О Моцарт, Моцарт!

Nay, even more: when the great Gluck appeared,
when he unveiled to us new marvels, deep
enchanting marvels—did I not forsake
all I had known, and loved so well and trusted?
Did I not follow him with eager stride,
obedient as one who'd lost his way
and met a passerby who knew the turning?
By dint of stubborn steadfast perseverance
upon the endless mountainside of art
I reached at last a lofty level. Fame
smiled on me; and I found in others' hearts
responses to the sounds I had assembled.
Came happy days; in quiet I enjoyed
work and success and fame—enjoying also
the works and the successes of my friends,
my comrades in that art divine we served.
Oh, never did I envy know. Nay, never!
Not even when Piccini found a way
to captivate the ears of savage Paris—
not even when I heard for the first time
the plangent opening strains of "Iphigenia."
Is there a man alive who'll say Salieri
has ever stooped to envy—played the snake
that, trampled underfoot, still writhes and bites
the gravel and the dust in helpless spite?
No one! . . . Yet now—I needs must say it—now
I am an envious man. I envy—deeply,
to agony, I envy.—Tell me, Heaven!
where now is justice when the holiest gift,
when genius and its immortality,
come not as a reward for fervent love,
for abnegation, prayer and dogged labor—
but light its radiance in the head of folly,
of idle wantonness? . . . Oh, Mozart, Mozart!

(Входит Моцарт.)

Моцарт

Ага! увидел ты! а мне хотелось
Тебя нежданной шуткой угостить.

Сальери

Ты здесь!—Давно ль?

Моцарт

     Сейчас. Я шел к тебе,
Нес кое-что тебе я показать;
Но, проходя перед трактиром, вдруг
Услышал скрыпку. . . Нет, мой друг, Сальери!
Смешнее отроду ты ничего
Не слыхивал. . . Слепой скрыпач в трактире
Разыгрывал voi che sapete. Чудо!
Не вытерпел, привел я скрыпача,
Чтоб угосить тебя его искусством.
Войди!

    (Входит слепой старик со скрыпкой.)

  Из Моцарта нам что-нибудь!

    (Старик играет арию из Дон-Жуана;
    Моцарт хохочет.)

Сальери

И ты смеяться можешь?

Моцарт

     Ах, Сальери!
Ужель и сам ты не смеешься?

Mozart enters.

Mozart

Aha! you saw me! I was just preparing
to take you by surprise—a little joke.

Salieri

You here?—When did you come?

Mozart

                                This minute. I
was on my way to you to show you something
when, passing near a tavern, all at once
I heard a fiddle . . . Oh, my dear Salieri!
You never in your life heard anything
so funny . . . That blind fiddler in a pothouse
playing *Voi che sapete*. Marvelous!
I simply had to bring him here to have you
enjoy his art.—Step in!

> *Enter a blind old man with a violin.*

                Some Mozart, please!

> *The old man plays the aria from "Don Giovanni";*
> *Mozart roars with laughter.*

Salieri

And you can laugh?

Mozart

                Oh, come, can't you?

Сальери

                Нет.
Мне не смешно, когда маляр негодный
Мне пачкает Мадону Рафаэля,
Мне не смешно, когда фигляр презренный
Пародией бесчестит Алигьери.
Пошел, старик.

Моцарт

                Постой же: вот тебе,
Пей за мое здоровье.

                (*Старик уходит.*)

                Ты, Сальери,
Не в духе нынче. Я приду к тебе
В другое время.

Сальери

                Что ты мне принес?

Моцарт

Нет—так; безделицу. Намедни ночью
Бессоница моя меня томила,
И в голову пришли мне две, три мысли.
Сегодня их я набросал. Хотелось
Твое мне слышать мненье; но теперь
Тебе не до меня.

Сальери

                Ах, Моцарт, Моцарт!
Когда же мне не до тебя? Садись;
Я слушаю.

Salieri

I cannot.
I am not amused by miserable daubers
who make a mess of Raphael's Madonna;
I am not amused by despicable zanies
whose parodies dishonor Alighieri.
Be off, old man.

Mozart

Wait: here's some money for you—
you'll drink my health.

The old man goes out.

It seems to me, Salieri,
You're out of sorts to-day. I'll come to see you
some other time.

Salieri

What have you brought?

Mozart

Oh, nothing—
a trifle. My insomnia last night
was troubling me, and one or two ideas
entered my head. Today I dashed them down.
I wanted your opinion; but just now
you're in no mood for me.

Salieri

Ah, Mozart! Mozart!
When is my mood averse to you? Sit down.
I'm listening.

Моцарт (*за фортепиано*)

              Представь себе. . . кого бы?
Ну, хоть меня—немного помоложе;
Влюбленного—не слишком, а слегка—
С красоткой, или с другом—хоть с тобой—
Я весел. . . Вдруг: виденье гробовое,
Незапный мрак иль что-нибудь такое. . .
Ну, слушай же.

            (*Играет.*)

Сальери

              Ты с этим шел ко мне
И мог остановиться у трактира
И слушать скрыпача слепого!—Боже!
Ты, Моцарт, недостоин сам себя.

Моцарт

Что ж, хорошо?

Сальери

             Какая глубина!
Какая смелость и какая стройность!
Ты, Моцарт, бог, и сам того не знаешь;
Я знаю, я.

Моцарт

           Ба! право? может-быть. . .
Но божество мое проголодалось.

Сальери

Послушай: отобедаем мы вместе
В трактире Золотого Льва.

Mozart (*at the piano*)

        I want you to imagine . . .
Whom shall we say? . . . well, let's suppose myself
a little younger—and in love—not deeply,
but just a little —sitting with a damsel
or with a bosom friend—yourself, let's say—
I am merry . . . All at once: a ghostly vision,
a sudden gloom, or something of the sort . . .
Well, this is how it goes.

        He plays.

  Salieri

          You were bringing this,
and you could stop to linger at a tavern
and listen to a blind man with a fiddle!
Ah, Mozart, you are unworthy of yourself.

  Mozart

You like it, do you?

  Salieri

        What profundity!
What daring and what grace! Why, you're a god,
and do not know it; but *I* know, *I* know.

  Mozart

What, really? Maybe so . . . If so, His Godhead
is getting to be hungry.

  Salieri

        Listen, Mozart:
Let's dine together at the Golden Lion.

Моцарт

                        Пожалуй;
Я рад. Но дай, схожу домой, сказать
Жене, чтобы меня она к обеду
Не дожидалась.

               (*Уходит.*)

Сальери

                    Жду тебя; смотри ж.
Нет! не могу противиться я доле
Судьбе моей: я избран, чтоб его
Остановить—не то, мы все погибли,
Мы все, жрецы, служители музыки,
Не я один с моей глухою славой. . .
Что пользы, если Моцарт будет жив
И новой высоты еще достигнет?
Подымет ли он тем искусство? Нет;
Оно падет опять, как он исчезнет:
Наследника нам не оставит он.
Что пользы в нем? Как некий херувим,
Он несколько занес нам песен райских,
Чтоб возмутив бескрылое желанье
В нас, чадах праха, после улететь!
Так улетай же! чем скорей, тем лучше!

Вот яд, последний дар моей Изоры.
Осьмнадцать лет ношу его с собою—
И часто жизнь казалась мне с тех пор
Несносной раной, и сидел я часто
С врагом беспечным за одной трапезой
И никогда на шопот искушенья
Не преклонился я, хоть я не трус,
Хотя обиду чувствую глубоко,
Хоть мало жизнь люблю. Всё медлил я.
Как жажда смерти мучила меня,

Mozart

A capital idea. But let me first
go home a moment: I must tell my wife
she's not to wait for me.

He goes.

Salieri

> Don't fail me now.
—Nay, now can I no longer fight with fate:
my destiny's to stop him—else we perish,
we all, the priests, the ministers of music,
not I alone with my dull-sounding fame . . .
What worth are we if Mozart lives and reaches
new summits still? Will this exalt our art?
Nay: art will sink so soon as he departs:
he will leave us no successor—will have served
no useful purpose. Like a seraph swooping,
he brought us certain songs from Paradise,
only to stab us, children of the dust,
with helpless wingless longing, and fly off!
—So fly away!—the sooner now, the better.
Here's poison: the last gift of my Isora.
For eighteen years I've kept it, let it season—
and often life would seem to me a wound
too bitter to be borne—I have often sat
with some unwary enemy at table,
yet never did that inward whisper win me;
though I'm no coward and feel insult deeply,
and care not much for life. Still did I tarry,
tormented by the thirst for death, yet brooding;

Что умирать? я мнил: быть может, жизнь
Мне принесет незапные дары;
Быть может, посетит меня восторг
И творческая ночь и вдохновенье;
Быть может, новый Гайден сотворит
Великое—и наслажуся им. . .
Как пировал я с гостем ненавистным,
Быть может, мнил я, злейшего врага
Найду; быть может, злейшая обида
В меня с надменной грянет высоты—
Тогда не пропадешь ты, дар Изоры.
И я был прав! и наконец нашел
Я моего врага, и новый Гайден
Меня восторгом дивно упоил!
Теперь—пора! заветный дар любви,
Переходи сегодня в чашу дружбы.

Сцена II: *Особая комната в трактире; фортепиано.*

Моцарт и Сальери за столом.

Сальери

Что ты сегодня пасмурен?

Моцарт

Я? Нет!

Сальери

Ты, верно, Моцарт, чем-нибудь расстроен?
Обед хороший, славное вино,
А ты молчишь и хмуришься.

Моцарт

Признаться,
Мой Requiem меня тревожит.

why should I die? Perchance the future yet
holds unexpected benefits; perchance
I may be visited by Orphic rapture,
my night of inspiration and creation;
perchance another Haydn may achieve
some great new thing—and I shall live in him . . .
While I was feasting with some hated guest,
perchance, I'd muse, I'll find an enemy
more hateful still; perchance a sharper insult
may come to blast me from a prouder eminence
—*then* you will not be lost, Isora's gift!
And I was right! At last I have encountered
my perfect enemy: another Haydn
has made me taste divine delight! The hour
draws nigh at last. Most sacred gift of love:
You'll pass to-night into the cup of friendship.

Scene II: *A private room in a tavern, with a piano,*

Mozart and Salieri at table.

Salieri

What makes you look so gloomy?

Mozart

Gloomy? No.

Salieri

Mozart, there's surely something on your mind.
The dinner's good, the wine is excellent,
but you, you frown and brood.

Mozart

I must confess it:
I'm worried about my Requiem.

Сальери

А!

Ты сочиняешь Requiem? Давно ли?

Моцарт

Давно, недели три. Но странный случай. . .
Не сказывал тебе я?

Сальери

Нет.

Моцарт

Так слушай.
Недели три тому, пришел я поздно
Домой. Сказали мне, что заходил
За мною кто-то. Отчего—не знаю,
Всю ночь я думал: кто бы это был?
И что ему во мне? Назавтра тот же
Зашел и не застал опять меня.
На третий день играл я на полу
С моим мальчишкой. Кликнули меня;
Я вышел. Человек, одетый в черном,
Учтиво поклонившись, заказал
Мне Requiem и скрылся. Сел я тотчас
И стал писать—и с той поры за мной
Не приходил мой черный человек;
А я и рад: мне было б жаль расстаться
С моей работой, хоть совсем готов
Уж Requiem. Но между тем я. . .

Сальери

Что?

Моцарт

Мне совестно признаться в этом. . .

Salieri

Oh, you're writing
a Requiem? Since when?

Mozart

Three weeks or so.
But the queer part . . . didn't I tell you?

Salieri

No.

Mozart

Well, listen:
three weeks ago I got home rather late—
they told me someone had been there to see me.
All night—I know not why—I lay and wondered
who it could be and what he wanted of me.
Next day the same thing happened: the man came;
I was not in. The third day—I was playing
upon the carpet with my little boy—
there came a knock: they called me, and I went;
a man, black-coated, with a courteous bow,
ordered a Requiem and disappeared.
So I sat down at once and started writing.
Now from that day to this my man in black
has never come again.—Not that I mind
I hate the thought of parting with my work,
though now it's done. Yet in the meantime I . . .

Salieri

You what?

Mozart

I am ashamed to say it.

Сальери

В чем же?

Моцарт

Мне день и ночь покоя не дает
Мой черный человек. За мною всюду
Как тень он гонится. Вот и теперь
Мне кажется, он с нами сам-третей
Сидит.

Сальери

И, полно! что за страх ребячий?
Рассей пустую думу. Бомарше
Говаривал мне: «Слушай, брат Сальери,
Как мысли черные к тебе придут,
Откупори шампанского бутылку,
Иль перечти Женитьбу Фигаро».

Моцарт

Да! Бомарше ведь был тебе приятель;
Ты для него Тарара сочинил,
Вещь славную. Там есть один мотив. . .
Я все твержу его, когда я счастлив. . .
Ла ла ла ла. . . Ах, правда ли, Сальери,
Что Бомарше кого-то отравил?

Сальери

Не думаю: он слишком был смешон
Для ремесла такого.

Моцарт

Он же гений,
Как ты, да я. А гений и злодейство—
Две вещи несовместные. Не правда ль?

Salieri

To say what?

Mozart

I am haunted by that man, that man in black.
He never leaves me day or night. He follows
behind me like a shadow. Even now
I seem to see him sitting here with us,
making a third.

Salieri

Come, come! what childish terrors!
Dispel these hollow fancies, Beaumarchais
was wont to say to me: "Look here, old friend,
when black thoughts trouble you, uncork a bottle
of bright champagne, or reread 'Figaro.'"

Mozart

Yes, you and Beaumarchais were boon companions,
of course—you wrote "Tarare" for Beaumarchais.
A splendid piece—especially one tune—
I always find I hum it when I'm gay:
ta-tá, ta-tá . . . Salieri, was it true
that Beaumarchais once poisoned someone?

Salieri

No:
I doubt it. He was much too droll a fellow
for such a trade.

Mozart

And then he was a genius
like you and me. And villainy and genius
are two things that don't go together, do they?

Сальери

Ты думаешь?

       (Бросает яд в стакан Моцарта.)

Ну, пей же.

Моцарт

       За твое
Здоровье, друг, за искренний союз,
Связующий Моцарта и Сальери,
Двух сыновей гармонии.

       (Пьет.)

Сальери

       Постой,
Постой, постой! . . Ты выпил? . . без меня?

Моцарт *(бросает салфетку на стол)*

Довольно, сыт я.

       (Идет к фортепиано.)

       Слушай же, Сальери,
Мой Requiem.

       (Играет.)

       Ты плачешь?

Сальери

       Эти слезы
Впервые лью: и больно и приятно,
Как будто тяжкий совершил я долг,
Как будто нож целебный мне отсек
Страдавший член! друг Моцарт, эти слезы. . .

Salieri

You think so?

He pours the poison into Mozart's glass.

Drink your wine.

Mozart

Your health, dear friend:
here's to the frank and loyal brotherhood
of Mozart and Salieri, sons of Music.

He drinks.

Salieri

Wait, wait! You've drunk it off. You've left me out.

Mozart (*throwing his napkin on the table*)

Enough:
I've eaten.

He goes to the piano.

Listen to this, Salieri:
my Requiem.

He plays.

Are you weeping?

Salieri

These are tears
I've never shed before—painful yet anodyne,
as if I had discharged a heavy debt,
as if the surgeon's knife had lopped away
a sick and throbbing limb! These tears, dear Mozart . . .

Не замечай их. Продолжай, спеши
Еще наполнить звуками мне душу. . .

Моцарт

Когда бы все так чувствовали силу
Гармонии! но нет: тогда б не мог
И мир существовать; никто б не стал
Заботиться о нуждах низкой жизни;
Все предались бы вольному искусству.
Нас мало избранных, счастливцев праздных,
Пренебрегающих презренной пользой,
Единого прекрасного жрецов.
Не правда ль? Но я нынче нездоров,
Мне что-то тяжело; пойду, засну.
Прощай же!

Сальери

До свиданья.

(*Один.*)

Ты заснешь
Надолго, Моцарт! но ужель он прав,
И я не гений? Гений и злодейство
Две вещи несовместные. Неправда:
А Бонаротти? или это сказка
Тупой, бессмысленной толпы—и не был
Убийцею создатель Ватикана?

1826—30

You must not mind them. Oh, play on, make haste,
flooding my soul with sound . . .

Mozart

                    If all could feel
like you the force of harmony! But no;
the world would crumble then; for none would care
to bother with the baser needs of life;
then all would seek art's franchise. We are few,
the chosen ones, the happy idlers, we
who have no use for what is merely useful,
who worship only beauty—do we not,
dear friend?—But I'm not well—some leaden languor . . .
I must have sleep. Adieu!

Salieri

               Until we meet.

Alone.

Your sleep will be a long one, Mozart!—Nay,
it cannot be that what he said was true,
and I no genius. "Villainy and genius,
two things that do not go together." Wait:
that's false—for surely there was Buonarroti.
—Or is that but a legend, but a lie,
bred by the stupid mob, by their inane
vulgarity, and that great soul who wrought
the Vatican had never sunk to murder?

                                        1941

ПИР ВО ВРЕМЯ ЧУМЫ
(Из Вильсоновой трагедии:
The City of the Plague)

(*Улица. Накрытый стол.
Несколько пирующих мужчин и женщин.*)

Молодой человек

Почтенный председатель! я напомню
О человеке, очень нам знакомом,
О том, чьи шутки, повести смешные,
Ответы острые и замечанья,
Столь едкие в их важности забавной,
Застольную беседу оживляли
И разгоняли мрак, который ныне
Зараза, гостья наша, насылает
На самые блестящие умы.
Тому два дня, наш общий хохот славил
Его рассказы; невозможно быть,
Чтоб мы в своем веселом пированьи
Забыли Джаксона! Его здесь кресла
Стоят пустые, будто ожидая
Весельчака—но он ушел уже
В холодные подземные жилища. . .
Хотя красноречивейший язык
Не умолкал еще во прахе гроба,
Но много нас еще живых, и нам
Причины нет печалиться. Итак
Я предлагаю выпить в его память
С веселым звоном рюмок, с восклицаньем,
Как будто б был он жив.

Председатель

         Он выбыл первый
Из круга нашего. Пускай в молчаньи
Мы выпьем в честь его.

A FEAST DURING THE PLAGUE

Pushkin's version of a scene in Wilson's tragedy
The City of the Plague

> *Several men and women making merry at a table
> laid in the middle of the street.*

A Young Man

Most honorable chairman! Let me now
remind you of a man we all knew well,
a man whose quiddities and funny stories,
smart repartees and pungent observations,
—made with a solemn air that was so pleasing—
lent such a sparkle to the table talk
and helped to chase the gloom which nowadays
our guest the Plague unfortunately casts
over the minds of our most brilliant wits.
Two days ago our rolling laughter greeted
the tales he told; 'twould be a sorry jest
if we forgot while banqueting to-day
our good old Jackson! Here his armchair gapes:
its empty seat still seems to be awaiting
the wag; but he, alas, has left already
for a cold dwelling-place beneath the earth.
Though never was so eloquent a tongue
doomed to keep still in a decaying casket,
we who remain are numerous and have
no reason to be sorrowful. And so
let me suggest a toast to Jackson's spirit,
a merry clash of glasses, exclamations,
as if he were alive.

The Chairman

     He was the first
to drop out of our ranks. In silence let us
drink to his memory.

Молодой человек

Да будет так!

(*Все пьют молча.*)

Председатель

Твой голос, милая, выводит звуки
Родимых песен с диким совершенством;
Спой, Мери, нам, уныло и протяжно,
Чтоб мы потом к веселью обратились
Безумнее, как тот, кто от земли
Был отлучен каким-нибудь виденьем.

Мери (*поет*)

Было время, процветала
В мире наша сторона;
В воскресение бывала
Церковь Божия полна;
Наших деток в шумной школе
Раздавались голоса,
И сверкали в светлом поле
Серп и быстрая коса.

Ныне церковь опустела;
Школа глухо заперта;
Нива праздно перезрела;
Роща темная пуста;
И селенье, как жилище
Погорелое, стоит,—
Тихо все—одно кладбище
Не пустеет, не молчит—

Поминутно мертвых носят,
И стенания живых
Боязливо Бога просят
Успокоить души их.

The Young Man

> Have it your own way.

> *All lift their glasses in silence.*

The Chairman (*to one of the women*)

Your voice, my dear, in rendering the accents
of native songs reveals a wild perfection:
sing, Mary, something dolorous and plaintive
that afterwards we may revert more madly
to merriment—like one who has been torn
from a familiar world by some dark vision.

> **Mary** (*sings*)
>
> In times agone our village
> was lovely to behold;
> our bonny church on Sundays
> was full of young and old;
> our happy children's voices
> rang in the noisy school;
> in sunny fields the reaper
> swung fast his flashing tool.
>
> But now the church is empty;
> the school is locked; the corn
> bends overripe and idle;
> the dark woods are forlorn;
> and like charred ruins the village
> stands stricken on its hill:
> no sound; alone the churchyard
> is full and never still.
>
> A new corpse every minute
> is carried in with dread
> by mourners loudly begging
> God's welcome for the dead.

Поминутно места надо,
И могилы меж собой,
Как испуганное стадо,
Жмутся тесной чередой.

Если ранняя могила
Суждена моей весне—
Ты, кого я так любила,
Чья любовь отрада мне,—
Я молю: не приближайся,
К телу Дженни ты своей;
Уст умерших не касайся,
Следуй издали за ней.

И потом оставь селенье,
Уходи куда-нибудь,
Где б ты мог души мученье
Усладить и отдохнуть.
И когда зараза минет,
Посети мой бедный прах;
А Эдмонда не покинет
Дженни даже в небесах!

Председатель

Благодарим, задумчивая Мери,
Благодарим за жалобную песню!
В дни прежние чума такая ж видно,
Холмы и долы ваши посетила,
И раздавались жалкие стенанья
По берегам потоков и ручьев,
Бегущих ныне весело и мирно
Сквозь дикий рай твоей земли родной;
И мрачный год, в который пало столько
Отважных, добрых и прекрасных жертв,
Едва оставил память о себе
В какой-нибудь простой пастушьей песне

A new hole every minute
is needed for their sleep,
and tombs and tombs together
huddle like frightened sheep.

So if an early gravestone
must crown my springtime bright,
you whom I loved so dearly,
whose love was my delight,—
to your poor Jenny's body,
I pray, do not come near,
kiss not her dead lips; follow
with lagging steps her bier.

And after I am buried,—
go, leave the village, find
some place where hearts are mended
and destiny is kind.
And when the Plague is over
visit my dust, I pray . . .
But, even dead, will Jenny
beside her Edmund stay.

The Chairman

We thank you, Mary, melancholy Mary,
we thank you all for this melodious moan.
In former days a similar infection
has visited, it seems, your hills and valleys,
and one could hear most piteous lamentations
sounding along the rivers and the brooks
which now so peacefully and gaily tumble
through the wild paradise of your dear land;
and that dark year in which so many perished,
so many gallant, good and comely souls,
has left but a vague memory that clouds
the elemental minstrelsy of shepherds

Унылой и приятной. . . нет! ничто
Так не печалит нас среди веселий,
Как томный, сердцем повторенный звук!

Мери

О, если б никогда я не певала
Вне хижины родителей своих!
Они свою любили слушать Мери;
Самой себе я, кажется, внимаю
Поющей у родимого порога—
Мой голос слаще был в то время: он
Был голосом невинности. . .

Луиза

                    Не в моде
Теперь такие песни! но всё ж есть
Еще простые души: рады таять
От женских слез и слепо верят им.
Она уверена, что взор слезливый
Ее неотразим—а если б то же
О смехе думала своем, то верно
Всё б улыбалась. Вальсингам хвалил
Крикливых северных красавиц: вот
Она и расстоналась. Ненавижу
Волос шотландских этих желтизну.

Председатель

Послушайте: я слышу стук колес!

               (Едет телега, наполненная мертвыми
                 телами. Негр управляет ею.)

Ага! Луизе дурно; в ней, я думал—
По языку судя, мужское сердце.
Но так-то—нежного слабей жестокой,

with pleasing plaintiveness. Nothing, I swear,
so saddens us amid life's animation
as dreamy sounds that dreamy hearts repeat.

Mary

Oh, had I never sung beyond the threshold
of the small cottage where my parents dwelt!
Dearly they used to love their Mary's voice.
Behind my song I felt as if I listened
to my old self singing in the bright doorway:
my voice was sweeter in those days: it was
the golden voice of innocence.

Louisa

       Such ditties
are nowadays old-fashioned; but one still
finds simple souls eager to melt when seeing
a woman weep: they blindly trust her tears.
She seems to be quite sure that her wet eyes
are most enchanting; and if just as highly
she ranked her laughter then you may be sure
she'd always titter. Walsingham had chanced
to praise the shrill-voiced Northern beauties; so
forthwith she wails her head off. I do hate
that yellow color of her Scottish hair.

The Chairman

Listen! I hear the sound of heavy wheels.

     A cart passes laden with dead bodies.
     It is driven by a Negro.

The Chairman

Aha, Louisa faints. I thought she had
a warrior's heart judging by her expressions—
but evidently cruelty is weaker

И страх живет в душе, страстьми томимой!
Брось, Мери, ей воды в лицо. Ей лучше.

Мери

Сестра моей печали и позора,
Приляг на грудь мою.

Луиза (*приходя в чувство*)

        Ужасный демон
Приснился мне: весь черный, белоглазый. . .
Он звал меня в свою тележку. В ней
Лежали мертвые—и лепетали
Ужасную, неведомую речь. . .
Скажите мне: во сне ли это было?
Проехала ль телега?

Молодой человек

        Ну, Луиза,
Развеселись—хоть улица вся наша
Безмолвное убежище от смерти,
Приют пиров ничем невозмутимых,
Но знаешь? эта черная телега
Имеет право всюду разъезжать—
Мы пропускать ее должны! Послушай
Ты, Вальсингам: для пресеченья споров
И следствий женских обмороков, спой
Нам песню—вольную, живую песню—
Не грустию шотландской вдохновенну,
А буйную, вакхическую песнь,
Рожденную за чашею кипящей.

Председатель

Такой не знаю—но спою вам гимн,
Я в честь чумы—я написал его
Прошедшей ночью, как расстались мы.
Мне странная нашла охота к рифмам,

than tenderness: strong passions shy at shadows.
Some water, Mary, on her face. She's better.

Mary

Dear sister of my sorrow and dishonor,
recline upon my breast.

Louisa (*regaining her senses*)

A dreadful demon
appeared to me: all black with white eyes rolling,
he beckoned me into his cart where lay
piled bodies of dead men who all were lisping
a horrible, a most unearthly tale.
Oh, tell me please—was it a dream I dreamt
or did the cart pass really?

The Young Man

Come, Louisa,
laugh it away. Though all the street is ours
—a quiet spot secure from death's intrusion,
the haunt of revelers whom none may trouble—
but . . . Well, you see, that black cart has the right
to roll and creak down any street it chooses
and we must let it go its way. Look here,
friend Walsingham: to cut short all discussions
that lead to women swooning, sing us something,
sing us a liberal and lively song,
—not one inspired by long mists of the Highlands
but some unbridled bacchanalian stuff
that sprung to life from wine-foam at a banquet.

The Chairman

Such songs I know not, but I have for you
a hymn in honor of the Plague. I wrote it
the other night as soon as we had parted:
I was possessed by a strange urge to rhyme

Впервые в жизни! Слушайте ж меня:
Охриплый голос мой приличен песне.—

Многие

Гимн в честь чумы! послушаем его!
Гимн в честь чумы! прекрасно! bravo! bravo!

Председатель (*поет*)

Когда могущая зима,
Как бодрый вождь, ведет сама
На нас косматые дружины
Своих морозов и снегов,—
На встречу ей трещат камины,
И весел зимний жар пиров.

Царица грозная, Чума
Теперь идет на нас сама
И льстится жатвою богатой;
И к нам в окошко день и ночь
Стучит могильною лопатой. . .
Что делать нам? и чем помочь?

Как от проказницы зимы,
Запремся также от Чумы!
Зажжем огни, нальем бокалы;
Утопим весело умы
И, заварив пиры да балы,
Восславим царствие Чумы.

Есть упоение в бою,
И бездны мрачной на краю,
И в разъяренном океане,
Средь грозных волн и бурной тьмы
И в аравийском урагане,
И в дуновении Чумы.

which never had I felt before. So listen.
My husky voice will suit this kind of poem.

Several Voices

A hymn! A hymn! Let's hear our chairman sing it!
In honor of the Plague? Good. Bravo, bravo!

The Chairman (*sings*)

When mighty Captain Winter swoops
upon us with his hoary troops,
leading against us all his grim
    legions of frost and snow,—
logs crackling brightly laugh at him
    and festive wine cups glow.

Her awful Majesty the Plague
now comes at us with nothing vague
about her aims and appetite;
    with a grave-digger's spade
she knocks at windows day and night.
    Where should we look for aid?

Just as we deal with Winter's pest
against *this* one it will be best
to stay in lighted rooms and drink
    and drown our minds, and jest.
Come, let us dance upon the brink
    to glorify Queen Pest!

There's bliss in battle and there's bliss
on the dark edge of an abyss
and in the fury of the main
    amid foam-crested death;
in the Arabian hurricane
    and in the Plague's light breath.

Всё, всё, что гибелью грозит,
Для сердца смертного таит
Неизъяснимы наслажденья—
Бессмертья, может быть, залог!
И счастлив тот, кто средь волненья
Их обретать и ведать мог.

Итак—хвала тебе, Чума!
Нам не страшна могилы тьма,
Нас не смутит твое призванье!
Бокалы пеним дружно мы,
И Девы-Розы пьем дыханье—
Быть может—полное Чумы.

(*Входит старый священник.*)

Священник

Безбожный пир, безбожные безумцы!
Вы пиршеством и песнями разврата
Ругаетесь над мрачной тишиной,
Повсюду смертию распространенной!
Средь ужаса плачевных похорон,
Средь бледных лиц молюсь я на кладбище—
А ваши нанавистные восторги
Смущают тишину гробов—и землю
Над мертвыми телами потрясают!
Когда бы стариков и жен моленья
Не освятили общей, смертной ямы—
Подумать мог бы я, что нынче бесы
Погибший дух безбожника терзают
И в тьму кромешную тащат со смехом.

Несколько голосов

Он мастерски об аде говорит!
Ступай, старик! ступай своей дорогой!

All, all such mortal dangers fill
a mortal's heart with a deep thrill
of wordless rapture that bespeaks
    maybe, immortal life,
—and happy is the man who seeks
    and tastes them in his strife.

And so, Dark Queen, we praise thy reign!
Thou callest us, but we remain
unruffled by the chill of death,
    clinking our cups, carefree,
drinking a rose-lipped maiden's breath
    full of the Plague, maybe!

An old Clergyman enters.

The Clergyman

What godless feast is this, you godless madmen?
Your revelry and ribald songs insult
the silent gloom spread everywhere by death!
Among the mourners and their moans, among
pale faces, I was praying in the churchyard
whither the thunder of your hateful orgies
came troubling drowsy graves and rocking
the very earth above the buried dead.
Had not the prayers of women and old men
blessed the dark pit of death's community
I might have thought that busy fiends to-night
were worrying a sinner's shrieking spirit
and dragging it with laughter to their den.

Several Voices

A masterly description of inferno!
Be gone, old priest! Go back the way you came!

Священник

Я заклинаю вас святою кровью
Спасителя, распятого за нас:
Прервите пир чудовищный, когда
Желаете вы встретить в небесах
Утраченных возлюбленные души—
Ступайте по своим домам!

Председатель

Домá
У нас печальны—юность любит радость.

Священник

Ты ль это, Вальсингам? Ты ль самый тот,
Кто три тому недели, на коленях
Труп матери, рыдая, обнимал
И с воплем бился над ее могилой?
Иль думаешь: она теперь не плачет,
Не плачет горько в самых небесах,
Взирая на пирующего сына
В пиру разврата, слыша голос твой,
Поющий бешеные песни, между
Мольбы святой и тяжких воздыханий?
Ступай за мной!

Председатель

Зачем приходишь ты
Меня тревожить? не могу, не должен
Я за тобой идти: я здесь удержан
Отчаяньем, воспоминаньем страшным,
Сознаньем беззаконья моего,
И ужасом той мертвой пустоты,
Которую в моем дому встречаю—
И новостью сих бешеных веселий,
И благодатным ядом этой чаши,

The Clergyman

Now I beseech you by the holy wounds
of One Who bled upon the Cross to save us,—
break up your monstrous banquet, if you hope
to meet in heaven the dear souls of all those
you lost on earth. Go to your homes!

The Chairman

                                   Our homes
are dismal places. Youth is fond of gladness.

The Clergyman

Can it be you—you, Walsingham? the same man
who but three weeks ago stood on his knees
and wept as he embraced his mother's corpse,
and writhed, and rocked, and howled over her grave?
Or do you think she does not grieve right now—
grieve bitterly, even in God's abode—
as she looks down at her disheveled son
maddened by wine and lust, and hears his voice
a voice that roars the wildest songs between
the purest prayer and the profoundest sigh?
Arise and follow me!

The Chairman

                     Why do you come
to trouble thus my soul? Here am I held
by my despair, by memories that kill me,
by the full knowledge of my evil ways,
and by the horror of the lifeless void
that meets me when I enter my own house,
and by the novelty of these wild revels,
and by the blessed poison of this cup,

И ласками (прости меня Господь)—
Погибшего—но милого созданья. . .
Тень матери не вызовет меня
Отселе—поздно—слышу голос твой,
Меня зовущий—признаю усилья
Меня спасти. . . старик! иди же с миром;
Но проклят будь, кто за тобой пойдет!

Многие

Bravo, bravo! достойный председатель!
Вот проповедь тебе! пошел! пошел!

Священник

Матильды чистый дух тебя зовет!

Председатель (*встает*)

Клянись же мне, с поднятой к небесам—
Увядшей, бледною рукой—оставить
В гробу навек умолкнувшее имя!
О, если б от очей ее бессмертных
Скрыть это зрелище! меня когда-то
Она считала чистым, гордым, вольным—
И знала рай в объятиях моих. . .
Где я? святое чадо света! вижу
Тебя я там, куда мой падший дух
Не досягнет уже. . .

Женский голос

     Он сумасшедший—
Он бредит о жене похороненной!

Священник

Пойдем, пойдем. . .

and by the light caresses (God forgive me)
of a depraved but fair and gentle creature.
My mother's soul can summon me no more;
my place is here; too late! . . . I hear your voice
calling my soul . . . I recognize your efforts
to save me . . . but, old man, depart in peace—
and cursed be anyone who goes with you.

Several Voices

Bravo, bravo! Well spoken, worthy chairman!
Now you have got your sermon, priest! Be gone!

The Clergyman

Mathilda's stainless spirit summons you!

The Chairman

No,—promise me,—with your pale withered hand
raised heavenward,—promise to leave unuttered
a name that death has silenced in the tomb.
Could I but hide from her immortal eyes
this sight, this banquet . . . Once upon a time
she thought me pure, free-spirited and proud,
and my embrace was paradise to her.
Where am I? Sacred child of light, I see you
above me, on a shore where my wrecked soul
now cannot reach you.

A Woman's Voice

                    Look, he has gone mad,
he raves about his wife who's dead and buried.

The Clergyman

Come, come with me.

Председатель

Отец мой, ради Бога,
Оставь меня!

Священник

Спаси тебя Господь!
Прости, мой сын.

(Уходит. Пир продолжается.
Председатель остается погруженный
в глубокую задумчивость.)

1830

The Chairman

> For God's sake, holy father,
leave me.

The Clergyman

> The Lord have mercy on your soul.
Farewell, my son.

> *The Clergyman departs. The feast continues. The
> Chairman remains plunged in deep meditation.*

1941

from
МЕДНЫЙ ВСАДНИК
Петербургская повесть

ВСТУПЛЕНИЕ
[. . .]
Люблю, военная столица,
Твоей твердыни дым и гром,
Когда полнощная царица
Дарует сына в царской дом,
Или победу над врагом
Россия снова торжествует,
Или, взломав свой синий лед,
Нева к морям его несет
И, чуя вешни дни, ликует.

[. . .]

ЧАСТЬ ПЕРВАЯ
Над омраченным Петроградом
Дышал ноябрь осенним хладом.
Плеская шумною волной
В края своей ограды стройной,
Нева металась, как больной
В своей постеле беспокойной.
Уж было поздно и темно;
Сердито бился дождь в окно,
И ветер дул, печально воя.
В то время из гостей домой
Пришел Евгений молодой. . .
Мы будем нашего героя
Звать этим именем. Оно
Звучит приятно; с ним давно
Мое перо к тому же дружно.

[. . .]

1833

from
THE BRONZE HORSEMAN
A Petersburg Tale

EXORDIUM

O, military capital, I love
the smoke and thunder of your fortress [gun]
when of the Midnight Realm the empress
gives the imperial house a son
or victory over the foe
Russia again is celebrating,
or having shattered her blue ice,
the Neva bears it to the seas
and, sensing vernal days, rejoices.

PART I

O'er the ensombered Town of Peter
November breathed with autumn chill.
Plashing with noisy wave against
the margins of her trim embankment,
the Neva tossed about
like a sick man upon his restless bed.
'Twas late and dark. The rain
beat crossly on the windowpane,
and the wind blew with a sad howl.
At this time from a visit
came home young Eugene.
We'll call our hero
by this name. It
sounds pleasingly. With it, moreover,
my pen somehow has long been friends.

1951–57

* * *

Пора, мой друг, пора! покоя сердце просит—
Летят за днями дни, и каждый час уносит
Частичку бытия, а мы с тобой вдвоем
Предполагаем жить, и глядь—как раз—умрем.
На свете счастья нет, но есть покой и воля.
Давно завидная мечтается мне доля—
Давно, усталый раб, замыслил я побег
В обитель дальную трудов и чистых нег.

1834

* * *

'Tis time, my dear, 'tis time. The heart demands repose.
Day after day flits by, and with each hour there goes
A little bit of life; but meanwhile you and I
Together plan to dwell . . . yet lo! 'tis then we die.
There is no bliss on earth: there's peace and freedom, though.
An enviable lot I long have yearned to know:
Long have I, weary slave, been contemplating flight
To a remote abode of work and pure delight.

1965

* * *

В мои осенние досуги,
В те дни, как любо мне писать,
Вы мне советуете, други,
Рассказ забытый продолжать.
Вы говорите справедливо,
Что странно, даже неучтиво
Роман не конча перервать,
Отдав уже его в печать,
Что должно своего героя
Как бы то ни было женить,
По крайней мере уморить,
И лица прочие пристроя,
Отдав им дружеский поклон,
Из лабиринта вывесть вон.

Вы говрите: «Слава Богу,
Покамест твой Онегин жив,
Роман не кончен—понемногу
Иди вперед; не будь ленив.
Со славы, вняв ее призванью,
Сбирай оброк хвалой и бранью—
[Рисуй и франтов городских
И милых барышень своих,
Войну и бал, дворец и хату,
И келью [. . .] и харем]
И с нашей публики [меж тем]
Бери умеренную плату,
За книжку по пяти рублей—
Налог не тягостный, ей[-ей]».

1835

* * *

During my days of autumn leisure—
those days when I so love to write—
you, friends, advise me to go on
with my forgotten tale.
You say—and you are right—
that it is odd, and even impolite,
to interrupt an uncompleted novel
and have it published as it is;
that one must marry off one's hero
in any case,
or kill him off at least, and, after having
disposed of the remaining characters
and made to them a friendly bow,
expel them from the labyrinth.

You say: thank God, while your Onegin
is still alive,
the novel is not finished; forward go
little by little, don't be lazy.
While heeding her appeal, from Fame
collect a tax in praise and blame.
[Depict the dandies of the town,
your amiable misses,
warfare and ball, palace and hut,
cell [. . .] and harem, meantime]
take from our public
a reasonable payment—
five rubles, for each published part·
really, 'tis not a heavy tax.

ca. 1956–57

* * *

. . .Вновь я посетил
тот уголок земли, где я провел
изгнанником два года незаметных.
Уж десять лет ушло с тех пор, и много
переменилось в жизни для меня,
и сам, покорный общему закону,—
переменился я,—но здесь опять
минувшее меня объемлет живо—
и кажется, вечор еще бродил
я в этих рощах.

       Вот опальный домик,
где жил я с бедной нянею моей.
уже старушки нет, уж за стеною
не слышу я шагов ее тяжелых,
ни кропотливого ее дозора,
а вечером при завываньи бури,
ее рассказов, мною затверженных
от малых лет, но никогда не скучных.

Вот холм лесистый, над которым часто
я сиживал недвижим—и глядел
на озеро, воспоминая с грустью
иные берега, иные волны. . .
Меж нив златых и пажитей зеленых
оно, синея, стелется широко:
через его неведомые воды
плывет рыбак и тянет за собой
убогой невод. По брегам отлогим
рассеяны лачуги; там за ними
скривилась мельница, насилу крылья
ворочая при ветре. . .

      На границе
владений дедовских, на месте том,

THE RETURN OF PUSHKIN

... I have seen again
that corner of the earth where once I spent
in banishment two years of time unnoticed.
Another ten have now gone by, and many
have been the turns and changes in my life,
and I to nature's law confirming also
in many ways have changed; but here again
the past envelops me, so near and vivid,
that I, meseems, but yesternight among
these groves have wandered.

Modest house of exile!
'Tis here we dwelt, my poor old nurse and I.
But now she is no more, and from my chamber
that heavy tread of hers I hear no longer;
gone are her fussiness and supervision,
and gone the nights, full of the blizzard's wailing,
when she would tell me stories that since childhood
I knew by heart but never tired of hearing.

That wooded hilltop was the place where often
I sat in meditation while I gazed
at yonder lake and with nostalgic sadness
remembered other waves, another shoreline ...
'Mid pastures green and cornfields ripe and tawny
again the lake spreads wide and blue before me.
Across that dreamy wilderness of water
a fisherman drifts by and pulls behind him
his wretched drag-net. Upon the slopes around
some peasant huts are scattered, and beyond them
awry, a wind-mill stands, its vanes in motion,
rotating with an effort ...

On the border
of my grandfather's land, right near the spot

где в гору подымается дорога,
изрытая дождями, три сосны
стоят—одна поодаль,—две другие
друг к дружке близко. Здесь, когда их мимо
я проезжал верхом при свете лунном,
знакомым шумом шорох их вершин
меня приветствовал. По той дороге
теперь поехал я и пред собою
увидел их опять. Они все те же,
все тот же их, знакомый уху шорох,
но около корней их устарелых,
где некогда все было пусто, голо,
теперь младая роща разрослась,
зеленая семья; кусты теснятся
под сенью их, как дети. А вдали
стоит один угрюмый их товарищ,
как старый холостяк, и вкруг него
по-прежнему все пусто!

      Здравствуй, племя
младое, незнакомое! не я
увижу твой могучий поздний возраст,
когда перерастешь моих знакомцев
и старую главу их заслонишь
от глаз прохожего. Но пусть мой внук
услышит ваш приветный шум, когда,
с приятельской беседы возвращаясь,
веселых и приятных мыслей полон,
пройдет он мимо вас во мраке ночи
и обо мне вспомянет. . .

      В разны годы
под вашу сень, Михайловские рощи,
являлся я. Когда вы в первый раз
увидели меня, тогда я был
веселым юношей. Беспечно, жадно

where, furrowed by the elements, the highway
goes toiling up the hill-side, three tall pines
arise—one at a distance, the two others
set close together. Here, whenever by them
alone I used to pass on horseback in the moonlight,
their friendly summits soughing in the wind
would greet me wistfully. Now I come riding
again along that road, and there before me
again I see them loom. They have not altered,
they greet me with the same familiar murmur,
but near the spread of roots already rotting
where formerly the ground was bare and lifeless,
there has come forth a thriving youthful grove,
a verdant progeny. The shrubs, like children
about their parents cluster—while apart
from them the third tree stands like an old bachelor
in gloomy solitude, and as before
the soil is bare around him . . .

       I salute you,
o young tribe! You are unknown to me. Not I
shall live to see your later years of vigor,
when having overtopped my three old comrades,
their venerable summits you will screen
from passing travelers. But let me hope
my grandson hears your gentle sigh when he,
returning from some friendly entertainment,
and brimming with delightful festive thoughts,
among the shades of night comes ambling by you
and thinks of me in passing . . .

       I remember
at various times, Mihaylovskoe, roaming
through your fair groves. The day I made my first
appearance in your midst I was a youth,
the soul of merriment. With carefree ardor

я приступал лишь только к жизни; годы
промчалися—и вы во мне прияли
усталого пришельца. Я еще
был молод, но уже судьба
меня борьбой неравной истомила;
я был ожесточен. В уныньи часто
я помышлял о юности моей,
утраченной в бесплодных испытаньях,
о строгости заслуженных упреков,
о дружбе, заплатившей мне обидой
за жар души доверчивой и нежной—
и горькие кипели в сердце чувства. . .

1835

I had but started on life's journey. Swiftly
the seasons flew, and 'twas a weary stranger
that later you befriended. Youth
by me still tarried, but my strength in fate's
unequal strife already had been wasted.
Envenomed was my heart. Morosely brooding,
I often thought of blooming years gone by,
of youth misspent in fruitless tribulations,
of censure well deserved, despite its harshness,
of friends that had repaid my trust by slighting
all that a keen and tender soul could offer—
and deep in me there welled most bitter feelings.

ca. 1947

ИЗ ПИНДЕМОНТЕ

Недорого ценю я громкие права,
От коих не одна кружится голова.
Я не ропщу о том, что отказали Боги
Мне в сладкой участи оспоривать налоги
Или мешать Царям друг с другом воевать;
И мало горя мне—свободно ли печать
Морочит олухов, иль чуткая Цензура
В журнальных замыслах стесняет балагура.
Все это, видите ль, *слова, слова, слова!**
Иные, лучшие, мне дороги права;
Иная, лучшая, потребна мне Свобода. . .
Зависеть от Властей, зависеть от народа—
Не все ли нам равно? Бог с ними! . . Никому
Отчета не давать; себе лишь самому
Служить и угождать; для власти, для ливреи
Не гнуть ни совести, ни помыслов, ни шеи;
По прихоти своей скитаться здесь и там,
Дивясь божественным Природы красотам,
И пред созданьями искусств и вдохновенья
Трепеща радостно в восторгах умиленья—
     Вот счастье! вот права! . .

1836

*Hamlet.

* * *

I value little those much-vaunted rights
that have for some the lure of dizzy heights;
I do not fret because the gods refuse
to let me wrangle over revenues,
or thwart the wars of kings; and 'tis to me
of no concern whether the press be free
to dupe poor oafs or whether censors cramp
the current fancies of some scribbling scamp.
These things are *words, words, words.* My spirit fights
for deeper Liberty, for better rights.
Whom shall we serve—the people or the State?
The poet does not care—so let them wait.
To give account to none, to be one's own
vassal and liege, to please oneself alone,
to bend neither one's neck nor inner schemes
nor conscience for obtaining that which seems
power but is a flunkey's coat; to stroll
in one's own wake, admiring the divine
beauties of Nature and to feel one's soul
melt in the glow of man's inspired design
—this is the blessing, these are *rights*!

1947

РОДОСЛОВНАЯ МОЕГО ГЕРОЯ
(Отрывок из сатирической поэмы)

I.

Над омраченным Петроградом
Осенний ветер тучи гнал,
Дышало небо влажным хладом,
Нева шумела. Бился вал
О пристань набережной стройной,
Как челобитчик беспокойный
Об дверь судейской. Дождь в окно
Стучал печально. Уж темно
Всё становилось. В это время
Иван Езерский, мой сосед,
Вошел в свой тесный кабинет. . .
Однако ж род его, и племя,
И чин, и службу, и года
Вам знать нехудо, господа.

II.

Начнем *ab ovo:* мой Езерский
Происходил от тех вождей,
Чей дух воинственный и зверской
Был древле ужасом морей.
Одульф, его начальник рода,
Вельми бе грозен воевода,
Гласит Софийский хронограф.
При Ольге сын его Варлаф
Приял крещенье в Цареграде
С рукою греческой княжны;
От них два сына рождены:
Якуб и Дорофей. В засаде
Убит Якуб; а Дорофей
Родил двенадцать сыновей.

from

THE PEDIGREE OF MY HERO
(Fragment of a Satirical Poem)

I

O'er the gloom-covered town of Peter
the autumn wind was driving clouds;
the sky was breathing humid chill,
4 the Neva boomed. The billow beat
against the trim embankment's wharf
like some restless petitioner
against the judge's door. The rain
8 tapped sadly on the windowpane.
'Twas darkling. At this time
Ivan Ezerski came, my neighbor,
into his narrow study.
12 However, his forebears and tribe,
his rank, his office, and his age,
you should know, gentlemen.

II

Let's start *ab ovo:* my Ezerski
was a descendant of those chiefs
whose spirit bellicose and savage
4 was once the terror of the seas.
The generator of the family,
Odulf "was a most awesome warlord"
—so says the Sophian chronograph.
8 In Olga's reign his son Varlaf
embraced the Gospel in Constantinople
together with the dot of a Greek princess.
Two sons were born to them, Yakub
12 and Dorofey; of these, in ambush
Yakub was slain; while Dorofey
fathered twelve sons.

III.

Ондрей, по прозвищу Езерский,
Родил Ивана да Илью.
Он в лавре схимился Печерской.
Отсель фамилию свою
Ведут Езерские.

[. . .]

IV.

В века старинной нашей славы,
Как и в худые времена,
Крамол и смуты в дни кровавы,
Блестят Езерских имена.
Они и в войске и в совете,
На воеводстве и в ответе

[. . .]

V.

Когда ж от Думы величавой
Приял Романов свой венец,
Когда под мирною державой
Русь отдохнула наконец,
А наши вороги смирились,
Тогда Езерские явились
В великой силе при дворе.
При императоре Петре. . .

[. . .]

XIII.

Зачем крутится ветр в овраге,
Подъемлет лист и пыль несет,
Когда корабль в недвижной влаге
Его дыханья жадно ждет?
Зачем от гор и мимо башен
Литет орел, тяжел и страшен,
На черный пень? Спроси его.

III

Ondrey surnamed Ezerski, fathered
Ivan and Ilya, and took vows
in the Pecherskiy Monastery.
4 Thence the Ezerskis
derive their family name

     [. . .]

IV

In centuries of our old glory
as well as in unhappy times,
in gory days of riots and uprisings,
4 the names of the Ezerskis glitter.
They're in the army and in council,
they are the governors and envoys

     [. . .]

V

But when from the majestic Council
Romanov had received his crown;
when under a pacific rule
4 at last Rus rested,
and our foes were subdued,
then the Ezerskis came
into great force at court
8 under the Emperor Peter.

     [. . .]

XIII

Why does the wind revolve in the ravine,
sweep up the leaves and bear the dust,
when avidly on stirless water
4 wait for his breath the galleon must?
From mountains and past towers, why
does the dread heavy eagle fly
to a sear stump? Inquire of him.

Зачем Арапа своего
Младая любит Дездемона,
Как месяц любит ночи мглу?
Затем, что ветру и орлу
И сердцу девы нет закона.
Гордись: таков и ты поэт,
И для тебя условий нет.

XIV.

Исполнен мыслями златыми,
Непонимаемый никем,
Перед распутьями земными
Проходишь ты, уныл и нем.
С толпой не делишь ты ни гнева,
Ни нужд, ни хохота, не рева,
Ни удивленья, ни труда.
Глупец кричит: *куда? куда?*
Дорога здесь. Но ты не слышишь,
Идешь, куда тебя влекут
Мечты златые; тайный труд
Тебе награда; им ты дышишь,
А плод его бросаешь ты
Толпе, рабыне суеты.

1832–36

8   Why does young Desdemona love
    her blackamoor as the moon loves
    the gloom of night? Because
    for wind and eagle
12 and maiden's heart no law is laid.
    Poet, be proud: thus are you too:
    neither is there a law for you.

           XIV
    Fulfilled with golden thoughts,
    but understood by none,
    before the crossroads of this world,
4   you pass, morose and mute.
    You share not with the crowd its wrath,
    its needs, its mirth, its roar,
    its wonder, or its toil.
8   The fool cries: "Whither? Whither?
    This is the road!" You do not hear.
    You go where you are urged
    by golden dreams. Your secret work
12 is your reward; 'tis what you breathe.
    Unto the crowd you throw its fruit
    —unto the slaves of vain pursuit.

                                    1951–57, 1966–67

* * *

Exegi monumentum

Я памятник себе воздвиг нерукотворный.
К нему не зарастет народная тропа.
Вознесся выше он главою непокорной
     Александрийского столпа.

Нет, весь я не умру—душа в заветной лире
Мой прах переживет и тленья убежит—
И славен буду я, доколь в подлунном мире
     Жив будет хоть один пиит.

Слух обо мне пройдет по всей Руси великой,
И назовет меня всяк сущий в ней язык:
И гордый внук Славян, и Фин, и ныне дикой
     Тунгуз, и друг степей Калмык.

И долго буду тем любезен я народу,
Что чувства добрые я лирой пробуждал,
Что в мой жестокий век восславил я Свободу
     И милость к падшим призывал.

Веленью Божию, о Муза, будь послушна:
Обиды не страшась, не требуя венца,
Хвалу и клевету приемля равнодушно,
     И не оспоривай глупца.

1836

EXEGI MONUMENTUM

"No hands have wrought my monument; no weeds
will hide the nation's footpath to its site.
Tsar Alexander's column it exceeds
    in splendid insubmissive height.

"Not all of me is dust. Within my song,
safe from the worm, my spirit will survive,
and my sublunar fame will dwell as long
    as there is one last bard alive.

"Throughout great Rus' my echoes will extend,
and all will name me, all tongues in her use:
the Slavs' proud heir, the Finn, the Kalmuk, friend
    of steppes, the yet untamed Tunguz.

"And to the people long shall I be dear
because kind feelings did my lyre extol,
invoking freedom in an age of fear,
    and mercy for the broken soul."

Obey thy God, and never mind, O Muse,
the laurels or the stings: make it thy rule
to be unstirred by praise as by abuse,
    and do not contradict the fool.

1941–43

EXEGI MONUMENTUM

"I've set up to myself a monument
not wrought by hands. The public path to it
will not grow weedy. Its unyielding head
soars higher than the Alexandrine Column.

"No, I'll not wholly die. My soul in the sacred lyre
is to survive my dust and flee decay;
and I'll be famed while there remains alive
in the sublunar world at least one poet.

"Tidings of me will cross the whole great Rus,
and name me will each tribe existing there:
proud scion of Slavs, and Finn, and the now savage
Tungus, and—friend of steppes—the Kalmuck.

"And to the nation long shall I be dear
for having with my lyre evoked kind feelings,
exalted freedom in my cruel age
and called for mercy toward the downfallen."

To God's command, O Muse, obedient be,
offense not dreading, and no wreath demanding;
accept indifferently praise and slander,
and do not contradict a fool.

1951–57, 1966–67

EVGENIY ABRAMOVICH BARATÏNSKI

(1800–1844)

ON EVGENIY BARATÏNSKI

If in the taxonomy of talent there exists a cline be-
tween minor and major poetry, Evgeniy Baratïnski (1800–44)
presents such an intermediate unit of classification. His elegies are
keyed to the precise point where the languor of the heart and the
pang of thought meet in a would-be burst of music; but a remote
door seems to shut quietly, the poem ceases to vibrate (although its
words may still linger) at the very instant that we are about to sur-
render to it. He had deep and difficult things to say, but never quite
said them. He was regarded by Pushkin with a tender and grave
respect: its tonality is unique in the annals of the greater poet's
literary sympathies.

Early in 1816, Baratïnski was expelled from the Corps-des-Pages
(a military school for young noblemen): with a schoolmate (Han-
ikov) he had stolen a valuable snuffbox and five hundred rubles
in bank notes from the bureau of Hanikov's uncle. After spending
three years in the country, Baratïnski returned to St. Petersburg in
1819 (where he became acquainted with Pushkin) and then served

in Finland, starting as a private, 1820–24. Attempts on the part of Soviet commentators to compare his fate with that of Pushkin in terms of political martyrdom are grotesque.

1951–57

A great intellectualist, he was the victim of intellect, of analytic knowledge. He saw the steady inexorable movement of mankind away from nature. This pessimistic philosophy, allying itself to his profound temperamental melancholy, produced poems of extraordinary dark majesty.

ca. 1948–49

from
ФИНЛЯНДИЯ

Громады вечных скал, гранитные пустыни!
Вы дали страннику убежище и кров;
        [. . .]
Златые призраки, златые сновиденья,
Желанья пылкие, слетитеся толпой!
Пусть жадно буду пить обманутой душой
Из чаши юности волшебство заблужденья.
Что нужды до былых иль будущих племен?
Я не для них бренчу незвонкими струнами:
Я, невнимаемый, довольно награжден
За звуки звуками, а за мечты мечтами.

1820

from
FINLAND

Great everlasting rocks, deserts of granite,
you gave the wanderer refuge and shelter
        [. . .]
O golden phantoms, golden visions,
ardent desires, come flying in a crowd!
Let my deluded soul drink avidly the magic
of error from the cup of youth!
What matter past or future races?
I strum my dull strings not for them.
Though heeded not, I am in full rewarded
for sounds by sounds, for dreams by dreams.

1951–57

ПИРЫ

[. . .]

В простые чаши бог похмелья
Роскошно лил сынам веселья
Свое любимое *Аи.*
В нем укрывается отвага,
Его звездящаяся влага
Души божественной полна,
Свободно искрится она;
Как гордый ум, не терпит плена,
Рвет пробку резвою волной,—
И брызжет радостная пена,
Подобье жизни молодой.

[. . .]

1821

from
FEASTS

Into plain cups the god of tippling
luxuriously to sons of glee
pours out his fondest drink, Ay:
courage within it is concealed;
its liquid, twinkling starrily,
is full of a celestial soul.
It sparkles free.
Like a proud mind, it cannot bear captivity;
it bursts its cork with sportive surf
and merrily its foam doth spurt
—a simile of youthful life . . .

1951–57

***

Своенравное прозванье
Дал я милой в ласку ей:
Безотчетное созданье
Детской нежности моей;
Чуждо явного значенья,
Для меня оно символ
Чувств, которым выраженья
В языках я не нашел.
Вспыхнув полною любовью
И любви посвящено,
Не хочу, чтоб суесловью
Было ведомо оно.
Что в нем свету? Но сомненье
Если дух ей возмутит,
О, его в одно мгновенье
Это имя победит;
Но в том мире за могилой,
Где нет образов, где нет
Для узнанья, друг мой милой,
Здешних чувственных примет,
Им бессмертье я привечу,
Им к тебе воскликну я,
И душе моей навстречу
Полетит душа твоя.

1831–32

TO HIS WIFE

I have given her a nickname,
just a fanciful caress,
the unconscious inspiration
of my childish tenderness.
Though it seems devoid of meaning,
'tis to me a symbol plain
of such feelings whose expression
languages do not contain.
Born of love, it is devoted
to my full love's fullest flame;
so I wish not idle gossip
to discover it,—a name
none would value; but whenever
doubt assails her, then, I know,
in a flash that word is victor
and away all troubles go.

In the world beyond the tombstone
where there are no forms, my dear,
and no signs of recognition
as our senses know them here,—
thus Eternity I'll welcome,
thus 'mid stars will I exclaim,
and your soul to mine will flutter
on the light wings of that name.

ca. 1949

* * *

На что вы, дни! Юдольный мир явленья
    Свои не изменит!
Все ведомы, и только повторенья
    Грядущее сулит.

Не даром ты металась и кипела,
    Развитием спеша;
Свой подвиг ты свершила прежде тела,
    Безумная душа!

И тесный круг подлунных впечатлений
    Сомкнувшая давно,
Под веяньем возвратных сновидений
    Ты дремлешь; а оно

Бессмысленно глядит, как утро встанет,
    Без нужды ночь сменя;
Как в мрак ночной бесплодный вечер канет,
    Венец пустого дня!

1840

* * *

What use are ye, Days! The earthly world will not change its phenomena. All are familiar and the future betokens nothing but repetition. Not in vain, oh my foolish soul, hast thou tossed and seethed, madly hurrying on in thy development: thou hast outrun the body in this race. Now, having long ago brought to a close the narrow circle of earthly impressions and lulled by the fanning motion of recurrent dreams, thou dozest, whilst the body stolidly, stupidly stares on, watching the morning come, which uselessly replaces the night; then watching the fruitless evening drop into night's darkness—crowning another empty day.

ca. 1949

Все мысль, да мысль! Художник бедный слова!
О жрец ее! тебе забвенья нет;
Все тут, да тут и человек, и свет,
И смерть, и жизнь, и правда без покрова.
Резец, орган, кисть! счастлив, кто влеком
К ним, чувственным, за грань их не ступая!
Есть хмель ему на празднике мирском!
Но пред тобой, как пред нагим мечом,
Мысль, острый луч!—бледнеет жизнь земная!

1840

* * *

Ideas and nothing but ideas! Poor artist of words, thou art their priest and thou canst have no oblivion. Man and the world, death and life, Truth without veils—these are always with you. The chisel, the organ, the brush! Happy is he who is attracted by them, the sensuous, and passes not their limits. He can get drunk at the feast of life. But before thee, Thought, trenchant as a naked sword, earthly life grows pale.

ca. 1949

FYODOR IVANOVICH TYUTCHEV
(1803–1873)

ON FYODOR TYUTCHEV

Neither Tyutchev's life (1803–1873) nor personality contains that romantic appeal which makes the biographies of Pushkin and Lermontov almost homogeneous with their muses. His poetry, however, has quite exceptional qualities and reveals (in the thirties!) elements which characterize the fin de siècle renaissance of Russian poetry (also called decadence, also called symbolism—the student ought not to bother much about these terms) which in its turn was partly influenced by similar trends in French poetry. This is a somewhat loose statement but too much space would be required to elaborate peculiarities and affinities.

In the early twenties the gentle Tyutchev entered the diplomatic service and spent the next twenty-two years mostly abroad and mostly in South Germany. He was on friendly terms with Schelling and Heine and both his wives were German. His only insubordination during those years seems to have been a trip to Switzerland without a proper leave from his Ambassador. When about fifty he had a pathetic liaison which lasted until his mistress's death in

1864. Politically he was a rather smug conservative with Slavophile leanings and a sentimental fondness for permanently anointed Tsardom. The batch of poems inspired by his political views makes rather painful reading. On the other hand, his short lyrics belong to the greatest ever written in Russian.

1941–43

CLASSIFYING TYUTCHEV

Classificators distinguish two main groups of [early modern Russian] poets: the Archaists (Derzhavin, Krïlov, Griboedov, Küchelbecker) and the Romanticists (Zhukovski, Pushkin, Baratïnski, Lermontov). In Tyutchev the two lines merged.

1952–57

СЛЕЗЫ

O, lacrimarum fons!
—Gray

Люблю, друзья, ласкать очами
Иль пурпур искрометных вин,
Или плодов между листами
Благоухающий рубин.

Люблю смотреть, когда созданье
Как бы погружено в весне,
И мир заснул в благоуханьи
И улыбается во сне!..

Люблю, когда лицо прекрасной
Весенний воздух пламенит,
То кудрей шелк взвевает сладострастный,
То в ямочки впивается ланит.

Но что́ все прелести пафосския царицы,
И гроздий сок, и запах роз
Перед тобой, святой источник слез,
Роса Божественной денницы.

Небесный луч играет в них
И, преломясь о капли огневые,
Рисует радуги живые
На тучах жизни громовых.

И только смертного зениц
Ты, ангел слез, дотронешься крылами,
Туман рассеется слезами,
И небо серафимских лиц
Вдруг разовьется пред очами.

1823

TEARS

O, lacrimarum fons.
—Gray

Friends, with my eyes I love caressing
the purple of a flashing wine,
nor do I scorn the fragrant ruby
of clustered fruit that leaves entwine.

I love to look around when Nature
seems as it were immersed in May;
when bathed in redolence she slumbers
and smiles throughout her dreamy day.

I love to see the face of Beauty
flushed with the air of Spring that seeks
softly to toy with silky ringlets
or deepen dimples on her cheeks.

But all voluptuous enchantments,
lush grapes, rich roses—what are you
compared to tears, that sacred fountain,
that paradisal morning dew!

Therein divinest beams are mirrored,
and in those burning drops they break,
and breaking—what resplendent rainbows
upon Life's thunderclouds they make!

As soon as mortal eyes thou touchest,
with wings, Angel of Tears, the world
dissolves in mist, and lo! a skyful
of Seraph faces is unfurled.

1941–43

ЛЕТНИЙ ВЕЧЕР

Уж солнца раскаленный шар
С главы своей земля скатила,
И мирный вечера пожар
Волна морская поглотила.

Уж звезды светлые взошли,
И тяготеющий над нами
Небесный свод приподняли
Своими влажными главами.

Река воздушная полней
Течет меж небом и землею,
Грудь дышит легче и вольней,
Освобожденная от зною.

И сладкий трепет, как струя,
По жилам пробежал природы,
Как бы горячих ног ея
Коснулись ключевые воды.

ca. 1826–28

NIGHTFALL

Down from her head the earth has rolled
the low sun like a redhot ball.
Down went the evening's peaceful blaze
and seawaves have absorbed it all.

Heavy and near the sky had seemed.
But now the stars are rising high,
they glow and with their humid heads
push up the ceiling of the sky.

The river of the air between
heaven and earth now fuller flows.
The breast is ridded of the heat
and breathes in freedom and repose.

And now there goes through Nature's veins
a liquid shiver, swift and sweet,
as though the waters of a spring
had come to touch her burning feet.

1941-43

SILENTIUM

Молчи, скрывайся и таи
И чувства и мечты свои!
Пускай в душевной глубине
И всходят и зайдут оне,
Как звезды ясные в ночи:
Любуйся ими и молчи!

Как сердцу высказать себя?
Другому как понять тебя?
Поймет ли он, чем ты живешь?
Мысль изреченная есть ложь.
Взрывая, возмутишь ключи:
Питайся ими и молчи!

Лишь жить в самом себе умей:
Есть целый мир в душе твоей
Таинственно-волшебных дум;
Их заглушит наружный шум,
Дневные ослепят лучи:
Внимай их пенью и молчи!

ca. 1825–29

SILENTIUM

Speak not, lie hidden, and conceal
the way you dream, the things you feel.
Deep in your spirit let them rise
akin to stars in crystal skies
that set before the night is blurred:
delight in them and speak no word.

How can a heart expression find?
How should another know your mind?
Will he discern what quickens you?
A thought once uttered is untrue.
Dimmed is the fountainhead when stirred:
drink at the source and speak no word.

Live in your inner self alone:
within your soul a world has grown,
the magic of veiled thoughts that might
be blinded by the outer light,
drowned in the noise of day, unheard . . .
take in their song and speak no word.

1941–43

* * *

Душа хотела б быть звездой,—
Но не тогда, как с неба полуно́чи
Сии светила, как живые очи,
Глядят на сонный мир земной,—
Но днем, когда, сокрытые как дымом
Палящих солнечных лучей,
Они, как божества, горят светлей
В эфире чистом и незримом.

1829

My soul would like to be a star—
not at midnight
when these luminaries, like eager eyes,
peer at the drowsy earth—
but in the day-time when veiled
by the burning rays of the sun as if by smoke
they glow like pale divinities
in the pure and invisible ether.

1948–51

УСПОКОЕНИЕ

Гроза прошла. Еще курясь, лежал
Высокий дуб, перунами сраженный,
И сизый дым с ветвей его бежал
По зелени, грозою освеженной.

А уж давно звучнее и полней,
Пернатых песнь по роще раздалася,
И радуга концом дуги своей
В зеленые вершины уперлася!..

1830

APPEASEMENT

The storm withdrew, but Thor had found his oak,
and there it lay magnificently slain,
and from its limbs a remnant of blue smoke
spread to bright trees repainted by the rain—

—while thrush and oriole made haste to mend
their broken melodies throughout the grove,
upon the crests of which was propped the end
of a virescent rainbow edged with mauve.

                                        1941–44

from
ЦИЦЕРОН

[. . .]
Блажен, кто посетил сей мир
В его минуты роковые:
Его призвали всеблагие
Как собеседника на пир.

[. . .]

1830

* * *

Blest is the mortal who has stayed
at fateful moments on this sphere,
for him the very gods have bade
sit on their banquct as their peer.

ca. 1949

* * *

Песок сыпучий по колени. . .
Мы едем поздно; меркнет день,
И сосен по дороге тени
Уже в одну слилися тень.

Черней и чаще бор глубокий. . .
Какие грустные места! . .
Ночь хмурая, как зверь стоокий,
Глядит из каждого куста.

1830

THE JOURNEY

Knee-deep, this powdery sand . . . We ride
    late in the murky day.

Shadows cast by the pines now merged to form
    one shadow across our way.

Blacker and denser the wildwood grows.
    What a comfortless neighborhood!

Moody night peers like a hundred-eyed beast
    out of every bush in the wood.

1941–44

THE JOURNEY

Soft sand comes up to our horses' shanks
    as we ride in the darkening day
and the shadows of pines have closed their ranks:
    all is shadow along our way.

In denser masses the black trees rise.
    What a comfortless neighborhood!
Grim night like a beast with a hundred eyes
    peers out of the underwood.

1941–44

* * *

The crumbly sand is knee-high.
We're driving late. The day is darkening,
and on the road the shadows of the pines
into one shadow have already fused.

Blacker and denser is the deep pine wood.
What melancholy country!
Grim night like a hundred-eyed beast
looks out of every bush.

1951–57

АЛЬПЫ

Сквозь лазурный сумрак ночи
Альпы снежные глядят;
Помертвелые их очи
Льдистым ужасом разят.
Властью некой обаянны,
До восшествия зари
Дремлют, грозны и туманны,
Словно падшие цари!

Но восток лишь заалеет,
Чарам гибельным конец:
Первый, в небе, просветлеет
Брата старшего венец.
И с главы большого брата
На меньших бежит струя,
И блестит в венцах из злата
Вся воскресшая семья.

1830

* * *

Through the azure haze of the night
the snowy Alps stare;
their dead glazed eyes
radiate icy horror.
Spellbound by some unknown power,
until sunrise
they slumber, terrible and misty,
like fallen kings.

But as soon as the east flushes
the perilous enchantment is dispelled:
the big brother's crown
is the first to become alive with light;
and from the elder's head
the liquid ray runs down upon the younger brothers,
and lo, in crowns of gold
wide awake stands the whole family.

1948–51

СУМЕРКИ

Тени сизые смесились,
Цвет поблекнул, звук уснул;
Жизнь, движенье разрешились
В сумрак зыбкий, в дальний гул. . .
Мотылька полет незримый
Слышен в воздухе ночном. . .
Час тоски невыразимой!
Всё во мне, — и я во всем. . .

Сумрак тихий, сумрак сонный,
Лейся в глубь моей души,
Тихий, томный, благовонный,
Все залей и утиши.
Чувства — мглой самозабвенья
Переполни через край! . .
Дай вкусить уничтоженья,
С миром дремлющим смешай!

ca. 1830–35

DUSK

Now the ashen shadows mingle,
tints are faded, sounds remote.
Life has dwindled to a single
vague reverberating note.
In the dusk I hear the humming
of a moth I cannot see.
Whence is this oppression coming?
I'm in all, and all's in me.

Gloom so dreamy, gloom so lulling,
flow into my deepest deep,
flow, ambrosial and dulling,
steeping everything in sleep.
With oblivion's obscuration
fill my senses to the brim,
make me taste obliteration,
in this dimness let me dim.

1941–44

СЛЕЗЫ

Слезы людские, о, слезы людские,
Льетесь вы ранней и поздней порой,
Льетесь безвестные, льетесь незримые,
Неистощимые, неисчислимые,
Льетесь, как льются струи дождевые
В осень глухую, порою ночной.

ca. 1849

TEARS

Human tears, O the tears! you that flow
when life is begun—or half-gone,
tears unseen, tears unknown, you that none
can number or drain, you that run
like the streamlets of rain from the low
clouds of Autumn, long before dawn . . .

1941–44

* * *

Святая ночь на небосклон взошла,
И день отрадный, день любезный,
Как золотой ковер она свила,—
Ковер, накинутый над бездной.
И, как виденье, внешний мир ушел. . .
И человек, как сирота бездомный,
Стоит теперь, и немощен и гол,
Лицом к лицу пред этой бездной темной.
На самого себя покинут он,
Упразднен ум и мысль осиротела,
В душе своей, как в бездне, погружен,
И нет извне опоры ни предела.
И чудится давно минувшим сном
Теперь ему все светлое, живое,
И в чуждом, неразгаданном ночном
Он узнает наследье родовое. . .

1850

THE ABYSS

When sacred Night sweeps heavenward, she takes
the glad, the winsome day, and folding it,
rolls up its golden carpet that had been
spread over an abysmal pit.

Gone vision-like is the external world,
and man, a homeless orphan, has to face
in utter helplessness, naked, alone,
the blackness of immeasurable space.

Upon himself he has to lean; with mind
abolished, thought unfathered, in the dim
depths of his soul he sinks, for nothing comes
from outside to support or limit him.

All life and brightness seem an ancient dream—
while in the very substance of the night,
unraveled, alien, he now perceives
a fateful something that is his by right.

1941–44

ПОСЛЕДНЯЯ ЛЮБОВЬ

О, как на склоне наших лет
Нежней мы любим и суеверней. . .
Сияй, сияй, прощальный свет
Любви последней, зари вечерней!

Полнеба обхватила тень,
Лишь там на западе брезжит сиянье,
Помедли, помедли, вечерний день,
Продлись, продлись, очарованье!

Пускай скудеет в жилах кровь,
Но в сердце не скудеет нежность. . .
О, ты, последняя любовь!
Ты и блаженство и безнадежность.

ca. 1852–54

LAST LOVE

Love at the closing of our days
is apprehensive and very tender.
Glow brighter, brighter, farewell rays
of one last love in its evening splendor.

Blue shade takes half the world away:
through western clouds alone some light is slanted.
O tarry, O tarry, declining day,
enchantment, let me stay enchanted.

The blood runs thinner, yet the heart
remains as ever deep and tender.
O last belated love, thou art
a blend of joy and of hopeless surrender.

1941–43

* * *

Есть в осени первоначальной
Короткая, но дивная пора:
Весь день стоит как бы хрустальный,
И лучезарны вечера. . .

Где бодрый серп гулял и падал колос,
Теперь уж пусто все—простор везде;
Лишь паутины тонкий волос
Блестит на праздной борозде.

Пустеет воздух, птиц не слышно боле;
Но далеко еще до первых зимних бурь,
И льется чистая и теплая лазурь
На отдыхающее поле.

1857

AUTUMN

When Autumn has just come, there is
most brief a lull: brief but divine.
All day 'tis like some precious prism,
and limpidly the evenings shine.

Where lusty sickles swung and corn-ears bent
the plain is empty now: wider it seems.
Alone a silky filament
across the idle furrow gleams.

The airy void, now birdless, is revealed,
but still remote is the first whirl of snow;
and stainless skies in mellow blueness flow
upon the hushed reposing field.

1941–43

***

Она сидела на полу
И груду писем разбирала,
И, как остывшую золу,
Брала их в руки и бросала.

Брала знакомые листы
И чудно так на них глядела,
Как души смотрят с высоты
На ими брошенное тело.

И сколько жизни было тут,
Невозвратимо пережитой,
И сколько горестных минут,
Любви и радости убитой.

Стоял я молча в стороне
И пасть готов был на колени,
И страшно грустно было мне,
Как от присущей милой тени.

са. 1858

* * *

She sat on the floor
and sorted out a heap of letters:
she took them up like handfuls of dead cold ashes
and let them drop.

She took those familiar pages
and passing strange was the way she looked at them:
so spirits look from above
at the bodies they have shed.

And what a profusion of life was contained there,
life gone for ever,
and how much grief lingered,
how much gladness and love that had been killed.

In silence I stood apart
and was ready to fall on my knees
full of awe and sadness,
as if I were in the presence of some dear ghost.

ca. 1948–51

***

Ночное небо так угрюмо
Заволокло со всех сторон:
То не угроза и не дума,
То вялый, безотрадный сон.
Одни зарницы огневые,
Воспламеняясь чередой,
Как демоны глухонемые,
Ведут беседу меж собой.

Как по условленному знаку,
Вдруг неба вспыхнет полоса,
И быстро выступят из мраку
Поля и дальние леса!
И вот опять все потемнело,
Все стихло в чуткой темноте,
Как бы таинственное дело
Решалось там—на высоте. . .

1865

The sky is overcast with slow
and sullen nightclouds: it might seem
to meditate or threaten . . . No—
'tis drooping in a dreary dream.
But flashes of sheet-lightning come
and vanish, and throughout the night
akin to demons deaf and dumb
converse in alphabetic light.

The blackness at a given sign
splits vividly, and then one sees
a rapidly advancing line
of meadow grass and distant trees.
Back into place the shadows swing:
expectant, motionless they lie,
as if some very secret thing
were being settled in the sky.

ca. 1948–51

**

Умом Россию не понять,
Аршином общим не измерить:
У ней особенная стать—
В Россию можно только верить.

1866

[RUSSIA]

One cannot understand her with the mind
Nor take her measure with a caliper:
Her state and stamp are of a special kind,—
All one can do is to believe in her.

ca. 1958–59

ALEKSEY VASILIEVICH KOLTSOV
(1809–1842)

ON ALEKSEY KOLTSOV

Koltsov . . . deserves being mentioned even in the most concise survey of the early nineteenth century on account of his not very strong but very authentic and original genius. . . . He has been often compared to Burns. I should rather compare him to Housman. . . .

Ordinarily [his poems] are written as if told or sung by a man or woman of the people. Their themes are melancholy, the plaintive song of a girl who has been married against her wish to a man she does not love, or that delightful poem addressed to "the little peasant"—"mujichok"—not a young peasant of course, but to a shabby, undersized poorish farmer who inexplicably sleeps through the spring when all farm work should be begun. The *domovoi*, the house goblin, manages the house, dusting the barns, giving away the peasant's horses for the debts he owes his neighbors. . . .

Mirsky rightly remarks that the two keywords of Koltsov's poetry are *prostor* and *privolie*. The best I can do to explain these two notions is this: *prostor* is the open endless spaces of the Russian steppes or of the American prairies. Endless open spaces are said to dwarf man, to make him feel insignificant before the vastness of nature. The feeling in "prostor" is the exact opposite of this notion: *prostor* makes man feel his soul as vast and free as the nature around him, makes him heave a deep sigh of content and wake up to the unlimited vitality instilled by God in man's strong healthy body and immortal soul. "Privolie" is a cosier notion, applying more to the practical aspects of life: the unconstrainedness in the distribution of time and effort amid free unhampered life conditions. I would say that prostor implies the immensity of the plains or of the ocean while privolie applies rather to a quiet glade in the forest with an oblique ray of the sun and the comfortable murmur of a shaded brook.

1948–49

* * *

Что ты спишь, мужичок?
Ведь весна на дворе;
Ведь соседи твои
Рабо́тают давно.

Встань, проснись, подымись,
На себя погляди:
Что́ ты был? и что́ стал?
И что́ есть у тебя?

На гумне—ни снопа;
В закромах—ни зерна;
На дворе, по траве—
Хоть шаром покати.

Из клетей домовой
Сор метлою посмел;
И лошадок, за долг,
По соседям развел.

И под лавкой сундук
Опрокинут лежит;
И погнувшись изба,
Как старушка, стоит.

Вспомни время свое:
Как катилось оно
По полям, и лугам,
Золотою рекой!

Со двора и гумна,
По дорожке большой,
По селам, городам,
По торговым людям!

* * *

Why do you sleep, little peasant,
when the season is spring?
Your neighbors
have been working for a long time.

Get up, wake up, come, get up
and look at yourself
consider what you used to be,
and what you have become, and what you possess.

Not a sheaf of wheat in the threshing barn,
in the granary not a seed
you could roll a ball through the empty yard
where there's nothing but weeds.

The house goblin
has swept the rubbish out of the sheds
and has distributed your shaggy little horses
among the neighbors whom you owed money.

Under the bench the trunk
lies upside down
and your log cabin stands all bent
like a little old woman.

Recall your best days
and the way they rolled
over meadow and field
like a flood of gold

out of courtyard and barn
along paths grown big
through village and town
among trading folks

И как двери ему
Растворяли везде,
И в почетном угле
Было место твое!

А теперь под окном
Ты с нуждою сидишь,
И весь день на печи
Без просыпу лежишь.

А в полях, сиротой,
Хлеб нескошен стоит.
Ветер точит зерно!
Птица клюет его!

Что ты спишь, мужичок?
Ведь уж лето прошло,
Ведь уж осень на двор
Через прясло глядит.

Вслед за нею зима
В теплой шубе идет,
Путь снежком порошит,
Под санями хрустит.

Все соседи на них
Хлеб везут, продают,
Собирают в казну,
Бражку ковшиком пьют.

1839

to be met everywhere
with wide open doors
and the place of honor
was yours in the room.

Now in misery
you sit at your window
or you sleep all day
asprawl on the straw

while the orphaned wheat
stands uncut in the fields
where the wind gnaws the grain
where the birds pick at it.

Still asleep, little peasant?
Why, the summer has gone
and autumn peers
through the picket fence.

Then winter comes,
in his furry coat;
he dusts the road with snow;
the snow sings under the sleighs.

All your neighbors on them
carry grain to the buyer,
heap the minted coins,
fill their dippers with ale.

1948–49

MIHAIL YURIEVICH LERMONTOV
(1814–1841)

ON MIHAIL LERMONTOV
THE LERMONTOV MIRAGE

Michael Lermontov was born when Pushkin was a lad of fifteen and he died four years after Pushkin's death, that is, at the quite ridiculous age of twenty-seven. Like Pushkin he was killed in a duel, but his duel was not the inevitable sequel of a tangled tragedy as in Pushkin's case. It belonged rather to that trivial type which in the eighteen-thirties and forties so often turned hot friendship into cold murder—a phenomenon of temperature rather than of ethics.

You must imagine him as a sturdy, shortish, rather shabby-looking Russian army officer with a singularly pale and smooth forehead, queer velvety eyes that "seemed to absorb light instead of emitting it," and a jerky manner in his demeanor and speech. Following both a Byronic fashion and his own disposition, he took pleasure in offending people, but there can hardly be any doubt that the bully in him was the shell and not the core, and that in many cases his attitude was that of a morbidly self-conscious, tender-hearted, somewhat childish young man building himself a sentiment-proof defense. He spent the best years of his short life in the Caucasus, taking part in dangerous expeditions against mountain tribes that kept rebelling against imperial domination. Finally, a quarrel with a fellow-officer, whom he had most methodically annoyed, put a stop to his not very happy life.

But all this is neither here nor there. What matters is that this very young, arrogant, not overeducated man, mixing with people who did not care a fig for literature, somehow managed, during the short period granted him by the typically perverse destiny which haunts geniuses, to produce verse and prose of such virility, beauty, and tenderness that the following generation placed him higher than Pushkin: the ups of poets are but seesaw reverses of their downs.

At fourteen he wrote a short lyrical poem "The Angel" which Russian critics have, not inadequately, described as coming straight from paradise; indeed, it contains a pure and truly heavenly melody brought unbroken to earth. At twenty-three he reacted to Pushkin's death by writing a poem which branded with its white fire the titled scoundrels who baited the greatest of all poets and kept fanning the flames of his African passions. And at twenty-five he resolutely turned to prose and would have achieved great things in that medium had not a perfectly avoidable bullet pierced his heart.

He was an ardent admirer of Byron, but his best work discloses hardly a trace of this influence. Superficially, this influence is quite clear in his earlier lyrics.

> Farewell! Nevermore shall we meet,
> we shall never touch hands—so farewell!
> [see p. 285 for full text]

Women prefer him to Pushkin because of the pathos and loveliness of his personality, singing so urgently through his verse. Radical critics, people who expect poets to express the needs of the nation, have welcomed in Lermontov the first bard of the revolution. Although he did not allude to politics in his works, what they admired in him was his violent pity for the underdog, and one pessimistic critic has suggested that had Lermontov lived he might have used his talent in the 'sixties and 'seventies to write novels with an obvious social message. Here and there, in the sobbing rhythm of some of his lines, I cannot help feeling that the tearful rhymsters of later generations, such as Nadson, who wallowed in civic lamentations, owe something to Lermontov's pathos in singing the death of a soldier or that of his own soul. Children in schools have been greatly tormented by being made to learn by heart yards and yards of Lermontov. He has been put to music by composers. There is a dreadful opera by Rubinstein based on his "Demon." A great painter treated his "Demon" in quite a different way and in terms of such peacock colors amid diamond-blazing eyes and purple clouds that Lermontov's genius ought to sleep content. Though decidedly patchy, he remains for the true lover of poetry a miraculous being whose development is something of a mystery.

It might be said that what Darwin called "struggle for existence" is really a struggle for perfection, and in that respect Nature's main and most admirable device is optical illusion. Among human beings, poets are the best exponents of the art of deception. Such poets as Coleridge, Baudelaire, and Lermontov have been particularly good at creating a fluid and iridescent medium wherein reality discloses the dreams of which it consists. A geological transverse section of the most prosaic of towns may show the fabulous reptile and the fossil fern fantastically woven into its foundation. Travellers have told us that in the mysterious wastes of Central Asia mirages are sometimes so bright that real trees are mirrored in the sham shimmer of optical lakes. Something of the effect of these manifold reflections is characteristic of Lermontov's poetry, and especially of that most fatamorganic poem of his which might bear the title: A Dream in a Dream of a Dream in a Dream. In this respect the poem is, as far as I know, perfectly unique. But curiously enough, none of Lermontov's contemporaries, least of all the poet himself, ever noticed the remarkable telescopic process of images that it contains. Here is this fourfold dream:

I dreamt that with a bullet in my side
in a hot gorge of Daghestan I lay . . .
[see p. 297 for full text]

Let us call the initial dreamer A^1, which will thus apply to the poetical personality of Lermontov, the live summary of the mirages involved. For simplicity's sake we shall ignore the argument that it was not he who really dreamt, but the poet he imagined dreaming. He dreams of his lifeless body lying among the yellow cliffs, and this second personality we shall call A^2. This A^2 dreams of a young woman in a distant land, and here is the central and deepest point of the whole image complex, which point we shall term A^3. In so far as the imagined existence of the young woman is implied, her dream of A^2 should be called A^4: however, this A^4 is a reversion to A^2, though not quite identical with it, and thus the circle is completed. The dreamer drifts back to the surface, and the full stop at the end of the poem comes with the exactitude of an alarm clock.

Incidentally, the poet got so thoroughly immersed in these dreams within dreams that in the last stanza he committed a solecism (omitted in my translation) which is also unique; for it is the solecism of a solipsist, and solipsism has been defined by Bertrand Russell as the *reductio ad absurdum* of subjective idealism: we dream our own selves. So, even in the methodical approach itself, we observe a quaint mirage of two terms which look almost alike. The solecism in question has been unconsciously retained (and aggravated) in John Pollen's translation of the poem in Leo Weiner's *Anthology of Russian Literature*. The young woman dreams that on that torrid sand "the well-known body lay." Lermontov has "the familiar corpse" ("znakomyi trup"), his intention having been evidently to say as tersely as possible: "the corpse of the young woman's good acquaintance." This "familiar corpse" or "well-known body" was unfortunately produced not merely as a phenomenon of bad grammar, but because in the poem itself the dead and the living got so hopelessly mixed. In a way, perhaps the poem would be less miraculous had not that blunder occurred, but I am afraid that what a Russian reader can skip, will not escape the humor of an

Anglo-Saxon, and anyway Pollen's "well-known body" is much too large. And I am reminded, too, of that Chinese poet who dreamt he was a butterfly and then, when he awoke, could not solve the problem whether he was a Chinese poet who had dreamt that entomological dream, or a butterfly dreaming that it was a Chinese poet.

To be a good visionary you must be a good observer. The better you see the earth the finer your perception of heaven will be; and, inversely, the crystal-gazer who is not an artist will turn out to be merely an old bore. Lermontov's long poem "The Demon" devoted to the lurid love-affair between a demon and a Georgian girl is built on a commonplace of mysticism. But it is saved by the bright pigments of definite landscapes painted here and there by a magic brush. There is nothing of an Oriental poet's passion for gems and generalizations here; Lermontov is essentially a European traveller, admiring distant lands, as all Russian poets have been, although they might never have left their hearths. The very love for the native countryside is with Lermontov (and others) European, in the sense that it is both irrational and founded on concrete sensual experience. "An unofficial English rose," or "the spires and farms" seen from a hilltop in Shropshire, or the little river at home which a Russian pilgrim, many centuries ago, recalled when he saw the Jordan, or merely those "green fields" a famous fat man babbled about as he died, offer a thrill of indescribable love for one's country that history books and statues in public gardens fail to provoke. But what is quite peculiar to "native land" descriptions in Russian poems is the atmosphere of nostalgia which sharpens the senses but distorts objective relationships. The Russian poet talks of the view from his window as if he were an exile dreaming of his land more vividly than he ever saw it, although at the moment he may be actually surveying the acres he owns. Pushkin longed to travel to Africa not because he was sick of Russian scenery but because he was eager to long for Russia when he would be abroad. Gogol in Rome spoke of the spiritual beauty of physical remoteness; and Lermontov's attitude to the Russian countryside implies a similar emotional paradox.

If I do love my land, strangely I love it:
'tis something reason cannot cure.
[see p. 291 for full text]

[see p. 291 for full text]

1941

LERMONTOV

Michael Lermontov was born when Pushkin was a lad of fifteen and he died four years after Pushkin's death, aged 27. Like Pushkin, he was killed in a duel but this was a casual rencontre—not the inevitable sequel of a tangled tragedy as in the master's case. He spent the best years of his short life in the Caucasus whither he had been banished twice—first for offending the Government by a piece of poetry on Pushkin's death (for which he rightly blamed the scoundrels surrounding the throne), then for a scrap with a lesser d'Anthès.

A moody young man with dark lusterless eyes, he tended to imitate Byron in his ways but was a greater poet than the latter. He was a brave soldier and seems to have enjoyed fighting the Caucasian tribes. His best poetry was written during the last three or four years of his life. As the critic Mirsky, whose work on Russian literature is the best on the market so far, puts it, "As a romantic poet he has . . . no rival in Russia and he had in him everything to become also a great realist—in the Russian sense." Of his longer pieces *The Demon* and *Mtsyri* are the most perfect. His highly original prose is terser, less velvety and even more sober than Pushkin's. Though decidedly patchy, Lermontov remains for the true lover of poetry a miraculous being whose development is something of a mystery.

1941–43

НЕБО И ЗВЕЗДЫ

Чисто вечернее небо,
Ясны далекие звезды,
Ясны, как счастье ребенка.
О, для чего мне нельзя и подумать:
Звезды, вы ясны, как счастье мое!

Чем ты несчастлив?—
Скажут мне люди.—
Тем я несчастлив,
Добрые люди, что звезды и небо—
Звезды и небо! а я—человек!..

Люди друг к другу
Зависть питают;
Я же, напротив,
Только завидую звездам прекрасным,
Только их место занять бы хотел.

1831

THE SKY AND THE STARS

Fair is the evening sky,
clear are the stars in the distance,
as clear as the joy of an infant.
Oh, why can't I tell myself even in thought:
The stars are as clear as my joy!

What is your trouble—
people might query.
Just this is my trouble,
excellent people: the sky and the stars
are the stars and the sky, whereas I am a man.

People are envious
of one another.
I, on the contrary,—
only the beautiful stars do I envy,
only to be in their place do I wish.

1944–47

АНГЕЛ

По небу полуночи ангел летел
    И тихую песню он пел;
И месяц, и звезды, и тучи толпой
    Внимали той песне святой.

Он пел о блаженстве безгрешных духов
    Под кущами райских садов;
О Боге великом он пел, и хвала
    Его непритворна была.

Он душу младую в объятиях нес
    Для мира печали и слез;
И звук его песни в душе молодой
    Остался без слов, но живой.

И долго на свете томилась она,
    Желанием чудным полна,
И звуков небес заменить не могли
    Ей скучные песни земли.

1831

THE ANGEL

An angel was crossing the pale vault of night,
    and his song was as soft as his flight,
and the moon and the stars and the clouds in a throng
    stood enthralled by this holy song.

He sang of the bliss of the innocent shades
    in the depths of celestial glades;
he sang of the Sovereign Being, and free
    of guile was his eulogy.

He carried a soul in his arms, a young life
    to the world of sorrow and strife,
and the young soul retained the throb of that song
    —without words, but vivid and strong.

And tied to this planet long did it pine
    full of yearnings dimly divine,
and our dull little ditties could never replace
    songs belonging to infinite space.

1944–46

ЖЕЛАНЬЕ

Отворите мне темницу,
Дайте мне сиянье дня,
Черноглазую девицу,
Черногривого коня.
Дайте раз по синю полю
Проскакать на том коне;
Дайте раз на жизнь и волю,
Как на чуждую мне долю,
Посмотреть поближе мне.

Дайте мне челнок дощатый
С полусгнившею скамьей,
Парус серый и косматый,
Ознакомленный с грозой.
Я тогда пущуся в море,
Беззаботен и один,
Разгуляюсь на просторе
И потешусь в буйном споре
С дикой прихотью пучин.

Дайте мне дворец высокой
И кругом зеленый сад,
Чтоб в тени его широкой
Зрел янтарный виноград;
Чтоб фонтан, не умолкая,
В зале мраморном журчал
И меня б в мечтаньях рая,
Хладной пылью орошая,
Усыплял и пробуждал. . .

1832

THE WISH

Open the door of my prison,
let me see the daylight again,
give me a black-eyed maiden
and a horse with a jet-black mane.
Over the wide blue grassland
let that courser carry me,
and just once, just a little closer,
let me glance at that alien portion—
that life and that liberty.

Give me a leaky sailboat
with a bench of half-rotten wood
and a well-worn sail all hoary
from the tempests it has withstood.
Then I shall launch on my voyage,
friendless and therefore free,
and shall have my fling in the open
and delight in the mighty struggle
with the savage whim of the sea.

Give me a lofty palace
with an arbor all around
where amber grapes would ripen
and the broad shade fleck the ground.
Let an ever-purling fountain
among marble pillars play
and lull me to sleep and wake me
in a halo of heavenly visions
and the cool dust of its spray.

1944–46

from
K *

1

Прости! мы не встретимся боле,
    Друг другу руки не пожмем;
Прости! твое сердце на воле,
    Но счастья не сыщет в другом.

[. . .]

3

Мгновение вместе мы были,
    Но вечность ничто перед ним;
Все чувства мы вдруг истощили,
    Сожгли поцелуем одним.
Прости! не жалей безрассудно,
    О краткой любви не жалей:
Расстаться казалось нам трудно,
    Но встретиться было б трудней.

1832

FAREWELL

Farewell! Nevermore shall we meet,
we shall never touch hands—so farewell!
Your heart is now free, but in none
will it ever be happy to dwell.

*

One moment together we came:
time eternal is nothing to this!
All senses we suddenly drained,
burned all in the flame of one kiss.

Farewell! And be wise, do not grieve:
our love was too short for regret,
and hard as we found it to part
harder still would it be if we met.

1941

ПАРУС

Белеет парус одинокой
В тумане моря голубом. . .
Что ищет он в стране далекой?
Что кинул он в краю родном?

Играют волны, ветер свищет,
И мачта гнется и скрыпит. . .
Увы! Он счастия не ищет,
И не от счастия бежит!

Под ним струя светлей лазури,
Над ним луч солнца золотой. . .
А он, мятежный, просит бури,
Как будто в бурях есть покой!

1832

THE SAIL

Amid the blue haze of the ocean
a sail is passing, white and frail.
What do you seek in a far country?
What have you left at home, lone sail?

The billows play, the breezes whistle,
and rhythmically creaks the mast.
Alas, you seek no happy future,
nor do you flee a happy past.

Below the mirrored azure brightens,
above the golden rays increase—
but you, wild rover, pray for tempests,
as if in tempests there was peace!

1944–46

БЛАГОДАРНОСТЬ

За всё, за всё Тебя благодарю я:
За тайные мучения страстей,
За горечь слез, отраву поцелуя,
За месть врагов и клевету друзей;
За жар души, растраченный в пустыне,
За всё, чем я обманут в жизни был.
Устрой лишь так, чтобы Тебя отныне
Недолго я еще благодарил.

1840

THANKSGIVING

For everything, for everything, O Lord,
I thank Thee—
for the secret pangs of passion,
the poisoned fangs of kisses,
the bitter taste
of tears;
for the revenge of foes
and for the calumny of friends,
and for the waste
of a soul's fervor burning in a desert,
and for all things that have deceived me here.
But please, O Lord,
henceforth let matters be arranged
in such a way
that I need not keep thanking Thee
much longer.

1944–46

ОТЧИЗНА

Люблю отчизну я, но странною любовью,
Не победит ее рассудок мой!
Ни слава, купленная кровью,
Ни полный гордого доверия покой,
Ни темной старины заветные преданья
Не шевелят во мне отрадного мечтанья.

Но я люблю—за что, не знаю сам—
Ее полей холодное молчанье,
Ее лесов дремучих колыханье,
Разливы рек ее, подобные морям;
Проселочным путем люблю скакать в телеге
И, взором медленно пронзая ночи тень,
Встречать по сторонам, вздыхая о ночлеге,
Дрожащие огни печальных деревень;
Люблю дымок спаленной жнивы,
В степи ночующий обоз
И на холме средь желтой нивы
Чету белеющих берез.
С отрадой, многим незнакомой,
Я вижу полное гумно,
Избу, покрытую соломой,
С резными ставнями окно;
И в праздник, вечером росистым,
Смотреть до полночи готов
На пляску с топаньем и свистом
Под говор пьяных мужичков.

1841

MY NATIVE LAND

If I do love my land, strangely I love it:
'tis something reason cannot cure.
Glories of war I do not covet,
but neither peace proud and secure,
nor the mysterious past and dim romances
can spur my soul to pleasant fancies.

And still I love thee—why I hardly know:
I love thy fields so coldly meditative,
native dark swaying woods and native
rivers that sea-like foam and flow.

In a clattering cart I love to travel
on country roads: watching the rising star,
yearning for sheltered sleep, my eyes unravel
the trembling lights of sad hamlets afar.

I also love the smoke of burning stubble,
vans huddled in the prairie night;
corn on a hill crowned with the double
grace of twin birches gleaming white.

Few are the ones who feel the pleasure
of seeing barns bursting with grain and hay,
well-thatched cottage-roofs made to measure
and shutters carved and windows gay.

And when the evening dew is glistening,
long may I hear the festive sound
of rustic dancers stamping, whistling
with drunkards clamoring around.

1941

СОСНА
(Из Гейне)

На севере диком стоит одиноко
    На голой вершине сосна
И дремлет качаясь, и снегом сыпучим
    Одета, как ризой, она.

И снится ей всё, что в пустыне далекой,
    В том крае, где солнца восход,
Одна и грустна на утесе горючем
    Прекрасная пальма растет.

1841

IMITATION OF HEINE

A pine there stands in the northern wilds
    alone on a barren bluff,
swaying and dreaming and clothed by the snow
    in a cloak of the finest fluff—

dreaming a dream of a distant waste,
    a country of sun-flushed sands
where all forlorn on a torrid cliff
    a lovely palm tree stands.

1944–46

УТЕС

Ночевала тучка золотая
На груди утеса великана;
Утром в путь она умчалась рано,
По лазури весело играя.

Но остался влажный след в морщине
Старого утеса. Одиноко
Он стоит, задумался глубоко,
И тихонько плачет он в пустыне.

1841

THE ROCK

The little golden cloud that spent the night
upon the breast of yon great rock, next day
rose early and in haste pursued its way
eager to gambol in the azure light.

A humid trace, however, did remain
within a wrinkle of the rock. Alone
and wrapt in thought, the old and gentle stone
sheds silent tears above the empty plain.

1944–46

СОН

В полдневный жар в долине Дагестана
С свинцом в груди лежал недвижим я;
Глубокая еще дымилась рана;
По капле кровь точилася моя.

Лежал один я на песке долины;
Уступы скал теснилися кругом,
И солнце жгло их желтые вершины
И жгло меня,—но спал я мертвым сном.

И снился мне сияющий огнями
Вечерний пир в родимой стороне.
Меж юных жен, увенчанных цветами,
Шел разговор веселый обо мне.

Но в разговор веселый не вступая,
Сидела там задумчиво одна,
И в грустный сон душа ее младая
Бог знает чем была погружена;

И снилась ей долина Дагестана;
Знакомый труп лежал в долине той;
В его груди дымясь чернела рана,
И кровь лилась хладеющей струей.

1841

THE TRIPLE DREAM

I dreamt that with a bullet in my side
in a hot gorge of Daghestan I lay.
Deep was the wound and steaming, and the tide
of my life-blood ebbed drop by drop away.

Alone I lay amid a silent maze
of desert sand and bare cliffs rising steep,
their tawny summits burning in the blaze
that burned me too; but lifeless was my sleep.

And in a dream I saw the candle-flame
of a gay supper in the land I knew;
young women crowned with flowers . . . And my name
on their light lips hither and thither flew.

But one of them sat pensively apart,
not joining in the light-lipped gossiping,
and there alone, God knows what made her heart,
her young heart dream of such a hidden thing . . .

For in her dream she saw a gorge, somewhere
in Daghestan, and knew the man who lay
there on the sand, the dead man, unaware
of steaming wound and blood ebbing away.

1941

THE TRIPLE DREAM

In noon's heat, in a dale of Dagestan,
With lead inside my breast, stirless I lay;
The deep wound still smoked on; my blood
Kept trickling drop by drop away.

On the dale's sand alone I lay. The cliffs
Crowded around in ledges steep,
And the sun scorched their tawny tops
And scorched me—but I slept death's sleep.

And in a dream I saw an evening feast
That in my native land with bright lights shone;
Among young women crowned with flowers,
A merry talk concerning me went on.

But in the merry talk not joining,
One of them sat there lost in thought,
And in a melancholy dream
Her young soul was immersed—God knows by what.

And of a dale in Dagestan she dreamt;
In that dale lay the corpse of one she knew;
Within his breast a smoking wound showed black,
And blood ran in a stream that colder grew.

ca. 1956–57

AFANASIY AFANASIEVICH FET
(SHENSHIN)
(1820–1892)

ON AFANASIY FET

Fet—the spirit of the air, a wispy cloud, a butterfly fanning its wings.

ca. 1948

Literary criticism in Russia, or at least that part of literary criticism that swayed the reader, was mainly a social force, occupied with social civic problems and to such critics, to critics immensely celebrated in Russia as champions of liberty, civilization, commonsense, popular science and the rest, to the Dobrolyubovs of the sixties and to the Mihaylovskis of the eighties, a poet who spent his time inventing new methods of making poems out of landscapes, or love, was a ridiculous freak, a heretic, a sinner against mankind. That, at a time when everything ought to be subordinated to action and action alone, a man dared to compose a poem in which there was not a single verb, but only nouns and adjectives, seemed monstrous. Fet was harried, spat at, spanked, mocked, insulted in such a thorough fashion that it is a wonder he never lost his head, never so much as replied to those attacks, ignoring absolutely his furious critics who in the long run made dreadful fools of themselves by raving at things they did not understand. And so it happened that up to the present day it is a good way to test whether a Russian understands poetry or not by finding out whether he appreciates Fet. . . .

The matter-of-fact critics who cursed Fet because he did not describe the sufferings of the Russian peasant in blunt manly measures, those critics were particularly maddened by Fet's verse slipping as it were between their fingers, verse which became intangible when placed in a coarse medium of their own world for in their world mental curves were as illegal as the roundness of the world was in the days of the flat-footed logicians who were firmly planted on a flat beach, where every grain of sand voiced, unheeded, the claim of its circular shape. A poem by Fet seemed to them meaningless, because for them the meaning of things was limited by the square angles of their immediate use—city squares where crowds gather with square flags, square shoes, square prison cells, square tombstones. But Fet looped his loop and was suddenly somewhere in the milky way just when he was expected to come home with some reasonable explanation of his behavior.

ca. 1947–49

* * *

Die Gleichmäßigkeit des Laufes der Zeit
in allen Köpfen beweist mehr, als irgend
etwas, daß wir Alle in denselben Traum
versenkt sind, ja daß es Ein Wesen ist,
welches ihn träumt.

—Schopenhauer

Измучен жизнью, коварством надежды,
Когда им в битве душой уступаю,
И днем и ночью смежаю я вежды
И как-то странно порой прозреваю.

Еще темнее мрак жизни вседневной,
Как после яркой осенней зарницы,
И только в небе, как зов задушевный,
Сверкают звезд золотые ресницы.

И так прозрачна огней бесконечность,
И так доступна вся бездна эфира,
Что прямо смотрю я из времени в вечность
И пламя твое узнаю, солнце мира.

И неподвижно на огненных розах
Живой алтарь мирозданья курится,
В его дыму, как в творческих грезах,
Вся сила дрожит и вся вечность снится.

И всё, что мчится по безднам эфира,
И каждый луч, плотской и бесплотный,—
Твой только отблеск, о солнце мира,
И только сон, только сон мимолетный.

И этих грез в мировом дуновеньи
Как дым несусь я и таю невольно,
И в этом прозреньи, и в этом забвеньи
Легко мне жить и дышать мне не больно.

ca. 1864

Die Gleichmässigkeit des Laufes der Zeit
in allen Köpfen beweist mehr, als irgend
etwas, dass wir Alle in denselben Traum
versenkt sind, ja dass es Ein Wesen ist,
welches ihn träumt.

—Schopenhauer, *Parerga,* II, 29.

When life is torture, when hope is a traitor,
when in the battle my soul must surrender,
then daily, nightly I lower my eyelids,
and all is revealed in a strange flash of splendor.

Like nights in autumn, life's darkness seems denser
between the distant and thunderless flashes.
Alone the starlight is endlessly friendly—
the stars that sparkle through golden bright lashes.

And all this lambent abyss is so limpid,
so close is the sky to my spirit's desire,
that, straight out of time into timelessness peering,
your throne I discern, empyrean fire.

And there the altar of all creation
stands still and smokes in a glory of roses.
Eternity dreams of itself, as the smoke-wreaths
vibrate with the forces and forms it composes.

And all that courses down cosmic channels,
and every ray of the mind or of matter
is but your reflection, empyrean fire,
dreams, only dreams that flit by and scatter.

And in that wind of sidereal fancies
I float like vapor, now dimmer now brighter—
and thanks to my vision, and thanks to oblivion,
with ease I breathe, and life's burden is lighter.

1943

ALTER EGO

Как лилея глядится в нагорный ручей,
Ты стояла над первою песней моей,
И была ли при этом победа, и чья,
У ручья ль от цветка, у цветка ль от ручья?

Ты душою младенческой всё поняла,
Что́ мне высказать тайная сила дала,
И хоть жизнь без тебя суждено мне влачить,
Но мы вместе с тобой, нас нельзя разлучить.

Та трава, что вдали на могиле твоей,
Здесь на сердце, чем старе оно, тем свежей,
И я знаю, взглянувши на звезды порой,
Что взирали на них мы как боги с тобой.

У любви есть слова, те слова не умрут.
Нас с тобой ожидает особенный суд;
Он сумеет нас сразу в толпе различить,
И мы вместе придем, нас нельзя разлучить!

1878

ALTER EGO

As a lily that looks at itself in a stream
so my very first song was your mirrored dream.
But whose was the triumph? Who gave and who took?
Was it brook from blossom or blossom from brook?

Your childish soul could so easily guess
the thoughts I was inwardly moved to express.
Though I live without you by a dreary decree,
we are one—for nothing can part you and me.

The grass on your grave in a distant clime
is here in my heart growing greener with time.
When I happen to glance at the stars, then I know
that together like gods we had looked at their glow.

Love has words of its own, these words cannot die.
Our singular case special judges will try:
in the crowd they will notice us right from the start—
for as one we will come—we whom nothing can part.

1943

ЛАСТОЧКИ

Природы праздный соглядатай,
Люблю, забывши все кругом,
Следить за ласточкой стрельчатой
Над вечереющим прудом.

Вот понеслась и зачертила—
И страшно, чтобы гладь стекла
Стихией чуждой не схватила
Молниевидного крыла.

И снова то же дерзновенье
И та же темная струя,—
Не таково ли вдохновенье
И человеческого я?

Не так ли я, сосуд скудельный,
Дерзаю на запретный путь,
Стихии чуждой, запредельной,
Стремясь хоть каплю зачерпнуть?

1884

THE SWALLOW

When prying idly into Nature
I am particularly fond
of watching the arrow of a swallow
over the sunset of a pond.

See—there it goes, and skims, and glances:
the alien element, I fear,
roused from its glassy sleep might capture
black lightning quivering so near.

There—once again that fearless shadow
over a frowning ripple ran.
Have we not here the living image
of active poetry in man—

of something leading me, banned mortal,
to venture where I dare not stop—
striving to scoop from a forbidden
mysterious element one drop?

1943

NIKOLAY ALEKSEEVICH NEKRASOV

(1821–1877)

ON NIKOLAY NEKRASOV

Nikolay Alekseevich Nekrasov, 1821–77, a famous poet who successfully transcended, in a few great poems, the journalist in him, who wrote topical jingles.

1970

Nekrasov's iambic pentameter enchants us particularly by its hortatory, supplicatory and prophetic force and by a very individual caesura after the second foot, a caesura which in Pushkin, say, is a rudimentary organ insofar as it controls the melody of the line, but which in Nekrasov becomes a genuine organ of breathing, as if it had turned from a partition into a pit, or as if the two-foot part of the line and the three-foot part had moved asunder, leaving after the second foot an interval full of music. . . . [T]his guttural, sobbing articulation—

> Oh, do not say the life you lead is dismal,
> And do not call a jailer one half-dead!

Before me Night yawns chilly and abysmal.
The arms of Love before you are outspread.

I know, to you another is now dearer,
It irks you now to spare me and to wait.
Oh, bear with me! My end is drawing nearer,
Let Fate complete what was begun by Fatc!

1934–38

Тяжелый крест достался ей на долю:
Страдай, молчи, притворствуй и не плачь!
Кому и страсть, и молодость, и волю,—
Все отдала—тот стал ее палач!

Давно ни с кем она не знает встречи;
Угнетена, пуглива и грустна,
Безумные, язвительные речи
Безропотно выслушивать должна:

«Не говори, что молодость сгубила
Ты, ревностью истерзана моей;
Не говори!.. близка моя могила,
А ты цветка весеннего свежей!

«Тот день, когда меня ты полюбила
И от меня услышала: "люблю"—
Не проклинай!.. близка моя могила:
Поправлю все, все смертью искуплю!

«Не говори, что дни твои унылы,
Тюремщиком больного не зови:
Передо мной—холодный мрак могилы,
Перед тобой—объятия любви!

«Я знаю: ты другого полюбила,
Щадить и ждать наскучило тебе...
О, погоди! близка моя могила—
Начатое и кончить дай судьбе!»..

Ужасные, убийственные звуки!..
Как статуя прекрасна и бледна,
Она молчит, свои ломая руки...
И что́ сказать могла б ему она?..

1855

* * *

A heavy cross is her allotted burden:
she hides her tears, dares hardly speak or stir;
some know the joys of passion, youth and freedom;
she gave him all—and now he tortures her!

Weeks have elapsed since she has talked to others;
oppressed, with bent and melancholy brow,
without a murmur, to the most fantastic
and galling speeches she must listen now:

"O do not say that your best years are crumbling
and that my jealousy is killing you.
O say not this! I know my end is coming,
and you—you bloom as fresh as April's dew.

"That distant day when first you felt you loved me,
and when you heard my words of love, that day
should not be cursed! I know my end is coming:
all will I mend, all shall my death repay!

"O do not say your days are dreary, do not
call a sick man your jailer, O enough!
In front of me I see the grave's cold darkness,
in front of you—the open arms of love.

"I know too well that now you love another:
it palls on you to spare me and to wait.
Delay the blow! I know my end is coming,
let fate complete what was begun by fate!" . . .

Most dreadful, demoniacal reproaches!
Like a fair marble form, pale with the dim
pallor of stone, she wrings her hands in silence
for there is nothing she could say to him.

1948–51

NIKOLAY NEKRASOV   311

Внимая ужасам войны,
При каждой новой жертве боя
Мне жаль не друга, не жены,
Мне жаль не самого героя. . .
Увы! утешится жена,
И друга лучший друг забудет;
Но где-то есть душа одна—
Она до гроба помнить будет!
Средь лицемерных наших дел
И всякой пошлости, и прозы,
Одни я в мире подсмотрел
Святые, искренние слезы—
То слезы бедных матерей!
Им не забыть своих детей,
Погибших на кровавой ниве,
Как не поднять плакучей иве
Своих поникнувших ветвей. . .

1855–56

* * *

As I hearken to the horrors of war,
at the news of every death
I pity not the friend, nor the wife,
nor even the hero himself.
Alas—the widow will be consoled
and the best friend will forget his friend,
but there is in the world one soul
that will remember for ever.
Amid our hypocritical affairs
and all kinds of matters, platitudinous and prosaic,
the only sacred and sincere tears I have observed
are the tears of unfortunate mothers.
For them to forget their children slain in battle
is as impossible as for a weeping willow
to lift its drooping branches.

1948–51

МОРОЗ, КРАСНЫЙ НОС
(Часть вторая, XXXVI)

Ни звука! Душа умирает
Для скорби, для страсти. Стоишь
И чувствуешь, как покоряет
Ее эта мертвая тишь.

Ни звука! И видишь ты синий
Свод неба, да солнце, да лес,
В серябряно-матовый иней
Наряженный, полный чудес,

Влекущий неведомой тайной,
Глубоко-бесстрастный. . . Но вот
Послышался шорох случайный—
Вершинами белка идет.

Ком снега она уронила
На Дарью, прыгнув по сосне.
А Дарья стояла и стыла
В своем заколдованном сне. . .

1863–64

from
RED-NOSED FROST
(last part, XXXVI)

(a young peasant woman is frozen to death in a winter forest)

Not a sound! The soul leaves the world
of sorrow and passion. You stand
and feel this dead stillness
overcoming you.

Not a sound! All you see
is the blue sky, the sun and the forest
festively clad in the lusterless silver of frost,
full of marvels,

mysteriously attractive
and deeply impassive. Then, suddenly—
a chance sound, a kind of little rustle:
it is a squirrel passing from tree-top to tree-top.

The squirrel as it leaps onto the next pine
causes a lump of snow to drop on Daria
—and Daria stands and freezes
in her enchanted sleep.

1948–51

РУСЬ
from
Кому на Руси жить хорошо

Битву кровавую
С сильной державою
Царь замышлял.
—Хватит ли силушки?
Хватит ли золота?—
Думал, гадал.

Ты и убогая,
Ты и обильная,
Ты и могучая,
Ты и бессильная,
Матушка-Русь!..

В рабстве спасенное
Сердце свободное—
Золото, золото
Сердце народное!

Сила народная,
Сила могучая—
Совесть спокойная,
Правда живучая!

Сила с неправдою
Не уживается,
Жертва неправдою
Не вызывается—

Русь не шелохнется,
Русь—как убитая!
А загорелась в ней
Искра сокрытая—

RUSSIA
from
Who Can Be Happy in Russia

A bloody battle
with a strong kingdom
The Tzar was planning.
Shall we have strength enough,
Shall we have wealth enough,
pondered the Tzar.

For thou art both beggarly
and inexhaustible
great is thy weakness
and great is thy force
Motherland-Russia

Saved despite slavery,
is thy free soul:
the soul of a nation
is a nation's gold.

The strength of a nation
its greatest might
is a clear conscience,
a keen sense of right.

Might and oppression
do not go together.
Oppression is something
not worth dying for.

Russia feigns death,
she does not stir,
but as soon as the secret spark
is kindled in her,

Встали—не бужены
Вышли—не прошены:
Жита по зернышку
Горы наношены.

Рать подымается
Неисчислимая,
Сила в ней скажется
Несокрушимая!

Ты и убогая,
Ты и обильная,
Ты и забитая,
Ты и всесильная,
Матушка-Русь!..

1876

Her ranks rise, though no trumpet sounds
They set out, though nobody calls them
Mountains of grain
Rise seed by seed.

They rise
in countless numbers.
Titanic, invincible.

For thou art both beggarly
and inexhaustible
great is thy weakness
and great is thy force,
Motherland-Russia.

1948–51

ALEKSANDR ALEKSANDROVICH BLOK
(1880–1921)

ON ALEKSANDR BLOK

Among major Russian poets, the greatest masters in the [iambic tetrameter] form were, in the nineteenth century, Pushkin and Tyutchev and, in the twentieth, Blok and Hodasevich.

1951–57

Blok . . . by far the greatest poet of the first two decades of this century.

1951–57

Blok "is one of those poets that get into one's system— and everything seems unblokish and flat. I, as most Russians, went through that stage some twenty-five years ago."

1943

How do you now regard the poets Blok and Mandelshtam and others who were writing in the days before you left Russia?

I read them in my boyhood, more than a half-century ago. Ever since that time I have remained passionately fond of Blok's lyrics. His long pieces are weak, and the famous *The Twelve* is dreadful, self-consciously couched in a phony "primitive" tone, with a pink cardboard Jesus Christ glued on at the end.

1966

НЕЗНАКОМКА

По вечерам над ресторанами
Горячий воздух дик и глух,
И правит окриками пьяными
Весенний и тлетворный дух.

Вдали, над пылью переулочной,
Над скукой загородных дач,
Чуть золотится крендель булочной,
И раздается детский плач.

И каждый вечер, за шлагбаумами,
Заламывая котелки,
Среди канав гуляют с дамами
Испытанные остряки.

Над озером скрипят улючины,
И раздается женский визг,
А в небе, ко всему приученный,
Бессмысленно кривится диск.

И каждый вечер друг единственный
В моем стакане отражен
И влагой терпкой и таинственной,
Как я, смирен и оглушен.

А рядом у соседних столиков
Лакеи сонные торчат,
И пьяницы с глазами кроликов
«In vino veritas!» кричат.

И каждый вечер, в час назначенный,
(Иль это только снится мне?)
Девичий стан, шелками схваченный,
В туманном движется окне.

THE STRANGE LADY

In the evenings, the sultry air above the restaurants
is both wild and torpid,
and drunken vociferations are governed
by the evil spirit of spring.

In the dusty vista of lanes
where reigns the suburban tedium of clapboard villas
the gilt sign of a bakery—a giant pretzel—glimmers,
and children are heard crying.

And every evening, beyond the town barriers,
in a zone of ditches,
wags of long standing, their jaunty derbies askew,
go for walks with their lady friends.

From the lake comes the sound of creaking oar locks,
and women are heard squealing,
while overhead, the round moon,
accustomed to everything, blankly mugs.

And every evening my sole companion
is reflected in my wineglass,
as tamed and as stunned as I am
by the same acrid and occult potion.

And nearby, at other tables,
waiters drowsily hover,
and tipplers with the pink eyes of rabbits
shout: *In vino veritas!*

And every evening, at the appointed hour
(or is it merely a dream of mine?),
the figure of a girl in clinging silks
moves across the misty window.

И медленно, пройдя меж пьяными,
Всегда без спутников, одна,
Дыша духами и туманами,
Она садится у окна.

И веют древними поверьями
Ее упругие шелка,
И шляпа с траурными перьями,
И в кольцах узкая рука.

И странной близостью закованный
Смотрю за темную вуаль,
И вижу берег очарованный
И очарованную даль.

Глухие тайны мне поручены,
Мне чье-то солнце вручено,
И все души моей излучины
Пронзило терпкое вино.

И перья страуса склоненные
В моем качаются мозгу,
И очи синие бездонные
Цветут на дальнем берегу.

В моей душе лежит сокровище,
И ключ поручен только мне!
Ты право, пьяное чудовище!
Я знаю: истина в вине.

1906

Slowly she makes her way among the drinkers,
always escortless, alone,
perfume and mists emanating from her,
and takes a seat near the window.

And her taut silks,
her hat with its tenebrous plumes,
her slender bejeweled hand
waft legendary magic.

And with a strange sense of intimacy enchaining me,
I peer beyond her dusky veil
and perceive an enchanted shoreline,
a charmed remoteness.

Dim mysteries are in my keeping,
the orb of somebody's day has been entrusted to me,
and the tangy wine has penetrated
all the meanders of my soul.

And the drooping ostrich feathers
sway within my brain,
and the dark-blue fathomless eyes
become blossoms on the distant shore.

A treasure lies in my soul,
and I alone have the keeping of its key.
Those drunken brutes are right:
indeed,—there is truth in wine . . .

1948–51

РОССИЯ

Опять, как в годы золотые,
Три стертых треплются шлеи,
И вязнут спицы росписные
В расхлябанные колеи. . .

Россия, нищая Россия,
Мне избы серые твои,
Твои мне песни ветровые,—
Как слезы первые любви!

Тебя жалеть я не умею,
И крест свой бережно несу. . .
Какому хочешь чародею
Отдай разбойную красу!

Пускай заманит и обманет,—
Не пропадешь, не сгинешь ты,
И лишь забота затуманит
Твои прекрасные черты. . .

Ну, что ж? Одной заботой боле—
Одной слезой река шумней,
А ты все та же—лес, да поле,
Да плат узорный до бровей. . .

И невозможное возможно,
Дорога долгая легка,
Когда блеснет в дали дорожной
Мгновенный взор из-под платка,
Когда звенит тоской острожной
Глухая песня ямщика! . .

1908

Again, as in my golden years,
three sets of well-worn harness thongs swing before me,
and the painted wheel spokes sink deep
in slushy ruts.

Russia, beggarly Russia,
your grey hovels,
your wind-borne songs
are to me like the first tears of love.

I know not how to pity you
but tenderly I carry my cross;
you may abandon your brigandish beauty
to any wizard you choose.

Let him entice you and deceive you—
perish you will not, nor disappear;
only care will becloud
your beautiful face.

Well, what of it? One care the more,
one more tear increases the noise of the river,
while you remain always the same—forest and meadowland,
and bright-patterned kerchief coming down to your eyebrows.

And the impossible is possible,
and the long road is made easy,
when in the dusty distance a swift glance flashes
from under that kerchief
or when a convict's note of dull anguish
rings through the dim song of the troika driver.

1948–51

НА ЖЕЛЕЗНОЙ ДОРОГЕ

Марии Павловне Ивановой

Под насыпью, во рву некошенном,
Лежит и смотрит, как живая,
В цветном платке, на косы брошенном,
Красивая и молодая.

Бывало, шла походкой чинною
На шум и свист за ближним лесом.
Всю обойдя платформу длинную,
Ждала, волнуясь, под навесом.

Три ярких глаза набегающих—
Нежней румянец, круче локон:
Быть может, кто из проезжающих
Посмотрит пристальней из окон. . .

Вагоны шли привычной линией,
Подрагивали и скрипели;
Молчали желтые и синие;
В зеленых плакали и пели.

Вставали сонные за стеклами
И обводили ровным взглядом
Платформу, сад с кустами блеклыми,
Ее, жандарма с нею рядом. . .

Лишь раз гусар, рукой небрежною
Облокотясь на бархат алый,
Скользнул по ней улыбкой нежною. . .
Скользнул—и поезд в даль умчало.

Так мчалась юность бесполезная,
В пустых мечтах изнемогая. . .
Тоска дорожная, железная
Свистела, сердце разрывая. . .

THE RAILROAD

At the foot of a railroad embankment, on the uncut grass of a hollow,
there she lies, her eyes open, as if alive.
A colored kerchief is thrown over her tresses;
she is beautiful, she is young.

It used to be her custom to step out demurely
at the rumble and whistle approaching from behind yonder wood.
She would walk the entire length of the platform
and wait, in a flutter, under its sloping roof.

As the three bright eyes swept nearer,
the flush of her cheek grew softer,
who knows, some passenger more observant than the rest,
might look out of the window.

The cars rolled by in their familiar array,
jolting a jot, and creaking:
the blue ones, and the yellow, were silent;
from the green cars came sobs and songs.

Drowsy travelers could be seen rising,
and through the glass their indiscriminate glance would survey
the boards of the station, the withered shrubs of its garden,
and her, and the local gendarme at her side.

Only once, a hussar,
leaning an indolent elbow upon red velvet,
smiled at her with fleeting tenderness,
smiled, and was whirled away.

Thus whirled her useless young life,
wearing itself out in hollow daydreams,
the dull anguish of distance and iron wheels
blowing its heartrending whistle.

Да что—давно уж сердце вынуто!
Так много отдано поклонов,
Так много жадных взоров кинуто
В пустынные глаза вагонов. . .

Не подходите к ней с вопросами,
Вам все равно, а ей—довольно:
Любовью, грязью иль колесами
Она раздавлена—все больно.

1910

Heart . . . ? Long since has the heart been squandered,
because too many have been the salutations,
the avid glances exchanged
with the vacant-eyed railway cars.

Stay away with your questions.
It does not matter to you, and she has had all she could stand.
Love, mud, wheels—whatever crushed her,
it hurts the same.

1948–51

from

РОЗА И КРЕСТ

«Всюду беда и утраты,
Что тебя ждет впереди?
Ставь же свой парус косматый,
Меть свои крепкие латы
Знаком креста на груди».

1913

* * *

All is disaster and loss.
What does the future conceal?
Set up your rough old sail
mark with the sign of the Cross
your breastplate of steel.

ca. 1948–49

***

Была ты всех ярче, верней и прелестней,
    Не кляни же меня, не кляни!
Мой поезд летит, как цыганская песня,
    Как те невозвратные дни. . .

Что было любимо,—все мимо, мимо. . .
    Впереди—неизвестность пути. . .
Благословенно, неизгладимо,
    Невозвратимо. . . прости!

1914

* * *

You were truer than others, and vivid, and sweet,—
oh, do not condemn me! My train
is as fleet as the song of a gypsy, as fleet
as those days that shall not come again.

Days of love that recede as I speed in the night
on a journey I cannot foretell . . .
Blest be the past, blest be its light,
blest be its loss . . . farewell!

1948–51

VLADISLAV FELITSIANOVICH HODASEVICH
(1886–1939)

ON VLADISLAV HODASEVICH

This century has not yet produced any Russian poet surpassing Vladislav Hodasevich.

1951–57

ON HODASEVICH

This poet, the greatest Russian poet of our time, Pushkin's literary descendant in Tyutchev's line of succession, shall remain the pride of Russian poetry as long as its last memory lives. What makes his genius particularly striking is that it matured in the years of our literature's torpescence, when the Bolshevist era neatly divided poets into established optimists and demoted pessimists, endemic hearties and exiled hypochondriacs; a classification which, incidentally, leads to an instructive paradox: inside Russia the dictate acts from outside; outside Russia, it acts from within. . . .

Even genius does not save one in Russia; in exile, one is saved by genius alone. No matter how difficult Hodasevich's last years were, no matter how sorely the banality of an émigré's lot irked him, no matter, too, how much the good old indifference of fellow mortals contributed to his mortal extinction, Hodasevich is safely enshrined in timeless Russia. Indeed, he himself was ready to admit, through the hiss of his bilious banter, through the "cold and murk" of the days predicted by Blok, that he occupied a special position: the blissful solitude of a height others could not attain . . .

Hodasevich seemed to have sensed in his very fingers the branching influence of the poetry he created in exile and therefore felt a certain responsibility for its destiny, a destiny which irritated him more than it saddened him. The glum notes of cheap verse struck him more as a parody than as the echo of his collection *Evropeyskaya Noch'* (European Night), where bitterness, anger, angels, the gulfs of adjacent vowels—everything, in short, was genuine, unique, and quite unrelated to the current moods which clouded the verse of many of those who were more or less his disciples.

To speak of his *masterstvo, Meisterschaft,* "mastery," *i.e.* "technique," would be meaningless and even blasphemous in relation to poetry in general. . . . [T]he perfect poem (at least three hundred examples of which can be found in Russian literature) is capable of being examined from all angles by the reader in search of its idea or only its sentiment, or only the picture, or only the sound (many things of that kind can be thought up, from "instrumentation" to "imaginization"), but all this amounts to a random selection of an entity's facet, none of which would deserve, really, a moment of our attention (nor could it of course induce in us any thrill except, maybe, obliquely, in making us recall some other "entity," somebody's voice, a room, a night), had not the poem possessed that resplendent independence in respect of which the term "masterly technique" rings as insulting as its antonym "winning sincerity."

What I am saying here is far from being new; yet one is impelled to repeat it when speaking of Hodasevich. There exists not quite exact verse (whose very blurriness can have an appeal of its own like that of lovely nearsighted eyes) which makes a virtue of approximation by the poet's striving toward it with the same precision in selecting his words as would pass for "mastery" in more picturesque circumstances. Compared to those artful blurrings, the poetry of Hodasevich may strike the gentle reader as an overpolishing of form—I am deliberately using this unappetizing epithet. But the whole point is that his poetry—or indeed any authentic poetry—does not require any definition in terms of "form" . . .

I should not be surprised if this person or that finds Hodasevich's posthumous fame inexplicable at first blush. Furthermore, he published no poems lately—and readers are forgetful, and our literary critics are too excited and preoccupied by evanescent topical themes to have the time or occasion to remind the public of important matters. Be it as it may, all is finished now: the bequeathed gold shines on a shelf in full view of the future, whilst the gold-miner has left for the region from where, perhaps, a faint something reaches the ears of good poets, penetrating our being with the beyond's fresh breath and conferring upon art that mystery which more than anything characterizes its essence.

Well, so it goes, yet another plane of life has been slightly displaced, yet another habit—the habit (one's own) of (another person's) existence—has been broken. There is no consolation, if one starts to encourage the sense of loss by one's private recollections of a brief, brittle, human image that melts like a hailstone on a window sill. Let us turn to the poems.

1939

(This article, signed "V. Sirin," the pen-name I used in the twenties and thirties, in Berlin and Paris, appeared in the émigré literary magazine *Sovremennyya zapiski*, LXIX, 1939, Paris. I have clung closely to my tortuous Russian text in the present translation into English.)

1972

A NOTE ON VLADISLAV HODASSEVICH

Vladislav Hodassevich was born in the late eighties in Moscow and died in Paris in 1939. He had been living in exile since 1922.

He was the finest poet that post-war Russia produced, and the influence of his "neo-classical" style upon the younger generation of Russian poets, both in Paris and in the Soviet Union, has been quite exceptionally strong though less fruitful, in the long run, than that of Alexander Blok's "neo-romantic" poetry. I use these shabby textbook terms because any more personal attempt to define Hodassevich's rhythms and methods would lead me too far.

A little book of some 175 pages published in Paris in 1927 (*Sobranye Stikhov—Collection of Poems*—which he calls "my discarded snake-skin" in his dedication on the copy he gave me) contains practically all such poems of his mature years as he wished to preserve, and it is curious to note that Tutchev, the great 19th century poet, with whom he seems to have had a marked spiritual connection, was equally sparing of his genius. Hodassevich has also written a remarkable *"Life of Derzhavin"* (18th century poet) which will be admired as long as Russian literature exists. His extensive studies of Pushkin's life and versification placed him in the foremost rank of Pushkinian scholars; and I have encountered when translating the three poems offered here the same special difficulties that I did when tackling Pushkin. Simplicity and fullness of verbal perfection allied to an almost mathematical precision of imagery are harder to render than the colorful effusiveness of less limpid or less vigorous poets.

1941

ОБЕЗЬЯНА

Была жара. Леса горели. Нудно
Тянулось время. На соседней даче
Кричал петух. Я вышел за калитку.
Там, прислонясь к забору, на скамейке
Дремал бродячий серб, худой и черный.
Серебряный тяжелый крест висел
На груди полуголой. Капли пота
По ней катились. Выше, на заборе,
Сидела обезьяна в красной юбке
И пыльные листы сирени
Жевала жадно. Кожаный ошейник,
Оттянутый назад тяжелой цепью,
Давил ей горло. Серб, меня заслышав,
Очнулся, вытер пот и попросил, чтоб дал я
Воды ему. Но чуть ее пригубив,—
Не холодна ли,—блюдце на скамейку
Поставил он, и тотчас обезьяна,
Макая пальцы в воду, ухватила
Двумя руками блюдце.
Она пила, на четвереньках стоя,
Локтями опираясь на скамью.
Досок почти касался подбородок,
Над теменем лысеющим спина
Высоко выгибалась. Так, должно быть,
Стоял когда-то Дарий, припадая
К дорожной луже, в день, когда бежал он
Пред мощною фалангой Александра.
Всю воду выпив, обезьяна блюдце
Долой смахнула со скамьи, привстала
И—этот миг забуду ли когда?—
Мне черную, мозолистую руку,
Еще прохладную от влаги, протянула. . .
Я руки жал красавицам, поэтам,
Вождям народа—ни одна рука

THE MONKEY

The heat was fierce. Great forests were on fire.
Time dragged its feet in dust. A cock was crowing
in an adjacent lot.
                    As I pushed open
my garden-gate I saw beside the road
a wandering Serb asleep upon a bench
his back against the palings. He was lean
and very black, and down his half-bared breast
there hung a heavy silver cross, diverting
the trickling sweat.
                    Upon the fence above him,
clad in a crimson petticoat, his monkey
sat munching greedily the dusty leaves
of a syringa bush; a leathern collar
drawn backwards by its heavy chain bit deep
into her throat.
                    Hearing me pass, the man
stirred, wiped his face, and asked me for some water.
He took one sip to see whether the drink
was not too cold, then placed a saucerful
upon the bench, and, instantly, the monkey
slipped down and clasped the saucer with both hands
dipping her thumbs; then, on all fours, she drank,
her elbows pressed against the bench, her chin
touching the boards, her backbone arching higher
than her bald head. Thus, surely, did Darius
bend to a puddle on the road when fleeing
from Alexander's thundering phalanges.

When the last drop was sucked the monkey swept
the saucer off the bench, and raised her head,
and offered me her black wet little hand.
Oh, I have pressed the fingers of great poets,
leaders of men, fair women, but no hand

Такого благородства очертаний
Не заключала! Ни одна рука
Моей руки так братски не коснулась!
И видит Бог, никто в мои глаза
Не заглянул так мудро и глубоко,
Воистину—до дна души моей.
Глубокой древности сладчайшие преданья
Тот нищий зверь мне в сердце оживил,
И в этот миг мне жизнь явилась полной,
И мнилось—хор светил и волн морских,
Ветров и сфер мне музыкой органной
Ворвался в уши, загремел, как прежде,
В иные, назапамятные дни.

И серб ушел, постукивая в бубен.
Присев ему на левое плечо,
Покачивалась мерно обезьяна,
Как на слоне индийский магараджа.
Огромное малиновое солнце,
Лишенное лучей,
В опаловом дыму висело. Изливался
Безгромный зной на чахлую пшеницу.

В тот день была объявлена война.

1919

had ever been so exquisitely shaped
nor had touched mine with such a thrill of kinship,
and no man's eyes had peered into my soul
with such deep wisdom . . . Legends of lost ages
awoke in me thanks to that dingy beast
and suddenly I saw life in its fullness
and with a rush of wind and wave and worlds
the organ music of the universe
boomed in my ears, as it had done before
in immemorial woodlands.
                  And the Serb
then went his way thumping his tambourine:
on his left shoulder, like an Indian prince
upon an elephant, his monkey swayed.
A huge incarnadine but sunless sun
hung in a milky haze. The sultry summer
flowed endlessly upon the wilting wheat.

That day the war broke out, that very day.

1941

БАЛЛАДА

Сижу, освещаемый сверху,
Я в комнате круглой моей.
Смотрю в штукатурное небо
На солнце в шестнадцать свечей.

Кругом—освещенные тоже,
И стулья, и стол, и кровать.
Сижу—и в смущеньи не знаю,
Куда бы мне руки девать.

Морозные белые пальмы
На стеклах беззвучно цветут.
Часы с металлическим шумом
В жилетном кармане идут.

О, косная, нищая скудость
Безвыходной жизни моей!
Кому мне поведать, как жалко
Себя и всех этих вещей?

И я начинаю качаться,
Колени обнявши свои,
И вдруг начинаю стихами
С собой говорить в забытьи.

Бессвязные, страстные речи!
Нельзя в них понять ничего,
Но звуки правдивее смысла,
И слово сильнее всего.

И музыка, музыка, музыка
Вплетается в пенье мое,
И узкое, узкое, узкое
Пронзает меня лезвие.

ORPHEUS

Brightly lit from above I am sitting
in my circular room; this is I—
looking up at a sky made of stucco,
at a sixty-watt sun in that sky.

All around me, and also lit brightly,
all around me my furniture stands,
chair and table and bed—and I wonder
sitting there what to do with my hands.

Frost-engendered white feathery palmtrees
on the window-panes silently bloom;
loud and quick clicks the watch in my pocket
as I sit in my circular room.

Oh, the leaden, the beggarly bareness
of a life where no issue I see!
Whom on earth could I tell how I pity
my own self and the things around me?

And then clasping my knees I start slowly
to sway backwards and forwards, and soon
I am speaking in verse, I am crooning
to myself as I sway in a swoon.

What a vague, what a passionate murmur
lacking any intelligent plan;
but a sound may be truer than reason
and a word may be stronger than man.

And then melody, melody, melody
blends my accents and joins in their quest,
and a delicate, delicate, delicate
pointed blade seems to enter my breast.

Я сам над собой вырастаю,
Над мертвым встаю бытием,
Стопами в подземное пламя,
В текучие звезды челом.

И вижу большими глазами—
Глазами, быть может, змеи—
Как пению дикому внемлют
Несчастные вещи мои.

И в плавный, вращательный танец
Вся комната мерно идет,
И кто-то тяжелую лиру
Мне в руки сквозь ветер дает.

И нет штукатурного неба
И солнца в шестнадцать свечей:
На гладкие черные скалы
Стопы опирает—Орфей.

1921

High above my own spirit I tower,
high above mortal matter I grow:
subterranean flames lick my ankles,
past my brow the cool galaxies flow.

With big eyes—as my singing grows wilder—
with the eyes of a serpent maybe,
I keep watching the helpless expression
of the poor things that listen to me.

And the room and the furniture slowly,
slowly start in a circle to sail,
and a great heavy lyre is from nowhere
handed me by a ghost through the gale.

And the sixty-watt sun has now vanished,
and away the false heavens are blown:
on the smoothness of glossy black boulders
this is Orpheus standing alone.

1941

* * *

Ни жить, ни петь почти не стоит:
В непрочной грубости живем.
Портной тачает, плотник строит:
Швы расползутся, рухнет дом.

И лишь порой сквозь это тленье
Вдруг умиленно слышу я
В нем заключенное биенье
Совсем иного бытия.

Так, провождая жизни скуку
Любовно женщина кладет
Свою взволнованную руку
На грузно пухнущий живот.

1922

POEM

What is the use of time and rhyme?
We live in peril, paupers all.
The tailors sit, the builders climb,
but coats will tear and houses fall.

And only seldom with a sob
of tenderness I hear . . . oh, quite
a different existence throb
through this mortality and blight.

Thus does a wife, when days are dull,
place breathlessly, with loving care,
her hand upon her body, full
of the live burden swelling there.

1941

«НЕ ЯМБОМ ЛИ ЧЕТЫРЕХСТОПНЫМ»

[. . .]

Из памяти изгрызли годы,
Кто и за что в Хотине пал;
Но первый звук Хотинской оды
Нам первым криком жизни стал.

[. . .]

1938

* * *

Years have from memory eroded
Who perished at Hotin, and why;
But the Hotinian ode's first sound
For us became our life's first cry.

1951–57

OSIP EMILIEVICH MANDELSHTAM
(1891–1938)

ON OSIP MANDELSHTAM

As to Mandelshtam, I also knew him by heart, but he gave me a less fervent pleasure [than Blok]. Today, through the prism of a tragic fate his poetry seems greater than it actually is.

1966

ON ADAPTATION

Here is a literal translation of a great poem by Mandelshtam (note the correct form of his name), which appears in the original Russian on pp. 142 and 144 of Olga Carlisle's anthology *Poets on Street Corners* (Random House, New York, 1968). It consists of sixteen tetrametric (odd) and trimetric (even) anapestic lines with a masculine rhyme scheme *bcbc*.

For the sake of the resonant valor of ages to come . . .
[see p. 357 for full text]

A number of details in the text are ambiguous (for example, the word translated as "coward" is a homonym of the old Russian *trus*, meaning "quaking" (thus "earthquake"), and the word translated as "injustice" has the additional meaning of "falsehood"), but I will limit myself to discussing some of the quite unambiguous passages misinterpreted, or otherwise mangled, by Robert Lowell in his "adaptation" on pp. 143 and 145 of the same collection.

Line 1, "resonant valor," *gremuchaya doblest'* (nom.): Mandelshtam improves here on the stock phrase "ringing glory" (*gremyashchaya slava*). Mr. Lowell renders this as "foreboding nobility," which is meaningless, both as translation and adaptation, and can be only explained by assuming that he worked out an ominous meaning from the "rumbling" improperly given under *gremuchiy* (see also *gremuchaya zmeya*, rattlesnake) by some unhelpful informer, *e.g.* Louis Segal, M.A., Ph.D. (Econ.), D.Phil., compiler of a Russian-English dictionary.

Line 5, "wolfhound," *volkodav:* lexically "wolf-crusher," "wolf-strangler"; this dog gets transformed by Mr. Lowell into a "cutthroat wolf," another miracle of misinformation, mistransfiguration, and misadaptation.

Line 6, "wear the hide of a wolf" (Lowell) would mean to impersonate a wolf, which is not at all the sense here.

Line 8, actually "of the Siberian prairie's hot furcoat," *zharkoy shuby sibirskih stepey*. The rich heavy pelisse, to which Russia's wild East is likened by the poet (this being the very blazon of its faunal opulence) is demoted by the adapter to a "sheepskin" which is "shipped to the steppes" with the poet in its sleeve. Besides being absurd in itself, this singular importation totally destroys the imagery of the composition. And a poet's imagery is a sacred, unassailable thing.

Lines 11–12: the magnificent metaphor of line 8 now culminates in a vision of the arctic starlight overhead, emblemized by the splendor of gray-blue furs, with a suggestion of astronomical heraldry (cf. Vulpecula, a constellation). Instead of that the adapter has "I want to run with the shiny blue foxes moving like dancers in the night," which is not so much a pretty piece of pseudo-Russian fairytale as a foxtrot in Disneyland.

Line 13: Why does the adaptation read "there the Siberian river is glass"? Perhaps, because the *techyot* (flows) of the text gives *tekla* in the past tense feminine, and its form *stekla* (flowed down) also happens to be the genitive case of *steklo* (glass)—a really outstanding howler, if my supposition is correct, and an inexplicable cliché, if it isn't.

Line 14, "pine," *sosna:* the adapter has "fir tree," another plant altogether. This is a mistake often committed on both sides of the Bering Strait (and condoned, I note, by Dr. Segal).

Line 16: "or slaver in the wolf trap's steel jaw" (Lowell)—an ending that snaps as it were the very backbone of Mandelshtam's poem.

I am well aware that laborious literal reproduction of one of the masterpieces of Russian poetry is prevented by the rigor of fierce fidelity from parading as a good English poem; but I am also aware that it is true translation, albeit stiff and rhymeless, and that the adapter's good poem is nothing but a farrago of error and improvisation defacing the even better poem it faces in the anthology. When I think that the American college student of today, so docile, so trustful, so eager to be led to any bright hell by an eccentric teacher, will mistake that adaptation for a sample of Mandelshtam's thought ("the poet compares the sheepskin sent him from abroad to the wolf hide he refuses to wear"), I cannot help feeling that despite the good intentions of adapters something very like cruelty and deception is the inevitable result of their misguided labors.

Although some of the English versions in Miss Carlisle's collection do their best to follow the text, all of them for some reason or other (perhaps in heroic protection of the main offender) are branded "Adaptations." What, then, is there especially adaptive or adaptational in an obvious travesty? This I wish to be told, this I wish to comprehend. "Adapted" to what? To the needs of an idiot audience? To the demands of good taste? To the level of one's own genius? But one's audience is the most varied and gifted in the world; no arbiter of genteel arts tells us what we can or can't say; and as to genius, nowhere in those paraphrases is the height of fancy made to fuse with the depth of erudition, like a mountain orbed by its reflection in a lake—which at least would be some consolation. What we do have are crude imitations, with hops and flutters of irresponsible invention weighed down by the blunders of ignorance. If this kind of thing becomes an international fashion I can easily imagine Robert Lowell himself finding one of his best poems, whose charm is in its concise, delicate touches (". . . splinters fall in sawdust from the aluminum-plant wall . . . wormwood . . . three pairs of glasses . . . leathery love") adapted in some other country by some eminent, blissfully monolingual foreign poet, assisted by some American expatriate with a not-too-extensive vocabulary in any language. An outraged pedant, wishing to inform and defend our poet, might then translate the adaptation back into English (". . . I saw dusty paint split and fall like aluminum stocks on Wall Street . . . six glasses of absinthe . . . the football of passion"). I wonder on whose side the victim would be.

Written on September 20, 1969, and published on December 4, 1969, in *The New York Review of Books*. I fervently hope that this little essay managed to reach the poet's widow in Soviet Russia.

1969, 1972

* * *

1   За гремучую доблесть грядущих веков,

     За высокое племя людей

     Я лишился и чаши на пире отцов,

4   И веселья и чести своей.

     Мне на плечи кидается век-волкодав,

     Но не волк я по крови своей,

     Запихай меня лучше, как шапку, в рукав

8   Жаркой шубы сибирских степей,—

     Чтоб не видеть ни труса, ни хлипкой грязцы,

     Ни кровавых костей в колесе,

     Чтоб сияли всю ночь голубые песцы

12   Мне в своей первобытной красе.

     Уведи меня в ночь где течет Енисей,

     Где сосна до звезды достает,

     Потому что не волк я по крови своей

16   И неправдой искривлен мой рот.

1931, 1935

1   For the sake of the resonant valor of ages to come,
     for the sake of a high race of men,
     I forfeited a bowl at my fathers' feast,
4   and merriment, and my honor.

     On my shoulders there pounces the wolfhound age,
     but no wolf by blood am I;
     better, like a fur cap, thrust me into the sleeve
8   of the warmly fur-coated Siberian steppes,

     —so that I may not see the coward, the bit of soft muck,
     the bloody bones on the wheel,
     so that all night blue-fox furs may blaze
12 for me in their pristine beauty.

     Lead me into the night where the Enisey flows,
     and the pine reaches up to the star,
     because no wolf by blood am I,
16 and injustice has twisted my mouth.

                                  1969

BULAT SHALVOVICH OKUDZHAVA
(1924–1997)

ON BULAT OKUDZHAVA
A NOTE ON "SPERANZA" BY OKUDZHAVA

Dear Bill,

You will observe three unusual features here: my
translating a Soviet poet; my doing so in rhyme;
and my thinking that you print that kind of stuff.
If you do, it might be a pretty idea to have the
transliteration and the translation side by side on
the same page. The note I append is (for me) the
most important part of the performance and please,
do not wilson the words "dit" and "scud"!

TRANSLATOR'S NOTE

There are three ways of translating poetry: 1. Para-
phrastic: offering a free version of the original with omissions, ad-
ditions and distortions prompted by the exigencies of form, the

conventions attributed to the consumer, and the translator's ignorance (ornamented bloom camouflaging plain bloomers; great pleasure domes erected on the morass of mistranslated everyday terms); 2. Lexical: rendering the basic meaning of words, without any concession to syntax (so that, for instance, in an English translation from the Russian the articles "the" and "a" would be omitted); and 3. Literal: rendering as closely as associative and syntactical capacities of the Into language allow, the exact contextual meaning of the poem in the From language. Only this is the true translation.

Except in a very few cases, the form of the original poem in From, and especially its rhymes, cannot be retained in a literal Into translation. Those few cases are fascinating.

Recently I have been so distressed by a well-known American poet's impossible travesty of Mandelshtam's logic and magic that I cast around for some Russian poem that I could still save from the enthusiastic paraphrast who strangles another man's muse with his own muse's strong hair. Could I render it in a form close to the original while preserving its literal meaning almost intact? I say "almost" because in my translation of the poem that I have now selected (a ballad by Bulat Shalvovich Okujava, born in 1924 in Moscow) I had to make several minute adjustments in order to preserve its throaty, guitar-like tonalities. It belongs to the popular Russian genre of sung poetry and is especially difficult to translate (which is why I chose it) because its impact upon the senses derives not from direct verbal originality but from an inspired combination of idiomatic clichés. The bilingual reader will note that I could not force myself either to use the name "Nadezhda" (unpronounceable in English) or turn it into the stiff, long-faced, long-aproned "Hope," hence my "Speranza" which reenacts dazzlingly the eloquent lilt of the original.

Other inaccuracies are the scanty rhymes (Okujava closes lines 2 and 6 of each stanza with additional rich feminine assonance) and such words as "should throw" "when war" which are not in the text. Despite these flaws my version is faithful enough to prove, I trust, that a translator's adequate knowledge of both From and Into languages and a couple of sleepless nights can sometimes help to render not only the meaning, but also most of the music of a heart-rending dit. The accents in the transliteration have been added in order that the non-Russian reader may scan properly the iambic tetrameter, which only in the last stanza contains an expressive accumulation of scuds.

1966

СЕНТИМЕНТАЛЬНЫЙ РОМАНС

Надежда, я вернусь тогда, когда трубач отбой сыграет,
когда трубу к губам приблизит и острый локоть отведет.
Надежда, я останусь цел: не для меня земля сырая,
а для меня—твои тревоги и добрый мир твоих забот.

Но если целый век пройдет и ты надеяться устанешь,
Надежда, если надо мною смерть развернет свои крыла,
ты прикажи, пускай тогда трубач израненный привстанет,
чтобы последняя граната меня прикончить не смогла.

Но если вдруг когда-нибудь мне уберечься не удастся,
какое новое сраженье ни покачнуло б шар земной,
я все равно паду на той, на той далекой, на Гражданской,
и комиссары в пыльных шлемах склонятся молча надо мной.

1957

SENTIMENTÁL'NÏY ROMÁNS

Nadézhda, yá vernús' togdá,
Kogdá trubách otbóy sygráet,
Kogdá trubú k gubám priblízit
I óstryy lókot' otvedyót.
Nadézhda, yá ostánus' tsél:
Ne dlya menyá zemlyá syráya,
A dlya menyá—tvoí trevógi
I dóbryy mír tvoíh zabót.

No ésli tsélyy vék proydyót,
I tý nadéyat'sya ustánesh',
Nadézhda, ésli nado mnóyu
Smert' razvernyót svoí krylá,
Ty prikazhí, puskáy togdá
Trubách izránennyy privstánet,
Chtoby poslédnyaya granáta
Menyá prikónchit' ne smoglá.

No ésli vdrúg kogdá-nibud'
Mne uberéch'sya ne udástsya,
Kakóe nóvoe srazhén'e
Ni pokachnúlo b shár zemnóy,
Ya vsyo ravnó padú na tóy,
Na tóy dalyókoy, na Grazhdánskoy,
I komissáry v pýl'nyh shlémah
Sklonyátsya mólcha nado mnóy.

A SENTIMENTAL BALLAD

Speranza, I'll be coming back
The day the bugler sounds retreat,
When to his lips he'll bring the bugle,
And outward his sharp elbow turn.
Speranza, I'll remain unharmed:
The clammy earth is not for me,
Because for me are your misgivings
And the kind world of your concern.

But if an entire century
Goes by, and you are sick of hoping,
Speranza, if it's over me
That death his outspread wings should throw
You must command: let then the bugler,
Sore wounded, raise himself a little
So that a last grenade may not
Dispatch me with a final blow.

But if I suddenly some day
Don't manage to protect myself,
When the terrestrial globe is jolted,
Whatever that new battle be,
I'll always fall in the same war,
The distant one, the Civil one,
And commissars in dusty helmets
Will bend in silence over me.

9 February 1966

PROGRAM NOTES

Montreux, May 25, 1973

Mee-tyú-shah

Here are the programme notes. I have put the po-
ets before the composers; you may transpose them if
you like. You may also wish to abridge the thing, but
please leave the Lermontov translation and Pushkin's
Night intact.

Ob-nee-máh-you
Vladimir Nabokov*

*In 1973 Nabokov's son Dmitri (diminutive: Mityusha), an operatic basso
profundo, recorded for BASF an album of nineteenth- and twentieth-century
Russian songs and poems set to music. Always supportive of his son's vocal
career, Vladimir Nabokov wrote the liner notes for the album.

PROGRAM NOTES

Program notes for a two-side record of twelve Russian songs in Dmitri Nabokov's rendition.

Side I

1

DARK EYES (*ÓCHI CHYÓRNYE*)

The beautiful word "*ochi*" (plural of "oko," compare Latin "*oculus*") is the Russian poetical term for "eyes" and the alliteration on "ch"—provided by "*chyornye*" ("black," "dark")—is especially pleasing to the Russian ear. This item is a hundred-year-old imitation of the tzigane type of song blending quick words with spasmodic strings. The anonymous gentleman in it is "adoring and abhorring" a pair of blazing dark eyes, belonging possibly to an authentic gypsy girl at a night club.

***

Выхожу один я на дорогу;
Сквозь туман кремнистый путь блестит;
Ночь тиха. Пустыня внемлет Богу,
И звезда с звездою говорит.

В небесах торжественно и чудно!
Спит земля в сиянье голубом. . .
Что же мне так больно и так трудно?
Жду ль чего? жалею ли о чем?

Уж не жду от жизни ничего я,
И не жаль мне прошлого ничуть;
Я ищу свободы и покоя!
Я б хотел забыться и заснуть! —

Но не тем холодным сном могилы. . .
Я б желал навеки так заснуть,
Чтоб в груди дремали жизни силы,
Чтоб дыша вздымалась тихо грудь;

Чтоб всю ночь, весь день мой слух лелея,
Про любовь мне сладкий голос пел,
Надо мной чтоб вечно зеленея
Темный дуб склонялся и шумел.

1841

2

I COME OUT ALONE UPON THE HIGHROAD
(*VYKHOZHÚ ODÍN YA NA DORÓGU*)

I come out alone upon the highroad;
Through the mist the flinty way gleams far.
The night's calm. The wilderness is harking
To the Lord, and star speaks unto star.

In the heavens all is grave and wondrous;
The earth sleeps, by bluish radiance lit.
Whence comes, then, this painful, irksome feeling?
Expectation? Heartache? What is it?

Yet from life I'm now expecting nothing
And I don't regret one bit the past.
All I want is liberty and quiet,
All I want is dreamless sleep at last.

Let it, though, not be the tomb's cold slumber;
I would wish to slumber in such wise
That in me life's forces would be dormant,
That my breast would gently fall and rise.

That all day, all night, in lulling accents
A sweet voice would sing to me of love,
That a somber oaktree, ever greening,
Would incline its rustling boughs above

In reading the wonderful lines written by Lermontov
(1814–1841) shortly before his death and listening to the music to
which they have been set by Miss Shashin, we should imagine Ler-
montov, a Russian army officer in the Caucasus, leaving his rowdy
companions in the roadside inn where he has dined, and walking
alone in the night to an oak above a mountain torrent. The music
comes, I suppose, in a sustained ripple from the inn he has left.

3

THE PEDDLER'S BOX (*KORÓBUSHKA*)

Part of a poem by Nekrasov (1821–77). In this part a dashing young fellow peddling "cottons and brocades" shows his bright wares to a girl with whom he meets in a grainfield. The music imitates a folk-tune, well-suited to the young peddler's rollicking discourse. The last strophe goes:

Only the deep night
Knows how they settled the deal.
So straighten up, high-stemmed rye,
And religiously keep their secret.

Знает только ночь глубокая,
Как поладили они.
Распрямись ты, рожь высокая,
Тайну свято сохрани!

1861

4

THE YOKE-BELL (*KOLOKÓL'CHIK*)

In a monotone tinkles the yoke-bell
And the roadway is dusting a bit

Однозвучно гремит колокольчик,
И дорога пылится слегка. . .

late 1840s or early 1850s

Thus begins this charming piece (verse by Makarov, music by Gurilev), whose lyrical lilt resembles tzigane, or pseudo-tzigane, ballads more than it does a viatic plaint on a road in the steppes. To the lone traveler in the open carriage the coachman's song brings back nostalgic visions of his native "fields and woods" in a more northern region of Russia.

Side I

5

TWO GUITARS (*DVE GITÁRY*)

The words are by Apollon Grigoriev (1822–1864), the music mimics a gypsy song. Many critics consider Grigoriev's poem to "rank with the most purely and beautifully inspired lyrics in the language." It begins:

> *Two guitars behind the wall*
>   *Plaintively start crooning.*
> *As a child I've known that tune;*
>   *Dear one, is it you there?*

> Две гитары за стеной
>   Жалобно заныли. . .
> С детства памятный напев,
>   Милый, это ты ли?

1857

Side I

6

MOSCOW COUNTRYSIDE EVENINGS
(*PODMOSKÓVNYE VECHERÁ*)

Words by Matusovski, music by Solovyov-Sedoy. A pleasant *romance* evoking the atmosphere of dachas and evening tea on the outskirts of present-day Moscow.

7

ALONG THE PETERSBURG HIGHWAY
(*VDOL' PO PÍTERSKOY*)

An old stylized folksong about a merrymaker picking up a drunken girl, with disjointed allusions to his troika, to various festivities, and to a wall-eyed pike. The road through that village is decidedly bumpy.

STEN'KA RAZIN AND THE PRINCESS
(*KNYAZHNÁ*)

A popular song with words by a minor poet (*c.* 1890)

Stepan ("Sten'ka") Razin, a Don Cossack, represented the blend of romantic banditry and rather vague social rebellion that plagued seventeenth century Russia. Two hundred years later a minor poet put one of Razin's adventures into verse. The poem begins (in prose translation):

> *From behind the island onto the fairway,*
> *into the expanse of the river's wave,*
> *float out the painted*
> *boats of* Sten'ka Razin

> Из-за острова на стрежень,
> На простор речной волны
> Выплывают расписные,
> Стеньки Разина челны.

The rest of the story concerns his throwing overboard a beloved concubine (the kidnapped daughter of a Persian prince) so as to pacify his gang who had been accusing him of "getting soft" (*báboy stal*).

2

AS THE KING WENT FORTH TO WAR
(*KAK KORÓL' SHYOL NA VOYNÚ*)

A song by Koenemann with text in Miss Konopnitski's Russian version. The king's exploits and victory are trumpeted with martial elation, while the plight of his troops is rendered in dirge-like tones.

3

FOR THE SHORES OF YOUR FAR COUNTRY
(*DLYA BEREGÓV OTCHÍZNY DÁL'NOY*)

Words by Pushkin (1799–1837), music by Borodin (1834–87).

In these famous stanzas written in 1830 in memory of a dead mistress Pushkin evokes their adieux when, ill with consumption, she was about to leave Odessa for Italy in 1824. She was Amalia Riznich, wife of a Dalmatian merchant. Her mother was Italian—hence the opening lines:

> *For the shores of your far country*
> *You were abandoning a foreign land*

> Для берегов отчизны дальной
> Ты покидала край чужой. . .

In the next stanzas he recalls her assuring him they would meet again in her native country "in the shade of olives," on the brink of "brilliant waters" lapping the cliffs. Now that she is dead he reminds her of the kiss of reunion that she has promised him, a debt he expects her to pay in another world.

НОЧЬ

Мой голос для тебя и ласковый и томный
Тревожит позднее молчанье ночи темной.
Близ ложа моего печальная свеча
Горит; мои стихи, сливаясь и журча,
Текут, ручьи любви; текут полны тобою.
Во тьме твои глаза блистают предо мною,
Мне улыбаются—и звуки слышу я:
Мой друг, мой нежный друг... люблю... твоя... твоя!..

1823

Side II

4

NIGHT (*NOCH'*)

A poem by Pushkin (1823) set to music by Anton Rubinstcin.

NIGHT

My voice that breathes for thee both tenderness and languor
disturbs at a late hour the silence of dark night.
Beside my bed a melancholy candle
sheds light. My verses, murmuring and merging,
flow, rills of love, flow, full of thee.
Thy eyes before me in the darkness shine,
they smile on me and I distinguish sounds:
"My dear, my dearest one . . . I love . . . I'm thine . . . I'm thine."

The identity of the lady, whose presence in his room the poet so vividly imagines, has not been established with any certainty.

Side II

5

DOUBT (*SOMNÉNIE*)

Words by Kukolnik (1809–68), music by Glinka (1804–57).

Subside, agitation of passion

Уймитесь, волнения страсти!

—thus starts this splendid piece. The incantational flow of the diction, the purity of its ample amphibrachic rhythm, are on a par with Glinka's plangent music. The poem undulates between torment and hope. At one moment—

I dream of a fortunate rival

Соперник мне снится счастливый. . .

and this is followed by a great surge of ecstasy:

The time of darkness will not tarry
Again we'll embrace one another
  And hotly and madly
The heart, resurrected, will throb.

Минует печальное время,
Мы снова обнимем друг друга.
  И страстно и жарко
Забьется воскресшее сердце. . .

1838

1973

III. FRENCH TO ENGLISH

RÉMI BELLEAU
(CA. 1528–1577)

from
AVRIL

[. . .]

Avril, la grace, et le ris
    De Cypris,
Le flair et la douce haleine:
Avril, le parfum des Dieux,
    Qui des cieux
Sentent l'odeur de la plaine.

C'est toy courtois et gentil,
    Qui d'exil
Retires ces passagères,
Ces arondelles qui vont,
    Et qui sont
Du printemps les messagères.

L'aubespine et l'aiglantin,
    Et le thym,
L'œillet, le lis et les roses
En ceste belle saison,
    A foison,
Monstrent leurs robes écloses.

[. . .]

1565–72

APRIL

April, Venus gives thee
    Grace and glee,
Fragrant breath and soft gale:
April, balm of the gods,
    Who the sod's
Odor cloud-high inhale.

Thou it is who with bland,
    Courteous hand
From their exile dost bring
Swallows, journeying far,
    Those that are
The forerunners of Spring.

Thyme and hawthorn are here;
    Eglatere,
Clove pink, lily and rose,
At this season so fair,
    Everywhere,
Their new raiments disclose.

1959

HENRI DE RÉGNIER

(1864–1936)

ODELETTE

Quelle douceur dans mes pensées
En ce clair, tendre et pur matin,
Devant ces barques balancées
Sans flamme à leur fanal éteint.

Le voyage de ma jeunesse
Avec sa course et ses éclairs
Est fini, et la paix caresse
Mon cœur las des ciels et des mers

Et qui, cessant d'être en partance,
Par trop de houles fatigué,
Désormais sage, se fiance
Aux anneaux de fer du vieux quai.

1921

PASSING OF YOUTH

Within my thoughts what sweetness flows
On this soft morning, pure and bright,
Before those rocking barks with those
Dead lanterns carrying no light.

The journey of my early days,
Its course, its thunders flashing by,
Are finished, and bland peace allays
The heart's surfeit of sea and sky.

And ceasing to be underway,
Worn by the surge's buffetings,
My heart, now sensible, will stay
Wed with the old quay's iron rings.

(translated by Sybil Shade)

PS. A prettier paraphrase of the first stanza, to cure the
tautological last line, would be:

What sweetness in my every thought
On this soft morning, pure and bright,
Before those rocking barks with nought
In their extinguished lamps but night.

December 25, 1962

NOTES

NWL	Simon Karlinsky, editor, *Dear Bunny, Dear Volodya: The Nabokov-Wilson Letters, 1940–1971*. 1979; 2nd ed., Berkeley and Los Angeles: University of California Press, 2001.
PLT	Vladimir Nabokov, *Pushkin, Lermontov, Tyutchev*. London: Lindsay Drummond, 1947. Includes all translations and notes from Nabokov's *Three Russian Poets* (TRP) plus additional translations.
PP	Vladimir Nabokov, *Poems and Problems*. New York: McGraw-Hill, 1971.
PRP	V. E. Gusev, editor, *Pesni russkih poetov*. Leningrad: Sovetskiy pisatel', 1998. 2 vols.
RR	*The Russian Review*
SO	Vladimir Nabokov, *Strong Opinions*. New York: McGraw-Hill, 1973.
TRP	Vladimir Nabokov, *Three Russian Poets*. Norfolk, CT: New Directions, 1944.
VéN	Véra Nabokov
VN	Vladimir Nabokov
VNA	Vladimir Nabokov Archive, Henry W. and Albert A. Berg Collection, New York Public Library
VNAM	Vladimir Nabokov Archive, Montreux, Switzerland

NOTE ON TRANSLITERATION

Vladimir Nabokov's transliteration system is used throughout the notes (see "Method of Transliteration," EO I: xix–xxviii).

INTRODUCTION

xxi: *proposed publishing three books:* . . . The Gift: page-a-day diary, November 11, 1958, VNA.

xxi: *agreement for an "Anthology of Russian Verse" in translation:* Jason Epstein to VN, December 2, 1958, VNA.

xxi: *"through Zhukovski, Batyushkov, Tyutchev, Pushkin, Lermontov, Fet, to Blok":* VéN to Jason Epstein, January 18, 1959, VNA.

xxi: *"the copious notes the first half has":* VN to Jason Epstein, June 6, 1959, VNA.

xxi: *"twice as many pages as that on* The Song*":* ibid.

xxi: *"An Anthology of Russian Poets" by mid-January 1970:* letter from VéN to Ray Mantle, October 22, 1968, VNA.

xxii: *"has at last become for readers abroad an established classic":* cited in Ljuba Tarvi, *Comparative Translation Assessment: Quantifying Quality* (Helsinki: University of Helsinki, 2004), 230.

xxiv: *three hundred perfect poems he believed had been written in Russian:* See p. 337.

xxv: *"fatally corrupted by the regime he faithfully served":* PP 133, in a note to the poem "O pravitelyakh" ("On Rulers"), a parody of Mayakovsky.

xxv: *thought marred by clumsy lapses:* Nabokov parodies Pasternak's "Nobel-evskaya premiya" ("Nobel Prize") in his "Kakoe sdelal ya durnoe delo" ("What Is the Evil Deed"), PP 146–47.

xxv: *compromised in her relationship to Stalin's Soviet Union:* unpublished letters from Véra Nabokov to Andrew Field, March 18, 1966, VNA; and to Simon Karlinsky, February 28, 1968, VNA.

xxv: *"definitely B-grade," and parodied in* Pnin: VN, cited in unpublished letter from Véra Nabokov to Andrew Field, March 18, 1966, VNA; *Pnin* (New York: Vintage, 1989): 56–57, 180–81.

xxv: *"what can be called the great debate on translation norms of the 1960s":* Tarvi 2004: 228.

xxv: *"'is the only modern poet in the class of Shakespeare and Dante'":* cited in Tarvi 2004: 234.

xxvi: *"goes way beyond bad taste":* Le Ton beau de Marot (New York: Basic Books, 1997), 548, 268, 270, 269.

xxvi: *"level of* Onegin's *harmonies":* VN, "Problems of Translation: 'Onegin' in English," *Partisan Review* XXII/4 (1955), 511–12.

xxvi: *an unmatched score for combined verbal and formal equivalence of 97 percent:* Tarvi 2004: 216.

xxvii: *"I tend to touch them up here and there":* unpublished, from TS note, VNA, perhaps the start of a talk that Nabokov was invited to deliver to the English Institute on September 14, 1954 (see note below to p. 14, "The Art of Translation [II]").

xxviii: *rhyme sequence possible within a three-quatrain frame: alternate, paired, and closed":* VN, "Problems of Translation, 498.

xxx: *a volume for the Folio Society:* Elaine Feinstein, editor, *After Pushkin* (London: Folio Society, 1999).

xxxiii: *who perhaps will love you so well:* Alexander Zholkovsky, "'Ya vas lyubil . . .' Pushkina: invarianty i struktura" ("Pushkin's 'I loved you . . .': Invariants and Structure"), http://www.usc.edu/dept/las/sll/rus/ess/bib21.htm

I. NABOKOV ON TRANSLATION

THE ART OF TRANSLATION (1)

2: *"Goldwin Smith Hall . . . Morrill Hall"*: at Cornell.

3: *"one old gentleman . . . head of a Slavic department"*: apparently Samuel Hazzard Cross of Harvard (1891–1946).

5: *"leave the Russian just as it stood"*: The following paragraph survives in the transcript prepared for LectsR in VNA, where it is marked "added by VN in an open space." Nabokov's intended position for it remains uncertain, but here seems more likely than most: "Under the dreadful conditions of compulsion, suspicion, physical danger that have surrounded writers in Soviet Russia during the last three decades, some of the best have turned to the comparatively safe business of translation, and this explains the heightening of the level of translations there—until they get caught translating the wrong books."

7: *"a famous Russian composer"*: Sergey Rakhmaninov.

11: *". . . my version . . ."*: No text of this translation survives.

  Text: The bulk of the text (from paragraph 6, "Three grades of evil . . . ," except for one other paragraph) dates from 1941, and was published in the *New Republic* on August 4, 1941. The first five paragraphs, added for a talk at Cornell, probably in 1951 or later, follow a TS, VNA.

PITY THE ELDERLY GRAY TRANSLATOR (12)

(Introduction)

 Unpublished, from a talk and reading, as part of the Morris Gray Fund poetry series, at Sever Hall, Harvard, 4:30 P.M., March 20, 1952; "The Translator," Haviaras/Milburn: 18.

Pity the elderly gray translator

 Unpublished poem, written March 17, 1952; in some versions, titled "Rimes." From MS and TS, VNA.

THE ART OF TRANSLATION
(II: "A KIND OF V MOVEMENT") (14)

 Unpublished, from TS, VNA. Perhaps this formed the beginning of a talk that Nabokov had been invited to deliver to the English Institute on September 14, 1954, as he wrote Edmund Wilson on July 30, "on the Art of Translation" (NWL: 317). The image in the first paragraph appears to have sparked the image of the first stanza of "On Translating *Eugene Onegin*," which Nabokov completed by the end of September 1954.

ON TRANSLATING "EUGENE ONEGIN" (16)

Written in 1954; published in the *New Yorker* on January 8, 1955, with last line cleansed to "The shadow of your monument"; reprinted, with the original last line restored, in EO I: 9–10; and in PP: 175.

ONE DAY, EXUBERANT AND GALLANT (18)

18: *scud:* In the "Notes on Prosody" that he included in his commentary to *Eugene Onegin,* Nabokov introduced the term *scud* to refer to "an unaccented stress" (EO III: 454) especially in iambic verse, a foot in which both the normally unstressed first syllable and the normally stressed second syllable are both unstressed. As he noted, this is a more frequent variation on metrical regularity in Russian than in English iambic verse.

LCNA Box 15, fol. 2.

II. NABOKOV: VERSES AND VERSIONS

MIHAIL VASILIEVICH LOMONOSOV

On Mihail Lomonosov (22)

EO III: 484–85, 488–89.

from *Краткое руководство к риторике* /
from *A Brief Manual of Rhetoric*

Pages 24–25.

Russian text from *Sochineniya M. V. Lomonosova,* edited by M. I. Suhomlinov (St. Petersburg: Tipografiya Imperatorskoy Akademii Nauk, 7 vols. 1891–1902), III, 36–37 (hereafter "Suhomlinov" followed by volume and page numbers).

English text from EO II: 522.

from *Пётр Великий, героическая поэма* /
from *Peter the Great, a Heroic Poem*

Pages 26–27.

"The best of the lot [of the numerous 'epics devoted to Peter I'] is Lomonosov's *Pyotr Velikiy, geroicheskaya poema,* in 1250 iambic hexameters (rhyming bbaaccee). It consists of an exordium (64 lines, dated Nov. 1, 1760) and two cantos (632 and 554 ll.). Ll. 171–73 of can. I are pleasantly prophetic: [quotes]" (EO II: 517).

Russian text from Suhomlinov II: 189.
English text and note from EO II: 517.

GAVRILA ROMANOVICH DERZHAVIN

On Gavrila Derzhavin (29)

EO II: 450; EO III: 139–40.

Памятник / I've set up to myself a monument

Pages 32–33.

"Derzhavin, imitating Horace ["Exegi monumentum," *Odes* III: XXX], produced in 1796 the following pieces in iambic hexameters alternatively rhymed (abab)" (EO II: 310); see Pushkin's response to this poem, pp. 214–16.

Russian text: *Sochineniya Derzhavina*, edited by Ya. Grot (St. Petersburg: V tipografii Imperatorskoi Akademii nauk, 9 vols. 1864–83), I, 785–88.

English text: EO II: 310.

NIKOLAY MIHAYLOVICH KARAMZIN

On Nikolay Karamzin (34)

EO III: 143, 144.

from *Два сравнения* / from *Two Similes*

Pages 36–37.

"One of the best Russian epigrams" (EO III: 145).

Russian text: *Sochineniya Karamzina*, edited by V. V. Sipovski (Petrograd: Izdanie Otdeleniya russkogo yazīka i slovesnosti Akademii Nauk, 1917), 227.

English text: EO III: 145.

VASILIY ANDREEVICH ZHUKOVSKI

On Vasiliy Zhukovski, Pushkin's Friend (38)

EO III: 145–47.

from *Певец* / from *The Bard*

Pages 40–41.

"A poet's tomb, with a wreath and lyre suspended from the branches over it, had been sung by Zhukovski in a famous elegy of 1811 entitled *The Bard* (*Pevets*). It consists of six stanzas of eight verses each, with rhymes abbaceec. Its meter is curious and was a great novelty in Russian prosody: four iambic pentameters are ful-

lowed in every stanza by three iambic tetrameters, and the closing
verse is a dactylic dimeter" (EO III: 75–76).

Russian text: V. A. Zhukovski, *Stihotvoreniya,* edited by Ts. Vol'pe
(Leningrad: Sovetskiy pisatel', 2 vols. 1939–40), I, 65 (hereafter
"Vol'pe" followed by volume and page numbers).

English text: EO III: 76.

from *Светлана* / from *Svetlana*

Pages 42–45.

"Zhukovski's masterpiece, *Svetlana* (1812)[is] . . . a ballad (*ballada*)
consisting of twenty stanzas of fourteen lines each, with a sonnet-
like rhyme sequence (babaceceddiffi) in two trochaic measures,
tetrameter (the eight lines with masculine rhymes b, c, d, f) and
trimeter (the six lines with feminine rhymes a, e, i). . . . This ballad
starts with girls divining . . . by means of wax . . . , 'golden rings,
emerald eardrops' . . . , and a 'mirror with candle.' . . . Thanks to
these conjurations, her lover appears—and the next nine stanzas
parody the equestrian and funereal theme of Bürger's *Lenore.* The
vision proves to be a harmless dream, and the ballad ends in a
delightful diurnal bathos: the light of blissful reality dispels the
chaotic nightmare as Svetlana's lover returns to her, safe and sound
after a year's absence" (EO II: 330–31).

"Svetlana engages in divination and conjuration before a can-
dlelit mirror at a table laid for two. Bright-eyed and uncanny, her
lover, after a year's absence, suddenly appears and, as in Bürger's
Lenore, carries her off—to his own grave. The whole event, however,
turns out to be a dream; and on the morrow, Svetlana's lover comes
home safely, and they are married" (EO II: 500).

Russian text: Vol'pe I: 136, 137, 142–43.

English text: EO II: 489 (A: "Lusterlessly shines the moon
/ . . . / silent is and sad"), 500–1.

Голос с того света / from *Thekla*

Pages 46–49.

"Zhukovski's treatment of Schiller's 'Thecla' theme . . . is, in art and
harmony, far superior to its model" (EO II: 235).

Russian text: Vol'pe I: 79.

English text: Unpublished TS, VNA.

from *К Гете* / from *To Goethe*

Pages 50–51.

Russian text: Vol'pe II: 264.

English text: EO II: 235.

Lord Ullin's Daughter, by Campbell [Thomas Campbell, 1777–1844]/
Уллин и его дочь / Oolleen and His Daughter

Pages 52–57.

> "Ryno, son of Fingal, Malvina, daughter of Toscar, and Ullin, chief
> of Fingal's bards, found their way into incongruous adaptations
> and are used by Zhukovski as mere evocative names ('Rino, the
> highland chief,' and 'Malvina,' daughter of Ullin) in his rather
> comical version of Campbell's second-rate ballad, *Lord Ullin's
> Daughter*" (EO II: 255).

> *the hardy Highland wight:* Véra Nabokov's typescript mistakenly
> read "whyte."

> Russian text: Vol'pe I: 326–27.
> English text: Unpublished TS, VNAM.

KONSTANTIN NIKOLAEVICH BATYUSHKOV

On Konstantin Batyushkov (58)

> EO III: 13–14.

Совет эпическому стихотворцу / Advice to an Epic Poet

Pages 60–61.

> "Among the half-dozen 'Petriads' (epics devoted to Peter I, miser-
> able imitations of miserable French 'Henriades') known to have
> circulated at the time, there was a grotesque *Lyric Hymn*, in eight
> cantos, by Prince Sergey Shihmatov, the publication of which (in
> 1810) provoked Batyushkov's witty epigram, 'Advice to an Epic
> Poet'" (EO II: 517).

> Russian text: *Sochineniya K. N. Batyushkova*, edited by L. N.
> Maykov and V. I. Saitov (St. Petersburg: P. N. Batyushkov, 3 vols.
> 1885–87), I, 110 (hereafter "Maykov/Saitov" followed by volume and
> page numbers).

> English text: EO II: 517.

«Ты помнишь что изрек» / Do you recall the cry / A later parody (Political)

Pages 62–63.

> Russian text: VN's transliteration of the Russian original (unpub-
> lished TS, VNA); Maykov/Saitov I: 298.

> English text, "Do you recall": Unpublished TS, VNA; see also
> EO III: 14; "A later parody": Unpublished TS, VNA.

VILGELM KARLOVICH KYUHELBEKER

On Vilgelm Kyuhelbeker (64)

> EO II: 445–47.

Commemorating Pushkin (65)

    EO III: 130–31, 305.

from *Участь русских поэтов* / from *Destiny of Russian Poets*

Pages 66–67.

    See Nabokov's comment on *Destiny of Russian Poets* in "On Vilgelm Kyuhelbeker" (p. 64). He adds, "I quote its last lines" (those cited above) then notes, "The bullet killed Pushkin, the rabble murdered Griboedov" (EO II: 446–47).

        Russian text: V. K. Kyuhel'beker, *Lirika i poemï*, edited by Yu. Tïnyanov (Leningrad: Sovetskiy pisatel', 2 vols. 1939), I, 207.

        English text: EO II: 446–47.

BARON ANTON ANTONOVICH DELVIG

On Anton Delvig (69)

    EO III: 23.

Пушкину / To Pushkin

Pages 70–71.

    Russian text: A. A. Del'vig, *Polnoe sobranie stihotvoreniy*, edited by B. Tomashevski ([Leningrad]: Izdatel'stvo pisateley v Leningrade, [1934]), 191.

        English text: EO III: 23–24.

ALEKSANDR SERGEEVICH PUSHKIN

On Aleksandr Pushkin (72)

    TRP 37; PLT 7–8.

On Pushkin's Idiom (73)

    LCNA box 15, fol. 5, from an abandoned appendix III, "Lexical Notes," to EO, a forerunner of the correlative lexicon in the revised 1975 edition.

from *Моему Аристарху* / from *To My Aristarch*

Pages 74–75.

    "As early as 1815, in a tetrametric poem *To My Aristarch* (his teacher of Latin at the Lyceum, N. Koshanski, 1785–1831), Pushkin had the wonderful lines [quotes from poem]" (EO II: 455).

        Russian text: A. S. Pushkin, *Polnoe sobranie sochineniy*, edited by D. D. Blagoy, S. M. Bondi, et al. (Moscow–Leningrad: Izdatel'stvo Akademii Nauk SSSR, 16 vols. 1937–59), I, 153 (hereafter "Blagoy/Bondi" followed by volume and page numbers).

        English text: EO II: 455 (A: "near still waters").

from *Сон* / from *The Dream*

Pages 76–77.

"'The Dream' (1816), one of his very first poems of real worth" (EO II: 544).

my mammy: not Pushkin's housekeeper, Arina Rodiovna, celebrated in other Pushkin poems. "Our poet's own nurse, his *mamushka,* in the years of his infancy was not Arina, but another woman, a widow named Uliana, of whom unfortunately very little is known" (EO II: 453).

Russian text: Blagoy/Bondi I: 189.

English text: EO II: 453–54.

Вольность / *Liberty: An Ode, 1817*

Pages 78–85.

"[T]he greatest poem of the first two decades of the nineteenth century is Pushkin's own ode, 'Liberty'" (EO II: 450). VN also calls it "the greatest ode in Russian" (EO III: 68).

mollitude: The roots of *iznezhennuyu,* the noun *nega,* and the adjective *nezhnïy* were Pushkin's favorites. Nabokov explains his unusual choice of translation: "*Nega* ranges from 'mollitude' (Fr. *mollesse*), i.e., soft luxuriousness, 'dulcitude,' through various shades of amorous pensiveness, *douce paresse,* and sensual tenderness to outright voluptuousness (Fr. *volupté*)" (EO II: 337).

Russian text: *Sochineniya Aleksandra Pushkina,* edited by M. L. Gofman (Berlin: Yubileynoe izdanie Pushkiskogo komiteta, 1937), 66–68 (hereafter "Gofman 1937" followed by page numbers); Blagoy/Bondi II (1): 45–48.

English text: TS, in Pushkin lecture notes, VNAM; a version of the translation Nabokov was preparing in the 1950s for his *Eugene Onegin* commentary (see EO III: 338–45), apparently used for teaching purposes around 1957.

from *К Щербинину* / from *To Shcherbinin*

Pages 88–89.

"[W]ritten in the summer of 1819 at Mihaylovskoe, addressed to Mihail Shcherbinin, a dashing friend of his in Petersburg" (EO III: 305).

Russian text: Blagoy/Bondi II (1): 88.

English text: EO III: 305.

from *Руслан и Людмила* / from *Ruslan and Lyudmila*

Pages 90–91.

"[H]is first long work, *Ruslan and Lyudmila,* [is] a mock epic in six cantos (*Ruslan i Lyudmila: Poema v shesti pesnyah,* St. Petersburg,

[August 10], 1820). This spirited fairy tale, bubbling along in freely rhymed iambic tetrameters, deals with the adventures of pleasantly Gallicized knights, damsels, and enchanters in a cardboard Kiev. Its debt to French poetry and to French imitations of Italian romances is overwhelmingly greater than the influence upon it of Russian folklore, but the purity of its diction and the verve of its colloquial modulations make of it, historically, the first Russian masterpiece in the narrative genre" (EO II: 96).

    Omér: "'Homer' is *Omír* in old-fashioned poetic Russian. Elsewhere our poet uses the correct Russian *Gomér.* Earlier (1818–20) he had completely Gallicized the name by writing it *Omér* [quotes lines from poem]" (EO II: 537–38).

    Parny: French poet Evariste Désiré Desforges, Chevalier de Parny (1753–1814).

    Russian text: Blagoy/Bondi IV: 54.

    English text: EO II: 538.

Наперсница волшебной старины /
from *The Bosom Friend of Magic Ancientry*

Pages 92–93.

    "In an elegy of 1822 composed in Kishinev . . . consisting of twenty-six freely rhymed iambic pentameters, Pushkin describes the two masks under which the Muse attended him: an old nurse (ll. 5–12) and a young enchantress (ll. 18–26) [quotes excerpt]. This again is Uliana. It seems evident to me that only beginning with the close of 1824 in Mihaylovskoe does Pushkin start to identify in retrospect Arina (now his housekeeper, formerly his sister's nurse) with a kind of collective 'my nurse.' Let us, by all means, remember Arina, but let us not forget good Uliana" (EO II: 454).

    For Arina, see p. 400.

    Russian text: Blagoy/Bondi II (1): 272.

    English text: EO II: 454.

Птичка / Little Bird

Pages 94–95.

    Russian text: Gofman 1937: 108; Blagoy/Bondi II (1): 280.

    English text: In *The Freud/Jung Letters,* edited by William McGuire, translated by Ralph Manheim and R. F. C. Hull (Princeton: Princeton University Press, 1974), 72 n2.

Демон / The Demon

Pages 96–97.

    "This 'demon' is connected with the 'Byronic' personality of Aleksandr Raevski (1795–1868), whom Pushkin first met in

Pyatigorsk in the summer of 1820. . . . When . . . this piece appeared under the title *My Demon* . . . , some readers thought they recognized Raevski, and Pushkin wrote, but did not publish, a refutation. In this MS note (1827) our poet, writing of himself in the third person, advises readers that his *Demon* is to be regarded not as the portrait of any particular individual but as the spirit influencing the morality of the age, a spirit of negation and doubt" (EO III: 163).

Russian text: Gofman 1937: 109–10; Blagoy/Bondi II (1): 299.

English text: EO III: 162–63 (*A:* "stirred my blood"; "with sudden anguish"; "the beautiful a fancy"; "love and freedom").

Свободы сеятель пустынный /
A lonely sower of liberty / Of freedom eremitic sower

Pages 98–99.

The epigraph is from Matthew 13:3.

Russian text: Gofman 1937: 111.

English text: "A lonely sower": Fragment from Pushkin lectures, Cornell, in VNAM; "Of freedom": EO II: 225 (A: "solitary sower").

from *Евгений Онегин, Глава первая /*
from *Eugene Onegin, Chapter 1*

Pages 100–103.

Russian text: EO IV: 21–23.

English text: RR 4/2 (1945): 38–39.

На Воронцова / Epigram (On Vorontsov)

Pages 104–5.

"General Vorontsov (1782–1856), son of Count Semyon Vorontsov, Russian ambassador in London, received an English education there. Since May 7, 1823, Vorontsov was the governor general of New Russia (Novorossiya, as the southern provinces of the empire were called) and vice-roy of the Bessarabian region . . . During the entire spring of 1824, Count Vorontsov . . . had been clamoring from Odessa to St. Petersburg, in letters to Count Nesselrode, Minister of Foreign Affairs, to rid him of the unpleasant and difficult Mr. Pushkin . . . 'a weak imitator of Byron'—but also the author of original epigrams and an admirer of the countess" (EO III: 193–94, 305–6).

Russian text: *Sobranie zapreshchyonnïh stihotvoreniy A. S. Pushkina* (Berlin: Izdanie I. P. Ladïzhnikova, [ca. 1920]), 45 (hereafter "Ladïzhnikov" followed by page numbers).

English text: PLT: 36.

from *Цыганы* / from *The Gypsies*

Pages 106–9.

> *his baffling name:* i.e., Publius Ovidius Naso. Ovid (43 B.C.–A.D. 17)
> was banished by Augustus in A.D. 8 to Tomis, on the Black Sea,
> where he remained until his death, and there wrote *Tristia* and
> *Epistulae ex Ponto* on the subject of his exile. In his own banishment
> by Alexander I in 1820 from St. Petersburg to the Crimea and
> the Caucasus, also on the Black Sea, Pushkin was conscious of his
> famous predecessor, as Nabokov, in flight from Petrograd to the
> Crimea in 1917–19, was conscious of both. Pushkin added a note to
> his reference to Ovid in *Eugene Onegin,* I, viii: "The contention that
> Ovid was banished to what is now Akkerman [Romanian Cetatea
> Albă, southwest of Odessa, Russia—VN's note] is baseless. In his ele-
> gies *Ex Ponto,* he clearly indicates that the place of his residence is
> the town of Tomi at the very mouth of the Danube" (EO II: 60–61).

> Russian text: Blagoy/Bondi IV: 186–87.

> English text: EO II: 59–60.

К Вяземскому / *To Vyazemski*

Pages 110–11.

> "Prince (*knyaz'*) Pyotr Vyazemski (1792–1878), a minor poet,
> was disastrously influenced by the French poetaster Pierre Jean
> Béranger; otherwise he was a verbal virtuoso, a fine prose stylist, a
> brilliant (though by no means always reliable) memoirist, critic, and
> wit. Pushkin was very fond of him and vied with him in scatologi-
> cal metaphors (see their letters). He was Karamzin's ward, Reason's
> godchild, Romanticism's champion, and an Irishman on his
> mother's side (O'Reilly)" (EO II: 27).

> "Vyazemski's florid and redundant style [is] full of definitions,
> and definitions of definitions" (EO II: 493).

> "Pushkin's esteem for Nikolay Turgenev—and for all freedom-
> loving, independent people as such—is evident from a marvelous
> epigram on Neptune . . . that heads a letter to Vyazemski, Aug. 14,
> 1826, from Mihaylovskoe to Petersburg: [quotes the poem]. This is
> an answer to a poem entitled *The Sea* that Vyazemski sent him in a
> letter of July 31, 1826, from Revel. Pushkin's epigram was prompted
> by rumors (which later proved false) to the effect that Great Brit-
> ain had surrendered the political émigré, Decembrist Nikolay
> Turgenev, to the Russian government" (EO III: 358).

> Russian text: Blagoy/Bondi III (1): 21.

> English text: EO III: 358.

Во глубине сибирских руд / Deep in Siberian mines

Pages 112–13.

> "In his poems directly related to the fate of the Decembrist move-
> ment [the abortive coup of December 14, 1825, planned by a 'secret
> union of cultured young noblemen opposed to tyranny and slavery'
> (EO III: 345)], Pushkin, while expressing a solemn sympathy for the
> exiled men, their families, and their cause, stressed his own artistic
> immunity, and this blend of participation and aloofness seems to have
> struck some of the Decembrists as slightly tasteless. In the beginning
> of January, 1827, Pushkin sent the following tetrametric stanzas . . . to
> Chita with the wife of the exiled Nikita Muravyov" (EO III: 349).
>> Russian text: Blagoy/Bondi III (1): 49.
>> English text: EO III: 349–50.

Ангел / The Angel

Pages 114–15.

> "[A] kind of amendment to *The Demon*. It is a not-uncolorful but on
> the whole mediocre little poem" (EO III: 164).
>> Russian text: Blagoy/Bondi III (1): 59.
>> English text: EO III: 164.

To Dawe, Esqr. / To Dawe, Esqr.

Pages 116–17.

> "Some time in the winter of 1828–29 Pushkin proposed to Annette
> Olenin and was refused" (EO III: 206).
>
> "Annette Olenin was at twenty a small graceful blonde, 'as cute
> and as quick as a mouse,' says Vyazemski (in a letter of May 3, 1828,
> to his wife)" (EO III: 202).
>> Russian text: Gofman 1937: 176; Blagoy/Bondi III (1): 101.
>> English text: EO III: 205.

from *Полтава / Dedication to the Long Poem* Poltava

Pages 118–19.

> "It is thought that this dedication . . . is addressed to Maria Volkon-
> ski. . . . The draft and the fair copy are headed with the words,
> written in English, 'I love this sweet name' (the heroine of *Poltava* is
> called Maria)" (EO II: 123–24).
>> Russian text: Blagoy/Bondi V: 17.
>> English text: EO II: 123–24.

Анчар / The Upas Tree

Pages 120–23.

>> Russian text: Gofman 1937: 177–78; "The Upas Tree, by Aleksandr
>> Pushkin," Haviaras/Milburn: 29 (recorded April 14, 1946).
>>> English text: TRP: 5–6.

На картинки к «Евгению Онегину» в «Невском Альманахе» /
On the Illustrations to Eugene Onegin *in the* Nevski Almanac

Pages 124–25.

> "The 1825 edition [of Canto One of *Eugene Onegin*] . . . appeared
> without the picture [which Pushkin had sketched as a guide for an
> illustrator]. It was redrawn eventually by the miserably bad artist
> Aleksandr Notbek or Nothbeck, and was one of a series of *EO* illus-
> trations, six engravings, published in January, 1829 (in the *Nevski
> Almanac,* ed. by Egor Aladyin)" (EO II: 177).
>> Russian text: Ladizhnikov: 46–47; Blagoy/Bondi III (1): 165.
>> English text: EO II: 177–78.

Зимнее утро / Winter Morning

Pages 126–27.

>> Russian text: Gofman 1937: 190; Blagoy/Bondi III (1): 183–84.
>> English text: PLT: 37.

Я вас любил: любовь еще, быть может /
I worshipped you. My love's reluctant ember /
I you loved: love yet, maybe

Pages 128–33.

> "According to B. Markevich, a toque of ponceau velvet was worn by
> the brilliant Caroline Sobanski (born Countess Rzhevuski, elder
> sister of Eva, Mme Hanski, whom Balzac was to marry in 1850) at
> social functions in Kiev, where Pushkin first saw her during a brief
> visit to that town in February, 1821. Three years later, in Odessa,
> he courted her, and they read *Adolphe* together. Still later, he fre-
> quented her Moscow salon and wrote her passionate letters and
> poems (*I Loved You,* 1829, and *What Is There in My Name for You,*
> 1830). She was a government spy" (EO III: 182).
>> Russian text: *Pushkin,* edited by S. A. Vengerov (St. Petersburg:
>> Brockhaus-Efron, 6 vols. 1907–15), III, 58 (hereafter "Vengerov"
>> followed by volume and page numbers).
>> English text: "I worshipped you": Unpublished; from EIN's tran-
>> script (Album 13, p. 193), VNA (*all men to worship you:* the phrase
>> "another to love you" appears as an alternative ending at the foot of
>> the page); note on "Ya vas lyubil," transliteration, and translations,
>> unpublished, from MS, VNA.

Что в имени тебе моем? / The Name

Pages 134–35.

>> Russian text: Gofman 1937: 194–95; Blagoy/Bondi III (1): 210.
>> English text: PLT: 36.

На Булгарина / Epigram

Pages 136–37.

Directed at Fadey Bulgarin (1789–1859), novelist, critic, journalist, and police agent. "The allusion is to François Eugène Vidocq (1775–1857), chief of the secret police in France, whose spurious *Memoirs* were such a hit in 1828–29. 'Figlyarin,' drawn from *figlyar* (zany) and rhyming with the subject's real name" (EO III: 226).

Russian text: Blagoy/Bondi III (1): 215.

English text: EO III: 226.

Труд / The Work (Trud)

Pages 138–39.

This poem marks the completion of EO. "Pushkin dated this poem: 'Boldino, Sept. 25, 1830, 3:15.' Translated one hundred and twenty-six years later, in Ithaca, New York" (EO III: 384).

Russian text: Blagoy/Bondi III (1): 230.

English text: EO III: 384.

from *Домик в Коломне* / from *A Small House in Kolomna*

Pages 140–41.

"His remarkable piece *A Small House in Kolomna* (forty octaves in iambic pentameter, 1829–30) opens with the petulant statement: [quotes the fragment]" (EO III: 515).

". . . at Boldino, where, from the first week of September, 1830, to the end of November, [Pushkin] spent the most fertile autumn in his entire life, owing partly to the consciousness of his impending marriage—a vague vista of financial obligations and humdrum obstacles to creative life. The estate of Boldino . . . belonged to Pushkin's father . . . who, however, had never visited it and was happy to have his elder son take charge of it. The old master house turned out to have no garden or park, but the environs were not devoid of the kind of bleak, gray grandeur that has inspired many a Russian poet" (EO III: 179–80).

Russian text: Blagoy/Bondi V: 83.

English text: EO III: 515.

from *Моя Родословная* / from *My Pedigree*

Pages 142–43.

"*My Pedigree,* an 84-line piece in iambic tetrameter, . . . was composed by Pushkin on Oct. 16 and Dec. 3, 1830, soon after he had completed the first draft of EO, Eight. Its composition was provoked by Fadey Bulgarin's coarse article in *Northern Bee* (*Severnaya pchela*), in which that critic made fun of Pushkin's keen interest in his Russian 'six-hundred-year-old' nobility and in his Ethiopian descent" (EO II: 33–34).

Abram Petrovich Gannibal, Pushkin's great-grandfather, was an African presented to Peter the Great, who became one of Peter's favorites and a famous general. Nabokov discusses the quest for the murky evidence of Gannibal's origins in Appendix I to EO.

Russian text: Blagoy/Bondi III (1): 262–63.

English text: EO II: 33; Post Scriptum from EO III: 495.

from *Скупой рыцарь* / A scene from *The Covetous Knight*

Pages 144–51.

Russian text: Gofman 1937: 783–86; Blagoy/Bondi VII: 110–13.

English text: TRP: 7–10.

Моцарт и Сальери / *Mozart and Salieri*

Pages 152–73.

Russian text: Gofman 1937: 792–99; Blagoy/Bondi VII: 123–34.

English text: *New Republic,* April 21, 1941: 559–60, 565; TRP: 20–29; PLT: 25–35.

Пир во время чумы / *A Feast during the Plague*

Pages 174–93.

Russian text: Gofman 1937: 800–807; Blagoy/Bondi VII: 175–84.

English text: TRP: 11–19.

from *Медный всадник* / from *The Bronze Horseman*

Pages 194–95.

"The most mature of his tetrametric masterpieces" (EO III: 515).

Eugene: "Another Eugene, however, is in the meantime losing his betrothed to the raging waters and being driven mad by the fancied gallop of an equestrian statue in the poem Pushkin devoted to that flood, *The Bronze Horseman* (composed 1833). The way Eugene Onegin, while hibernating, lends his first name to this unfortunate man is very amusing" [quotes beginning of part I] (EO III: 232).

"Pushkin employed the same device in his long poem *The Bronze Horseman: A Petersburg Tale* (1833), pt. II, l. 188, where the animated statue of Tsar Peter, with a ponderous reverberation, gallops (I again give the *o* its positional value) '*pa patryasyónnoy mastovóy.* / over the shaken pavement.' Here the two rapid identical *pa*'s, detonating the line, make it still more sonorous (in keeping with the beat of the bronze hoofs)" (EO II: 166).

Russian text: Blagoy/Bondi V: 137, 138.

English text: EO III: 232–33.

Пора, мой друг, пора! / 'Tis time, my dear, 'tis time

Pages 196–97.

Russian text: Blagoy/Bondi III (1): 330.

English text: From the foreword to *Despair* (New York: Vintage, 1989), xiv. Translated in EO as "'Tis time, my dear, 'tis time, for peace the heart is asking" (EO III: 253).

В мои осенние досуги / During my days of autumn leisure

Pages 198–99.

"Several times during the ensuing years he dallied with the idea of continuing the novel. Thus, in the course of his penultimate visit to Mihaylovskoe, soon after his arrival there on Sept. 7, 1835, he began a verse epistle to Pletnyov, who had urged him to continue EO. He began his epistle . . . in iambic pentameters . . . but then thought better of it and (about Sept. 16) switched to his old EO stanza" (EO III: 376).

Russian text: Blagoy/Bondi III (1): 397–98.

English text: EO III: 377–78.

. . .Вновь я посетил / The Return of Pushkin

Pages 200–205.

In a radio talk for the BBC, April 3, 1954, Nabokov introduced his translation: "The place is the Pushkin country seat Mihaylovskoe, in the province of Pskov, north-western Russia. He visited the place several times during his short life; he lived there in banishment in the middle twenties; and then saw it not long before his death. I have followed here very closely the cut of Pushkin's unrhymed iambic pentameter."

In EO, Nabokov notes that Pushkin's great-grandfather Abram Gannibal "spent a few years as a country squire on a piece of acquired land, and then went on building fortresses. In 1742, Elizabeth, Peter I's younger daughter, made him a major general and four years later granted him the countryseat Mihaylovskoe in the province of Pskov, which was to be forever linked up with Pushkin's name" (EO III: 434–35).

". . . in his admirable elegy in blank verse beginning . . . *Vnov' ya posetíl* . . . , dedicated to Mihaylovskoe (Sept. 26, 1835): '[Mihaylovskoe!] I've revisited [*Vnóv' ya posetíl*] / That little corner of the earth where I / Spent as an exile two unnoticed years.' The bracketed 'Mihaylovskoe' is, I suggest, the word, omitted by Pushkin, that most logically fills the first five divisions of the opening line" (EO II: 219).

my poor old nurse: "Arina (or Irina) Rodionovna (1758–1828), Pushkin's housekeeper in Mihaylovskoe, whither he removed, or rather was removed, from Odessa in 1824. She should not be confused . . . with the nurse he had as a child. . . . [H]e remembers her as sharing his years of exile in the country (1824–26) and telling him tales 'that since childhood' he 'knew by heart but never tired of hearing,' in his poem *Mihaylovskoe Revisited* (as it might be entitled . . .), composed there in 1835" (EO II: 452–53).

their friendly summits soughing in the wind: At Harvard on March 20, 1952 (Haviaras/Milburn: 19), Nabokov commented at this point.

> (Or even closer to the poet's text:
> "So old a sound—the soughing of their crests" . . .
> Here, incidentally, to interrupt
> my version for an instant, I have tried
> to match Pushkinian alliteration—
> "znakómïm shúmom shóroh ih vershín
> menyá privétstvoval . . ." or in my version:
> "So old a sound—the soughing of their crests").

The same interpolation is to be found in "Radio talk for BBC. On April 3, 1954 (Talk No. 3)" (VNA). In another version of this talk, Nabokov added after "alliteration": "a sibilant susurrus in this case" (VNA).

Russian text: M. L. Gofman, "Posmertnïe stihotvoreniya Pushkina" (1833–1836 gg.) in *Pushkin i ego sovremenniki. Materialï i issledovaniya,* XXXIII–XXXV ([St.] Petersburg: Rossiyskaya Gosudarstvennaya Akademicheskaya Tipografiya, 1922), 392–400.

In "The Return of Pushkin" VN makes extensive use of Pushkin's drafts no longer reproduced within the body of the poem (cf. Vengerov IV: 38–39 and Gofman 1937: 269–70; Blagoy/Bondi III [1]: 399–400, [2]: 995–1008).

English text: translation by VN for Nicholas Nabokov's *The Return of Pushkin: Elegy in Three Parts, for High Voice and Orchestra,* LCNA.

Из Пиндемонте / I value little those much-vaunted rights

Pages 206–7.

Russian text: Gofman 1937: 274.
English text: PLT: 35.

from *Родословная моего героя /*
from *The Pedigree of My Hero*

Pages 208–13.

"In . . . 1948, Bondi . . . publishes under an arbitrary title (*Ezerski*) a set of fifteen stanzas of the *Onegin* type, of which II–VI, fragments of VII, VIII and IX (combined to form two stanzas), and X were published by Pushkin in *Sovremennik,* 1836, under the title *The Pedigree of My Hero* (*Rodoslovnaya moego geroya*), with the subtitle 'Fragment of a Satirical Poem.' This hero is Pushkin's contemporary, the scion of a thousand-year-old line of warriors and boyars, originating with the Norman chiefs who, according to tradition, invaded Russia in the ninth century and gave her her first princes. The poem is an absolutely stunning performance, one of Pushkin's greatest master-pieces, and reflects the historiographic interests of Pushkin's last years. It was begun at the very end of 1832 and was taken up again in 1835 and 1836 . . .

"Ivan Ezerski's grandfather had 12,000 slaves, and his father had only one eighth of that number, and these 'had long been mortgaged.' Ezerski lives on a salary and is a *chinovnik* (official, functionary, civil servant, clerk) with a drab job as 'collegiate registrar' (the fourteenth and lowest rank in the service) in some government bureau in St. Petersburg" (EO III: 378–79).

Russian text: Blagoy/Bondi V: 97–99, 102–3.

English text: EO III: 379–81 (A: I: "O'er the ensombered"; "'Twas getting dark. Ivan Ezerski, / my neighbor, entered at this time"; IV: "names of the Ezerskis shine"; XIII: "the wind twists in a gully").

Я памятник себе воздвиг нерукотворный /
"No hands have wrought my monument" / Exegi monumentum

Pages 214–16.

"In 1836, in one of the most subtle compositions in Russian liter-ary history, Pushkin parodied Derzhavin [see pp. 32–33] stanza by stanza in exactly the same verse form. The first four have an ironic intonation, but under the mask of high mummery Pushkin smuggles in his private truth. They should be in quotation marks, as Burtsev pointed out some thirty years ago in a paper I no lon-ger can trace. The last quatrain is the artist's own grave voice repudiating the mimicked boast. His last line, although ostensibly referring to reviewers, slyly implies that only fools proclaim their immortality" (EO II: 310–11).

"Throughout great Rus' . . . untamed Tunguz": Nabokov translates this quatrain more literally in the notes to PP:

> Tidings of me will cross the whole great Rus,
> and name me will each tribe existing there:
> proud scion of Slavs, and Finn, and the now savage
> Tungus, and—friend of steppes—the Kalmuck
> (PP: 113).

accept indifferently . . . do not contradict a fool (216): This translation takes into account the emendations made in Blagoy/Bondi III (1):

424, where the last two lines read: "Hvalu i klevetu priemli ravnodu-shno, / I ne osporivay gluptsa."

Russian text: Gofman 1937: 275–76; "Exegi monumentum, by Aleksandr Pushkin," Haviaras/Milburn: 29 (recorded April 14, 1946).

English texts: "No hands have wrought," TRP: 5; "Exegi Monumentum," Haviaras/Milburn: 29 (recorded April 14, 1946); "I've set up to myself a monument," EO II: 311 (A; "in the fond lyre").

EVGENIY ABRAMOVICH BARATÏNSKI

On Evgeniy Baratïnski (218)

EO II: 380.

"A great intellectualist . . ." (219)

Unpublished; excerpt from a lecture on Baratïnski in a survey of Russian literature; from TS, VNAM.

from *Финляндия* / from *Finland*

Pages 220–21.

"It was in Finland that Baratïnski wrote the first poem that revealed his talent to discriminating readers. This is *Finlyandiya,* first published, 1820 . . . This Ossianic elegy consist[s] of seventy-two free iambics" (EO II: 383).

Russian text: *Polnoe sobranie sochineniy E. A. Boratïnskogo,* edited by M. L. Gofman (St. Petersburg: Izdanie Imperatorskoy Akademii Nauk, 2 vols. 1914–15), I, 16–18 (hereafter "Gofman 1914" followed by volume and page numbers).

English text: EO II: 383.

from *Пиры* / from *Feasts*

Pages 222–23.

his fondest drink, Ay: "The name of this glorious champagne comes from Aï or Ay, a town in the Marne Department, northern France" (EO II: 481).

Russian text: Gofman 1914 II. 10.

English text: EO II: 481.

Своенравное прозванье / To His Wife

Pages 224–25.

Russian text: *Baratïnski. Izbrannïe sochineniya,* edited by M. L. Gofman (Berlin: Izdatel'stvo Z. I. Grzhebina, 1922), 124 (hereafter "Gofman 1922" followed by page numbers).

English text: Unpublished; from TS, VNA; filed by VN under "miscellaneous translations" (1941–1966).

На что вы, дни! /
What use are ye, Days!

Pages 226–27.

Russian text: Gofman 1922: 141.

English text: Unpublished prose translation, part of a lecture on Baratïnski in a survey of Russian literature. From TS, VNAM.

Все мысль, да мысль! /
Ideas and nothing but ideas!

Pages 228–29.

Russian text: Gofman 1922: 142.

English text: Unpublished prose translation, part of a lecture on Baratïnski in a survey of Russian literature. From TS, VNAM.

FYODOR IVANOVICH TYUTCHEV

On Fyodor Tyutchev (230)

TRP: 37; PLT: 49.

Classifying Tyutchev (231)

EO II: 450.

Слезы / Tears

Pages 232–33.

The epigraph is from "Alcaic Fragment" ("O lachrymarum Fons, tenero sacros") by Thomas Gray (1716–1771).

Russian text: F. I. Tyutchev, *Stihotvoreniya* (Berlin: Slovo, 1921), 44–45 (hereafter "Tyutchev 1921" followed by page numbers).

English text: TRP: 32–33; PLT: 51; Harvard TS: 2.

Летний вечер / Nightfall

Pages 234–35.

Russian text: Tyutchev 1921: 66–67.

English text: TRP: 32; PLT: 50; Harvard TS: 1.

Silentium (Молчи, скрывайся и таи) /
Silentium (Speak not, lie hidden, and conceal)

Pages 236–37.

Russian text: Tyutchev 1921: 90; "Silentium, by Fyodor Tyutchev," Haviaras/Milburn: 24 (recorded April 14, 1946).

English text: The *Atlantic Monthly,* January 1944: 81; TRP: 33–34; PLT: 52; Harvard TS: 3.

Душа хотѣла б быть звѣздой / My soul would like to be a star

Pages 238–39.

        Russian text: Tyutchev 1921: 61–62.

        English text: Unpublished; Harvard TS: 14.

Успокоение / Appeasement

Pages 240–41.

        Russian text: Tyutchev 1921: 82.

        English text: RR 4/1 (1944): 45; TRP: 36; PLT: 55.

from *Цицеронъ* / Blest is the mortal who has stayed

Pages 242–43.

        Russian text: *Polnoe sobranie sochineniy F. I. Tyutcheva*, edited by P. V. Bïkov (St. Petersburg: A. F. Marks, 1913), 78 (hereafter "Bïkov 1913" followed by page numbers).

        English text: Unpublished MS note, in Mihail Karpovich Collection, CB.

Песок сыпучий по колени /
The Journey (Knee-deep, this powdery sand) /
The Journey (Soft sand comes up to our horses' shanks) /
The crumbly sand is knee-high

Pages 244–47.

        "As has been pointed out by Russian critics, the image in ll. 7–8 is an improvement upon a metaphor in Goethe's *Willkommen und Abschied:* 'Wo Finsternis aus dem Gesträuche mit hundert schwarzen Augen sah'" (EO II: 328–29).

        Russian text: Tyutchev 1921: 74; "The Journey, by Fyodor Tyutchev," Haviaras/Milburn: 26 (recorded April 14, 1946).

        English texts: ("Knee-deep"): RR 4/1 (1944): 45; ("Soft sand"): TRP: 33; PLT: 52; "The Journey, by Fyodor Tyutchev," Haviaras/Milburn: 26 (recorded April 14, 1946); "The crumbly sand": EO II: 328–29.

Альпы / Through the azure haze of the night

Pages 248–49.

        Russian text: Tyutchev 1921: 71.

        English text: Unpublished; from Harvard TS: 13.

Сумерки / Dusk

Pages 250–51.

        Russian text: Tyutchev 1921: 54–55.

        English text: RR 4/1 (1944): 46; TRP: 34–35; PLT: 53; Harvard TS: 4.

Слезы (Слезы людские, о, слезы людские) /
Tears (Human tears, O the tears!)

Pages 252–53.

        Russian text: Tyutchev 1921: 119; "Tears, by Fyodor Tyutchev,"
Haviaras/Milburn: 20 (recorded March 20, 1952), 27 (recorded
April 14, 1946).

            English text: RR 4/1 (1944): 46; TRP: 36; Harvard TS: 10.

Святая ночь на небосклон взошла / The Abyss

Pages 254–55.

        Russian text: Tyutchev 1921: 119–20.

            English text: TRP: 35; PLT: 54; Harvard TS: 7.

Последняя любовь / Last Love

Pages 256–57.

        Russian text: Tyutchev 1921: 146–47; "Last Love, by Fyodor
Tyutchev," Haviaras/Milburn: 25 (recorded April 14, 1946).

            English text: TRP: 34; PLT: 53; Harvard TS: 6.

            In an earlier version in "Poems of Fëdor Tyutchev" (*Atlantic
Monthly,* January 1944: 81), lines 6 and 8 read "alone a westerly radi-
ance is roaming / . . . / keep me enchanted in the gloaming"; lines
10 and 12, "its tenderness has not expended / . . . / Endless bliss
and hopelessness blended."

Есть в осени первоначальной / Autumn

Pages 258–59.

        Russian text: Tyutchev 1921: 156.

            English text: The *Atlantic Monthly,* January 1944: 81; TRP:
35–36; PLT: 55; Harvard TS: 8.

Она сидела на полу / She sat on the floor

Pages 260–61.

        Russian text: Tyutchev 1921: 158–59.

            English text: Unpublished; Harvard TS: 12.

Ночное небо так угрюмо / The sky is overcast

Pages 262–63.

        Russian text: Tyutchev 1921: 187–88.

            English text: Unpublished, "The Art of Translation," VNA;
Harvard TS: 11; "The Deaf-Mute Demons, by Fyodor Tyutchev,"
Haviaras/Milburn: 22 (recorded March 20, 1952).

Умом Россию не понять / *[Russia] One cannot understand her with the mind*

Pages 264–65.

> Russian text: Bïkov 1913: 202.

> English text: Unpublished; from Mihail Karpovich Collection, CB.

ALEKSEY VASILIEVICH KOLTSOV

On Aleksey Koltsov (266)

> Unpublished; part of a Koltsov–Nekrasov lecture in a survey of Russian literature. From TS, VNA.

Что ты спишь, мужичок? / *Why do you sleep, little peasant . . . ?*

Pages 268–71.

> *Under the bench the trunk:* "Where a farmer stores his wealth" (VN's note).

> Russian text: *Polnoe sobranie sochineniy A. V. Kol'tsova,* edited by A. I. Lyashchenko (St. Petersburg: Izdanie razryada izyashchnoy slovesnosti Imperatorskoy Akademii Nauk, 1911), 119–21.

> English text: Unpublished translation; part of a Koltsov–Nekrasov lecture (TS, VNA).

MIHAIL YURIEVICH LERMONTOV

The Lermontov Mirage (272)

> 277:   RR 1/1 (1941), 31–39.

Lermontov (277)

> *critic Mirsky:* D. S. Mirsky's (1890–1939) *A History of Russian Literature from the Earliest Times to the Death of Dostoevsky* (1881), published 1926–27, and his *Contemporary Russian Literature, 1881–1925* (1925), were combined by Francis J. Whitfield in 1949 into *A History of Russian Literature: From Its Beginnings to 1900,* still in print.

> TRP: 37–38; PLT: 39.

Небо и звезды / *The Sky and the Stars*

Pages 278–79.

> Russian text: *Polnoe sobranie sochineniy M. Yu. Lermontova* (Berlin: Slovo, 4 vols. 1921), I, 306 (hereafter "Lermontov 1921" followed by volume and page numbers).

> English text: PLT: 43.

Ангел / The Angel

Pages 280–81.

      Russian text: Lermontov 1921 I: 310–11.

        English text: RR 5/2 (1946): 50; PLT: 47.

Желанье / The Wish

Pages 282–83.

      Russian text: Lermontov 1921 II: 19–20.

        English text: PLT: 44.

from *K * / Farewell*

Pages 284–85.

      Russian text: Lermontov 1921 II: 20–21.

        English text: RR 1/1 (1941): 32; TRP: 30; PLT: 40.

Парус / The Sail

Pages 286–87.

      Russian text: Lermontov 1921 II: 7.

        English text: RR 5/2 (1946): 50; PLT: 45.

Благодарность / Thanksgiving

Pages 288–89.

      Russian text: Lermontov 1921 II: 255.

        English text: The *Atlantic Monthly*, November 1946: 108; PLT: 46.

Отчизна / My Native Land

Pages 290–91.

      Russian text: Lermontov 1921 II: 300–301.

        English text: RR 1/1 (1941): 35; TRP: 30–31; PLT: 41.

Сосна (Из Гейне) / Imitation of Heine

Pages 292–93.

      Russian text: Lermontov 1921 II: 264.

        English text: RR 5/2 (1946): 51; PLT: 43.

Утес / The Rock

Pages 294–95.

      Russian text: Lermontov 1921 II: 312.

        English text: RR 5/2 (1946): 51; PLT: 47.

Сон / The Triple Dream

Pages 296–98.

      Russian text: Lermontov 1921 II: 311–12; M. Yu. Lermontov, *Polnoe sobranie sochineniy*, edited by B. M. Eyhenbaum (Moscow–Leningrad:

OGIZ, 4 vols. 1947–48), I, 85 (hereafter "Eyhenbaum" followed by volume and page numbers).

English text: (*I dreamt that with a bullet in my side*): RR 1/1 (1941): 33; TRP: 31; PLT: 42; (In noon's heat, in a dale of Dagestan): Lermontov, *A Hero of Our Time,* translated by Vladimir Nabokov with Dmitri Nabokov (Garden City, NY: Doubleday Anchor, 1958), v–vi.

AFANASIY AFANASIEVICH FET (SHENSHIN)

On Afanasiy Fet (300)

> *"Fet—the spirit of the air . . .":* Unpublished lecture on Baratïnski for survey of Russian Literature, VNAM.

> *"Literary criticism in Russia . . .":* Unpublished, from Russian Survey Lectures, folder 17, VNA.

Измучен жизнью, коварством надежды / When life is torture

Pages 302–3.

> "The uniformity of the passage of time in the minds of all men proves more conclusively than anything else that we all plunged in the same dream; indeed, that it is one Being that dreams it" (VN's translation of the epigraph).

> Russian text: A. A. Fet, *Polnoe sobranie stihotvoreniy,* edited by B. Ya. Buhshtab (Leningrad: Sovetskiy pisatel', 1937), 98 (hereafter "Buhshtab 1937" followed by page numbers).

> English text: RR 3/1 (1943): 32; Harvard TS: 20.

Alter Ego (Как лилея глядится в нагорный ручей) /
Alter Ego (As a lily that looks at itself in a stream)

Pages 304–5.

> Russian text: Buhshtab 1937: 96.

> English text: RR 3/1 (1943): 31; Harvard TS: 19.

Ласточки / The Swallow

Pages 306–7.

> Russian text: Buhshtab 1937: 107–8.

> English text: RR 3/1 (1943): 33; Harvard TS: 21.

NIKOLAY ALEKSEEVICH NEKRASOV

On Nikolay Nekrasov (308)

> *"Nikolay Alekseevich Nekrasov, 1821–77 . . .":* PP 125n.

> *"Nekrasov's iambic pentameter . . .":* Vladimir Nabokov. *The Gift,* translated by Michael Scammell and Dmitri Nabokov (New York: Putnam, 1963), 263–64.

Тяжелый крест достался ей на долю /
A heavy cross is her allotted burden

Pages 310–11.

"Не говори, что дни твои унылы / . . . / Перед тобой—объятия
любви!": Nabokov parodied this verse in a jocular inscription to his
wife in the first Danish edition of *Pnin:*

Верочке

Не говори что дни твои—уроды,
Тюремщиком Володю не зови!
Передо мной—другие переводы,
Перед тобой—все бабочки мои!

В. Сирин

Монтре
январь
1965

(reproduced in the auction catalog of the Nabokov Library, Tajan: *Bib-*
liothèque Nabokov, Genève, May 5, 2004: 71–72). Following Nabokov's
version of Nekrasov's original, we could translate this inscription:

To Véra

O do not say your days are monstrous,
And do not call Volodya a jailor!
Before me I see other translations
Before you, all my butterflies!

V. Sirin

Montreux
January
1965

Russian text: *Stihotvoreniya N.A. Nekrasova,* edited by K. I. Chu-
kovsky ([St.] Petersburg: Gosudarstvennoe Izdatel'stvo, 1920), 70
(hereafter "Chukovsky 1920" followed by page numbers).
English text: Unpublished; Harvard TS: 15.

Внимая ужасам войны / As I hearken to the horrors of war
Pages 312–13.

Russian text: Chukovsky 1920: 48.
English text: Unpublished; Harvard TS: 16.

from *Мороз, Красный нос / from Red-Nosed Frost*
Pages 314–15.

Russian text: Chukovsky 1920: 158.
English text: Unpublished; Harvard TS: 18.

Русь (from *Кому на Руси жить хорошо*) /
Russia (from *Who Can Be Happy in Russia*)

Pages 316–19.
    Russian text: Chukovsky 1920: 346.
    English text: Unpublished; Harvard TS: 17.

ALEKSANDR ALEKSANDROVICH BLOK

On Aleksandr Blok (320)

    "Among major Russian poets": EO III: 495n.

    "Blok . . . by far the greatest poet": EO III: 525.

    Blok *"is one of those poets"*: VN to Edmund Wilson, January 12, 1943
    (NWL: 103).

    "How do you now regard the poets Blok and Mandelshtam": SO: 97.

Незнакомка / The Strange Lady

Pages 322–25.
    "Probably the most famous short poem in long rhyme (alternating
with masculines) is Blok's *The Incognita* (*Neznakomka*), a set of iambic
tetrameters in which the rhymal concatenation of extra syllables
looks like reflection of lights in the suburban puddles of the poem's
locus" (1957, EO III: 539).
    Russian text: *Sobranie sochineniy Aleksandra Bloka* (Berlin:
Alkonost, 5 vols. 1923), II, 162–64 (hereafter "Blok 1923" followed
by volume and page numbers).
    English text: Unpublished; Harvard TS: 22.

Россия / Again, as in my golden years

Pages 326–27.
    Russian text: Blok 1923 III: 229–30.
    English text: Unpublished; Harvard TS: 26.

На железной дороге / The Railroad

Pages 328–31.
    Russian text: Blok 1923 III: 233–35.
    English text: Unpublished; Harvard TS: 25.

from *Роза и Крест / All is disaster and loss*

Pages 332–33.
    Russian text: Blok 1923 V: 243.
    English text: Unpublished; from MS, filed by VN under "Miscel-
laneous translations (1941–1966)," VNA.

Была ты всех ярче, верней и прелестней /
You were truer than others

Pages 334–35.

> Russian text: Blok 1923 III: 192–93.
>
> > English text: Unpublished; Harvard TS: 24.

VLADISLAV FELITSIANOVICH HODASEVICH

On Vladislav Hodasevich (336)

> EO III: 478.

On Hodasevich (336)

> In Russian, *Sovremennïe zapiski* LXIX (1939), 262–64; in English, *Triquarterly* 27 (Spring 1973), 83–87; SO: 223–27.

A Note on Vladislav Hodassevich (339)

> NDPP: 596.

Обезьяна / The Monkey

Pages 340–43.

> Alexander Zholkovsky plausibly suggests in "Poem, Problem, Prank," *The Nabokovian* 47 (Fall 2001), 19–28, that Nabokov has paid a stylized homage to Hodasevich's poem in his account of his own "first poem," in chapter 11 of *Speak, Memory*. There Nabokov places the scene of his composing his first poem in the shadow of World War I's approach and with the possible sound of a barrel organ in the wings. The tribute seems likely, and Nabokov's point is perhaps, as Zholkovsky suggests, to contrast his unconscious aping (monkeying) of others then with his conscious allusiveness in his prose account of his first poem, and with Hodasevich's masterful relation to his poetic traditions.
>
> > Russian text: Vladislav Hodasevich, *Sobranie stihov* (Paris: Vozrozhdenie, 1927), 49–51 (hereafter "Hodasevich 1927").
> >
> > English text: NDPP: 597–98; Harvard TS: 28.

Баллада / Orpheus

Pages 344–47.

> Russian text: Hodasevich 1927: 118–19.
>
> > English text: NDPP: 599–600; Harvard TS: 27.

Ни жить, ни петь почти не стоит / Poem

Pages 348–49.

> Russian text: Hodasevich 1927: 117.
>
> > English text: NDPP: 598–99; Harvard TS: 29.

from *«Не ямбом ли четырехстопным»* /
Years have from memory eroded

Pages 350–51.

Russian text: V. F. Hodasevich, *Sobranie stihov (1913–1939)*, edited by
Nina Berberov (Münich: I. Baschkirzew, 1961), 206. VN evidently
cites Hodasevich's poem from memory, as the second line of the
quoted stanza reads: "Za chto i kto v Hotine pal,—" (ibid.).

English text: EO III: 478. See p. 26, "On Gavrila Derzhavin."

OSIP EMILIEVICH MANDELSHTAM

On Osip Mandelshtam (352)

SO: 97.

On Adaptation (352)

SO: 280–82.

За гремучую доблесть грядущих веков /
For the sake of the resonant valor of ages to come

Pages 356–57.

Russian text: Nabokov follows the text reproduced in *Poets on Street
Corners: Portraits of Fifteen Russian Poets* by Olga Carlisle (New York:
Random House, 1968), 142–43. In Carlisle's anthology, the Russian
text of "Za gremuchuyu doblest' gryadushchih vekov" was placed
side by side with "In the name of the higher tribes of the future," an
English version of Mandelshtam's poem as "adapted by Robert Lowell" (ibid.: 143–45).

English text: SO: 280–81.

BULAT SHALVOVICH OKUDZHAVA

A Note on "Speranza" by Okudzhava (359)

Unpublished, draft letter to William Maxwell, editor of the *New
Yorker*, February 1966; VNA. Nabokov's former friend the critic
Edmund Wilson had attacked Nabokov's choice of arcane words in
his 1964 translation of Pushkin's *Eugene Onegin* in a review, "The
Strange Case of Nabokov and Pushkin," in the *New York Review of
Books*, July 15, 1965, 3–6. Nabokov replied in "Nabokov's Reply,"
Encounter, February 1966, 80–89 (see SO 241–67).

Translator's Note (359)

"the non-Russian reader may scan properly the iambic tetrameter": In the
original, VN has it as "pentameter."

Сентиментальный романс /
Sentimentál'nïy románs / A Sentimental Ballad

Pages 362–64.

Russian text: Nabokov follows the text reproduced in Bulat Okudzhava, *Bud' zdorov, shkolyar. Stihi* (Frankfurt: Posev, 1964 [2nd ed. 1966]), 106. In all subsequent authorized editions Okudzhava's poem is entitled "Sentimental'nïy marsh." Transliteration by VN.

English text: Unpublished MS, VNA. *"Don't manage to protect myself"*: *"Fail to* protect myself" (variant).

PROGRAM NOTES (366)

Unpublished, VNA, VNAM.

Cover letter addressed to Dmitri Nabokov, the writer's son and translator.

Dark Eyes

Page 367.

Words by Evgeniy Grebyonka (1821–98)

Выхожу один я на дорогу /
I come out alone upon the highroad

Pages 368–69.

"I have used everywhere the simplest of the three standard transliterations to render the Cyrillic script. A crude approximation to the actual sounds of the language would give: 'Vi-ha-zhóo ah-déen ya nah darógoo,' but this is too subjective and variable to be of much use. A scientific phonetic transcript involving fancy signs, etc. would, of course, mean nothing to the general reader" (VN).

Russian text: Lermontov 1921 II: 319; Eyhenbaum II: 93–94.

The Peddler's Box / Koróbushka

Page 370.

Russian text: PRP 2: 63.

The Yoke-Bell / Kolokól'chik

Page 371.

Words by Ivan Makarov (dates unknown).

Russian text: PRP 2: 341.

Two Guitars / Dve gitáry

Page 372.
> Russian text: PRP 2: 13.

Moscow Countryside Evenings / Podmoskóvnye vecherá

Page 373.
> Words by Mihail Matusovski (1915–90)

Sten'ka Razin and the Princess / Knyazhná

Page 375.
> Words by Dmitriy Sadovnikov (1847–83)
>> Russian text: PRP 2: 249.

As the King Went Forth to War / Kak koról' shyol na voinú

Page 376.
> Words by Maria Konopnicka (Polish, 1842–1910), translated into
> a Russian version by Andrey Koltonovski and sung by the great
> Russian bass Fyodor Shalyapin (1873–1938).

For the shores of your far country / Dlya beregóv otchízny dál'noy

Page 377.
> Russian text: Blagoy/Bondi III (1): 257.

Ночь / Night

Pages 378–79.
> Russian text: Blagoy/Bondi II (1): 289.

Doubt / Somnénie

Page 380.
> Russian text: PRP 1: 522.

III. FRENCH TO ENGLISH

RÉMI BELLEAU

from *Avril / April*

Pages 384–85.
> French text: From *La Bergerie*, in Rémi Belleau, *Oeuvres complètes*,
> edited by A. Gouverneur (Paris: A. Gouverneur, 3 vols. 1867), II, 44.
> English text: Unpublished, from TS, VNA, sent as entry in a
> *Sunday Times* translation competition, announced March 29, 1959
> ("Easter Competitions: April in the South"), submitted April 4,
> 1959, with a "P.S. Regarding the deadline; please take the Atlantic
> into consideration."

HENRI DE RÉGNIER

Odelette / Passing of Youth

Pages 388–89.

French text: Nabokov encountered this poem in a translation competition in the *Sunday Times* December 23, 1962: 25. From: Henri de Régnier, *Vestigia Flammae. Poèmes* (Paris: Mercure de France, 1921), 114.

English text: Unpublished, VNA.

PERMISSIONS
ACKNOWLEDGMENTS

INDEX OF POETS

In the following indices, page numbers listed in italics indicate additional references to the listed poem or poet; the poem itself or the poet's work is listed in roman characters.

УКАЗАТЕЛЬ ЗАГЛАВИЙ И ПЕРВЫХ СТРОК

Небо и звезды, 278, *416п*

«Недорого ценю я громкие права», 206, *409п*

Незнакомка, 322, *419п*

«Ни жить, ни петь почти не стоит», 348, *421п*

«Ни звука! Душа умирает», 314, *419п*

«Ночевала тучка золотая», 294, *417п*

«Ночное небо так угрюмо», 262, *415п*

Ночь, 378, *423п*

«О, как на склоне наших лет», 256, *414п*

Обезьяна, 340, *420–21п*

Ода на взятие Хотина, 23, *421п*

«Однозвучно гремит колокольчик», 371, *422п*

«Она сидела на полу», 260, *414п*

«Опять, как в годы золотые», 326, *420п*

«Отворите мне темницу», 282, *416п*

Отчизна, *276–77, 290, 416п*

Памятник, 32, *396п, 410п*

Парус, 286, *416п*

Певец, 40, *396–97п*

«Песок сыпучий по колени. . .», 244, *413п*

Петр Великий, героическая поэма, 26, *395п*

Пир во время чумы, 72, 174, *407п*

Пиры, 222, *411п*

«По вечерам над ресторанами», 322, *419п*

«По небу полуночи ангел летел», 273, 280, *416п*

«Под насыпью, во рву некошенном», 328, *420п*

Podmoskóvnye vecherá, 373, *423п*

Полтава. Посвящение, 72, 118, *404п*

«Полу-милорд, полу-купец», 104, *402п*

«Пора, мой друг, пора! покоя сердце просит», 196, *408п*

Последняя любовь, 256, *414п*

«Почтенный председатель! я напомню», 174, *407п*

«Природы праздный соглядатай», 306, *418п*

«Прости! мы не встретимся боле», 284, *461*

Птичка, 94, *401п*

Пушкину, *69, 70, 399п*

Родословная моего героя (Отрывок из сатирической поэмы), 208, *410п*

Роза и Крест, 332, *420п*

Россия, 326, *420п*

Руслан и Людмила, 90, *400–401п*

Русь, 316, *419п*

INDEX OF TITLES AND FIRST LINES

"Fair is the evening sky," 279, *416n*
Farewell, 285, *461*
"Farewell! Nevermore shall we meet," 273, 285, *416*
Feast During the Plague, A, 72, 175, *407n*
Feasts, 223, *411n*
Finland, 221, *411n*
"For everything, for everything, O Lord," 289, *416n*
"For the sake of the resonant valor of ages to come," 352, 357, *421n*
For the shores of your far country (*Dlya beregóv otchízny dál'noy*), 377, *423n*
"From behind the island onto the fairway," 375, *423n*
"From golden fields descends Aurora," 25, *395n*

"Great everlasting rocks, deserts of granite," 221, *411n*
"Gone is the bard, and from these haunts his traces," 41, *396–97n*
Gypsies, The, 72, 107, *403n*

"Half-merchant and half-prince," 105, *402n*
"He—a swan born in blooming Ausonia," 69, 71, *399n*
"Here, after crossing Bridge Kokushkin," 125, *405n*
Hotinian Ode, The, 22–23, 23, *421n*

"I come out alone upon the highroad" (*Vykhozhú odín ya na dorógu*) 369,
    422–23n
"I dreamt that with a bullet in my side," 274–76, 297, *417n*
"I have given her a nickname," 225, *412n*
". . . I have seen again," 201, *408–9n*
"I loved you: love, perhaps, is yet," *xxix, xxix-xxxv*, 131
"I'm not Omér; in lofty verses," 91, *400–401n*
"I value little those much-vaunted rights," 207, *409n*
"I've set up to myself a monument" (Derzhavin), 33, *396n, 410n*
"I've set up to myself a monument" (Pushkin), 216, *396n, 410–11n*
"I worshipped you. My love's reluctant ember," *xxxiii-xxxiv*, 129, *405n*
"I you loved: love yet, maybe," *xxix*, 133, *405n*
"Ideas and nothing but ideas!," 229, *412n*
"If I do love my land, strangely I love it," 276–77, 291, *416n*
Imitation of Heine, 203, *416n*
"In a monotone tinkles the yoke-bell," 371, *422n*
"In a remote boreal world," 51, *397n*
"In a strange country I religiously observe," 95, *401n*
"In noon's heat, in a dale of Dagestan," 274–76, 298, *417n*
"In the evenings, the sultry air above the restaurants," 323, *419n*
"In those days when to me were new," 97, *401–2n*
"Into plain cups the god of tippling," 223, *411n*

Journey, The, 245, 246, *413n*

"Just as a mad young fellow frets awaiting," 145, *407n*

"Knee-deep, this powdery sand... We ride," 245, *413n*

Last Love, 257, *414n*
Later parody (Political), A, 63, *398n*
Liberty: An Ode, 79, *86–87, 400n*
"Life? A Romance. By whom? Anonymous," 37, *396n*
Little Bird, 95, *401n*
Lord Ullin's Daughter, 52, *398n*
"Love at the closing of our days," 257, *414n*

Monkey, The, 341, *420–21n*
Moscow Countryside Evenings (Podmoskóvnye vecherá), 373, *423n*
"Most honorable chairman! Let me now," 175, *407n*
Mozart and Salieri, 72, 153, *407n*
My Native Land, 276–77, 291, *416n*
My Pedigree, 143, 406–7n
"My soul would like to be a star," 239, *413n*
"My voice that breathes for thee both tenderness and languor," 379, *423n*

Name, The, 135, *405n*
Night, 379, *423n*
Nightfall, 235, *412n*
"No hands have wrought my monument; no weeds," 215, 216, *396n, 410–11n*
"Not a sound! The soul leaves the world," 315, *419n*
"Now the ashen shadows mingle," 251, *414n*

Odelette, 388, *424n*
"O'er the gloom-covered town of Peter," 209, *410n*
"Of freedom eremitic sower," 99, *402n*
"Of the four-foot iambus I've grown tired," 72,141, *406n,*
"Oh, do not say the life you lead is dismal," *308–9, 308–9*
On the Illustrations to Eugene Onegin *in the* Nevski Almanac, 125, *405n*
On Translating "Eugene Onegin," 16, *395n*
"O, military capital, I love," 195, *407n*
"One cannot understand her with the mind," 265, *415n*
"One day, exuberant and gallant," *18,* 19, *395n*
"Only the deep night," 370, *422n*
Oolleen and His Daughter, 55, *398n*
"Open the door of my prison," 283, *416n*
Orpheus, 345, 421n